A
Manual for
Officer Training

By

David W. Hall

© 2011, 2018
David W. Hall
648 Goldenwood Court
Powder Springs, GA 30127
770.424.9005
david.hall@midwaypca.org

Includes Bibliographical References and Appendixes

ISBN: 9781717390127
First Edition 2002; Second Edition 2011; Third edition 2018
Printed in the United States of America

To order additional copies, contact The Covenant Foundation
648 Goldenwood Court
Powder Springs, GA 30127
770.424.9005
david.hall@midwaypca.org

TABLE OF CONTENTS

Preface

Welcome to an exploration of your gifts, your church, and your calling to serve the Lord. This course is designed for use in the local church, specifically those Presbyterian churches that follow the Westminster Confession of Faith (hereafter WCF). Parts of this, nonetheless, lend themselves to other uses and to other churches. It also reflects one particular situation and is by no means the final word on all subjects. We offer it to others, though, as a humble and faithful testimony of what our Lord has taught us.

This training manual includes:
- handouts used in our course;
- supplemental articles, essays, and sermons;
- additional resources for denominational work;
- For more study, we recommend a small book on the Westminster Assembly, *Windows on Westminster* (order from Great Commissions Publication, http://www.gcp.org/);
- All that is needed is a copy of the WCF and the *Book of Church Order*, which is revised regularly. These can be obtained from the Christian Education and Publications Bookstore (1700 North Brown Road, Suite 102, Lawrenceville, GA 30043-8122. Fax: 678.825.1101. Email: cep@pcanet.org.)

Each Session lasts approximately 90 minutes and can easily be divided in half to fit in a normal Sunday School period if desired.

Acknowledgments

We are grateful to the following publishers who have granted us permission to reprint material:

- Portions of *Windows on Westminster*, Copyright © 1993, Great Commission Publications, Suwanee, Georgia.
- *Officer Training Manual* of the First Presbyterian Church, Jackson, Mississippi (Session Three, p. 10).
- Abridgement of John Murray's *Redemption Accomplished and Applied* (Grand Rapids, MI: Eerdmans Publishing Company, 1955).
- Abridgement of W. J. Seaton's, "The Five Points of Calvinism," (Edinburgh: Banner of Truth Trust, 1970).
- "The Importance and Relevance of the Westminster Confession," John Murray, *Collected Writings of John Murray,* The Banner of Truth Trust, Edinburgh, Scotland, 1976, Vol. 1: *The Claims of Truth*, chapter 43, pp. 316-322.
- "Presbyterianism" in *Always Reformed: A Dialogue of Differences within the Reformed Tradition*, David G. Hagopian, ed. (Phillipsburg, NJ: Presbyterian & Reformed Publishing Co., forthcoming).
- Portions of David W. Hall & Joseph H. Hall, *Paradigms in Polity* (Oak Ridge, TN: The Covenant Foundation).

Session #1: Well Grounded Leaders

Serving as an ordained leader in Christ's church is one of the highest, most fulfilling, and most challenging callings in all of life. While all Christians are called to serve their Lord with their gifts and in different ministries, not everyone is called to ordained office. The qualifications for ecclesiastical office are, thankfully, set forth in Scripture for us. God cared enough to leave a blueprint for churches in all ages.

Before we look at those qualifications for the regular offices—Deacons and Elders—two prerequisites should be acknowledged. Although these are obvious to some, for the sake of clarity and completeness, we comment on these below.

A Christian Walk: The Foundation

First, the Officer in the church must be able to relate his own spiritual testimony. For those who are more retiring in temperament, this may have some difficulty. Still, an awareness of Christian experience is so essential and so normal for those who are called to serve in God's church that it is a beginning point to state that the Elder or Deacon must be able to briefly and comfortably share his own spiritual autobiography.

Some guidelines and points for discussion are listed below. Candidates should read this thoughtfully, and the class leader may wish to emphasize other aspects at this time.

GUIDELINES for your PROFESSION of FAITH

I.   *Attitudes*
a. Be yourself.
b. Use your own words.
c. Witness (Grk. – *martyreo*) = "to tell the truth and nothing but the truth."
d. How do *you* know these things?

II.   *Content*: Your testimony may wish to include the answers to some of these questions:
a. Can you tell how Christ was with you when growing up?
b. When did Jesus Christ come into your life? What happened?
c. Who is Jesus Christ?
d. How has Christ remained with you?
e. What difference does the presence of Christ make in your daily life?
f. Is the Holy Spirit real to you? How?
g. When do you feel close and far away from God?
h. Do you have a pattern for devotions? What is it?

III.   An *Example*: The following questions were used by Sessions in some Presbyterian churches at the turn of the twentieth century. Hopefully they may prove helpful. Inquiries should be made as to:
a. The time when a desire was first felt by the candidate to confess Christ;
b. The influences which led to this desire;

   c. The motives impelling to union with the church;

   d. The habits of the candidates with respect to prayer and reading of the Scriptures;

   e. The acceptance by the candidates of the Scriptures as the Word of God;

   f. The extent of their realization of sin and consequent need of a Savior;

   g. Their dependence upon the Lord Jesus Christ alone for salvation;

   h. Their knowledge of fundamental Christian doctrine;

   i. Their purpose to obey and serve Christ in their life;

   j. Their purpose to perform faithfully their duties as church members.

(Source: Roberts, PCUSA *Manual* [1910], p. 139)

Second and following on the heels of a clear testimony, the Officer must have assurance about his own salvation. It would be impossible to represent God's people adequately or to function consistently as a leader in crucial situations without this. Officers should be able to comfort people and themselves with some of the following verses or others (see also the footnotes to WCF 17-18):

   John 10:27-30
   Philippians 1:6
   Romans 8:28-39
   2 Timothy 2:19

Once candidates are assured of their salvation and able to share their testimonies, their attention should turn to the qualifications of respective offices.

Divine Qualifications: Indicators of Calling

The qualifications for office1 are set forth in several key passages in Scripture:
   (a) the qualifications for Elders are located in 1 Timothy 3:1-7 and Titus 1:5-9;
   (b) the qualifications for Deacons occur in 1 Timothy 3:8-13.

All Christians, unfortunately, do not view these passages as norms for all times and places. After much study and experience, we have come to the conclusion that these are superb—divinely inspired—indicators for who should serve. Accordingly, we have three presuppositions as we interpret and apply these qualifications.

Presuppositions for applying the qualifications for Officers
   (1) These qualifications are not ideal or unreal (nor were they merely for Paul's time). Some interpreters sacrifice this part of the Bible by making these verses culturally relative. The view that these only applied in Paul's time (beside being contrary to 2 Tim. 3:16) leaves the church devoid of crucial guidance in this key area of leadership qualifications.
   (2) These qualifications present the minimum required of a mature Christian man (Note all are in the masculine gender, whenever a gender is specified). One is not considered a super-spiritual person if he has but one wife, is not a drunkard, or if his children are not

---

1 Additional sermons on this passage are forthcoming in the *Lectio Continua* Commentary series; or may be accessed from our SermonAudio.com page or via www.midwaypca.org/sermons.

scandalous rebels. Maturity, not angelic perfection, is expected and depicted here. God did not pitch these qualifications at an unattainable level.

(3) These qualifications apply absolutely where relevant but do not apply to all candidates in a few areas. Nowhere does the Bible require that a minister or Officer *be married*, but if he is married, his marriage must meet these qualifications. The same is true for having children. The Bible does not require offspring as a qualification for office, but if a man has children, they must meet these qualifications. While some churches *require* an Officer to be married and have children, and while most Officers will, there are other passages that exhibit men serving without wives. There is also no age qualification specified in Scripture, leaving the determination of maturity to the local church. Thus, *if* the shoe fits, the Officer *must* wear it; but he is not prevented from serving if the shoe does not fit certain family states. All moral qualifications (in contrast to family qualifications) apply absolutely.

Accordingly, these qualifications may be viewed as a bull's-eye type target with three concentric spheres: (1) the innermost sphere is the home; (2) the second sphere is the church; and (3) the third sphere is the world. The Officer's reputation must meet these qualifications in these three areas. The innermost, the home, is the proving ground for office. As 1 Timothy 3:4-5 common-sensically argues, if a man cannot shepherd this small flock, he cannot reasonably be expected to guide the larger flock.

Essential Beliefs (cf. BCO 24-5 [1] & [2], ordination vows

Our church is a confessional church. This means that many issues have already been studied well and are largely settled. Officers, as a rule of thumb, should agree with what the Westminster Confession of Faith (WCF) states in each individual chapter, as well as consent to the integrated system of doctrine put forth. The reason for this, other than biblical faithfulness, is quite practical: if the leadership corps disagrees on fundamentals, the flock will be confused, and painful division will result. Certainly, every Christian is in process or not fully arrived in doctrinal maturity; however, Officers are to have reached a large and healthy agreement—most will find the Westminster Confession to be impressive in capturing biblical truth—with the Reformed faith. In our particular setting, there are several main areas that must be agreed to:

1. The unqualified belief in the inerrancy of the Scriptures (WCF1)
2. The Trinitarian nature of God (WCF 2)
3. Predestination (as per WCF 3)
4. God is the Creator of all things *ex nihilo* (WCF 4
5. All persons are sinful and in need of the Savior (WCF 6)
6. Covenantal perspective (WCF 7)
7. The Person and Work of Christ (as per WCF 8)
8. The order of relation between Effectual Calling (10) and Saving Faith (14)
9. The meaning of Justification (11), Sanctification, and Saving Faith (14)
10. The perseverance of the Saints (17)
11. The Church (25)
12. Baptism (28) and the Lord's Supper (29)
13. Presbyterian Polity (30 & 31)

In an earlier pamphlet (*The Ruling Elder* by the Rev. Leonard Van Horn), the following helpful questions (and references to appropriate WCF sections) elucidate most of the fundamentals. *Note: these could form questions for exams in association with those in Appendix E below.*

The Doctrine of Inspiration

What is meant by "the infallible, verbally inspired Word of God"?	Chapter 1:2, 3, 8
How do we know that the Bible is true?	Chapter 1:5
What is the difference between General and Special Revelation?	Chapter 1:1
Why should the Bible be received as the only rule of faith and practice?	Chapter 1:2, 4
Why is the Bible the authoritative Word of God?	Chapter 1:4

The Doctrine of God

Who are the persons of the Godhead?	Chapter 2:3
How can we "prove" the existence of God? (Note: Heb. 11:6)	Chapter 2:1
What do we mean by the attributes of God?	Chapter 2:1
Why is the sovereignty of God important?	Chapter 3:1
Can you define predestination?	Chapter 3:3-5
Is the doctrine of election unfair?	Chapter 3:7

The Doctrine of Man

Who were involved in the creation of man?	Chapter 4:1
Why was the world and man created?	Chapter 4:1
How would you define the doctrine of providence?	Chapter 5:1
What is a definition of sin?	Chapter 6:6
What was the effect of the first sin?	Chapter 6:2-4
Can you distinguish between the Covenant of Works and the Covenant of Grace?	Chapter 7:2, 3

The Doctrine of Christ

Why is the virgin birth and bodily resurrection of Christ important?	Chapter 8:2, 4
What are the three offices of Christ?	Chapter 8:1
What is meant by the "particular atonement of Christ?"	Chapter 8:5
What do we mean by the *"ordo salutis"* (the order of how God applies redemption to the elect) and can you state it?	Chapter 10:1, 2
Why is this order so important for us to understand?	Chapters 14-18

The Law of God

Can you name the Ten Commandments in order?	Chapter 19:2
How is the law summarized by our Lord Jesus Christ?	
Why is the law of God important to believers?	Chapter 19:6, 7

The Worship of God

Can you summarize what part prayer, Scripture reading, hearing

God's Word, fasting and the giving of offerings are to play in the
   worship of God?   Chapter 21:1-6
Why do we worship on Sunday?   Chapter 21:7, 8

The Doctrine of the Church

How would you define the invisible and visible church?   Chapter 25:1, 2
Why is the Church important?   Chapter 25:3
What constitutes membership in the visible Church?   Chapter 25:2
Can you distinguish between ruling and teaching Elders?
What are the types of Church government and what type do Presbyterians follow?

The Sacraments

What do we mean when we say that the sacraments are "signs and seals?"   Chapter 27:1, 2
What are the sacraments and can you define them?   Chapters 27–29
What does the "covenant" have to do with baptism?   Chapter 28:1
Can you distinguish between the Roman Catholic, Lutheran,
   and Reformed view of the Lord's Supper?   Chapter 29

The Doctrine of Christ's Return

What will happen to the unjust and the justified at the Last Day?   Chapters 32–33
How will Christ come again?   Chapter 33
How should we as believers prepare for that Day?   Chapter 33:3

****

Van Horn comments: "The Elders of the Church have certain qualifications outlined in the Scripture. All men are not qualified who are in the Church just as all citizens are not qualified to be president or governor. The qualifications listed below should be approached with a definite attitude on the part of the man involved: 'I do not look at them with the attitude of seeking glory for myself but rather I see a grave responsibility before me.' We shall list the qualifications as they are listed from God's Word with a simple definition after each one. . . . The first qualification is that the Elder is a male member of the Church. There is no warrant in Scripture for women ordained Officers."

Exercise: After reviewing the various terms (most definitions are taken from Van Horn), in the left-hand margin of the table below, mark "H" for home, "C" for church, or "W" for world to apply the scope of the qualification. Of course, there may be some overlap. Use this exercise to identify the primary scope of the qualification.

H/C/W?	KJV	Definition	NIV
	blameless	not open to censure	above reproach
	husband of one wife	having a faithful marriage	husband of one wife (a one woman-man)
	vigilant	sober minded, circumspect	temperate
	sober	one who follows sound reasoning	self-controlled
	of good behavior	moral excellence toward others	respectable
	given to hospitality	love of strangers	hospitable
	apt to teach	capable of grasping/instructing truth	able to teach
	not given to wine	not a drunkard	not given to drunkenness
	no striker	not physically belligerent	not violent
	patient	kind demeanor	gentle
	not a brawler	adverse to useless fighting	not quarrelsome
	not greedy of filthy lucre	not seeking shameful gain	not lover of money
	rules his own house well	has children nurtured	manage own family well
	not a novice	not a neophyte in the faith	not a recent convert
	good report: without	outsiders respect his life	good reputation

Additional from Titus 1

	not self-willed	not complacent or arrogant	not overbearing
	a lover of the good	lover of good	a lover of the good
	just	upright in his dealings	upright
	holy	faithful to honor God	holy
	holding fast to the Word	holding scriptural doctrine	hold the trustworthy message firmly; and able to correct those who do not.

For More Study: Samuel Miller on *The Ruling Elder*[2]
Samuel Miller (1769-1850) was a distinct link from the American colonial church to the Princeton School. Miller served as Pastor of Presbyterian Churches in New York for twenty years prior to being called to be the second professor at Princeton Seminary in 1813. After serving for nearly a generation as Professor of Ecclesiastical History and Church Government, Miller authored the classic text on the Ruling Elder entitled, *An Essay On The Warrant, Nature and Duties of the Office of the Ruling Elder, in the Presbyterian Church* in 1832.

---

2 This manual attempts to provide fuller information on certain critical subjects than others; thus several studies, extracts, or abridgments are imported for the candidate's ease of access. We also have attempted not to overburden the average student. If one is already familiar with the subjects marked by the vertical border, or if time does not permit, users may simply skip the sections marked with such border. We have found these helpful over the years and do recommend them to readers. The outside margins are also intentionally left wide for taking notes or other glosses.

The following is an abridgement, which appeared in *Paradigms in Polity* (available from The Covenant Foundation).3 This selection provides one of the best expositions available on the Biblical qualifications for that office. In addition to being very practical and devotional in its language, these pages could be useful information to inform a congregation as a whole about the office and duties of the Ruling Elder.

****

THE NATURE AND DUTIES OF THE OFFICE OF THE RULING ELDER

The essential character of the Officer of whom we speak is that of an *ecclesiastical ruler*. 'He that ruleth, let him do it with diligence,' is the summary of his appropriate functions, as laid down in Scripture. The *Teaching Elder* is, indeed, also a *ruler*. In addition to this, however, he is called to preach the gospel and administer [the] sacraments. But the particular department assigned to the Ruling Elder is to cooperate with the pastor in spiritual inspection and government. The Scriptures, as we have seen, speak not only of 'Pastors and Teacher,' but also of 'governments'—of 'Elders that rule well, but do not labor in the word and doctrine.'

There is an obvious analogy between the office of a ruler in the Church, and in the civil community. A Justice of the Peace in the latter has a wide and important range of duties. Besides the function which he discharges when called to take his part on the bench of the judicial court in which he presides, he may be, and often is, employed every day (though less publicly) in correcting abuses, compelling the fraudulent to do justice, restraining, arresting, and punishing criminals, and, in general, carrying into execution the laws formed to promote public tranquility and order, which he has sworn to administer faithfully.

Strikingly analogous to this are the duties of the ecclesiastical ruler. He has no power, indeed, to employ the secular arm in restraining or punishing offenders against the laws of Christ. The kingdom under which he acts, and the authority which he administers, are not of this world. He has, of course, no right to fine, imprison, or externally molest the most profligate offenders against the Church's purity or peace—unless they are guilty of what is technically called 'breaking the peace,' that is, violating the civil rights of others and thus rendering themselves liable to the penalty of the civil law. And even when this occurs, the ecclesiastical ruler, as such, has no right to proceed against the offender. He has no other than moral power [Cf. BCO 3; this is the heart of church power as ministerial and declarative]. He must apply to the civil magistrate for redress, who can only punish for breaking the civil law. Still there is an obvious analogy between his office and that of the civil magistrate. Both are alike an ordinance of God. Both are necessary to social order and comfort. And both are regulated by principles, which commend themselves to the good sense and the conscience of those who wish well to social happiness.

The Ruling Elder, no less than the Teaching Elder (or Pastor), is to be considered as acting under the authority of Christ in all that he rightfully does. If the office of which we speak was appointed in the apostolic Church by infinite wisdom—if it is an ordinance of Jesus Christ, just as much as that of the minister of the gospel—then the former, equally with the latter, is

Christ's Officer. He has a right to speak and act in his name; and though elected by the members of the Church (and representing them, in the exercise of ecclesiastical rule), yet he is not to be considered as deriving his authority to rule from them, any more than he who 'labors in the word and doctrine' derives his authority to preach and administer other ordinances from the people who make choice of him as their teacher and guide.

There is a reason to believe that some, even in the Presbyterian Church, take a different view of this subject. They regard the Teaching Elder as an Officer of Christ and listen to his official instructions as to those of a man appointed by him [Christ], and coming in his name. But with respect to the Ruling Elder, they are wont to regard him as one who holds an office instituted by human prudence alone, and, therefore, as standing on very different ground in the discharge of his official duties from that which is occupied by the 'ambassador of Christ.' This is undoubtedly an erroneous view of the subject, and a view which, so far as it prevails, is adapted to exert the most mischievous influence. The truth is, if the office of which we speak is of apostolic authority, we are just as much bound to sustain, honor, and obey the individual who fills it, and discharges its duties according to the Scriptures, as we are to submit to any other Officer or institution of our Divine Redeemer.

We are by no means, then, to consider Ruling Elders as a mere ecclesiastical *convenience*, or as a set of counsellors whom the wisdom of man alone has chosen, and who may, therefore, be reverenced and obeyed as little or as much as human caprice may think proper; but as bearing an office of divine appointment—as the 'ministers of God for good' to his Church—and whose lawful and regular acts ought to command our conscientious obedience.

The Ruling Elders of each Church are called to attend to a public and formal, or to a more private, sphere of duty.

With regard to the first, of the PUBLIC and FORMAL duties of their office, they form, in the Church to which they belong, a bench or judicial court, called among us the Church Session, and in some other Presbyterian denominations, the consistory: both expressions importing a body of ecclesiastical men sitting and acting together, as the representatives, and for the benefit of the Church. This body of Elders, with the Pastor at their head and presiding at their meetings, forms a judicial assembly, by which all the spiritual interests of the congregation are to be watched over, regulated, and authoritatively determined.

Although, in ordinary cases, the Pastor of the Church may be considered as vested with the right to decide whom he will invite to occupy his pulpit (either when he is present, or occasionally absent), yet, in cases of difficulty or delicacy—and especially when ministers of other denominations apply for the use of the pulpit—it is the prerogative of the Church Session to consider and decide on the application. And if there is any fixed difference of opinion between the Pastor and the other members of the Session in reference to this matter, it is the privilege and duty of either party to request advice of their Presbytery in the case.

In the Church Session, whether the Pastor is present and presiding or not, every member has an equal voice. The vote of the most humble and retiring Ruling Elder is of the same avail as that of his Minister, so that no Pastor can carry measure unless he can obtain the concurrence of a majority of the Eldership. And as the whole spiritual government of each Church is committed to its bench of Elders, the Session is competent to regulate every concern, and to correct everything which they consider amiss in the arrangements or affairs of the Church which admits of correction. Every individual of the Session is, of course, competent to propose any new service plan, or measure which he believes will be for the benefit of the congregation; and if a majority of the Elders concur with him in opinion, it may be adopted. If, in any case, however, there should be a difference of opinion between the Pastor and the Elders (as to the propriety or practicability of any measure proposed) and insisted on by the latter, there is an obvious and effectual constitutional remedy—a remedy, however, which ought to be resorted to with prudence, caution, and prayer. The opinions and wishes of the Pastor ought, undoubtedly, to be treated with the most respectful delicacy. Still, they ought not to be suffered, when it is possible to avoid it, to stand in the way of great and manifest good. When such an alternative occurs, the remedy alluded to may be applied. On an amicable reference to the Presbytery, that body may decide the case between the parties.

And as the members of the Church Session, whether assembled in their judicial capacity or not, are the Pastor's counsellors and colleagues in all matters relating to the spiritual rule of the Church, so it is their official duty to encourage, sustain and defend him in the faithful discharge of his duty. It is deplorable, when a minister is assailed for his fidelity by the profane or the worldly, if any portion of the Eldership either takes part against him, or shrinks from his active and determined defense. It is not meant, of course, that they are to consider themselves bound to sustain him in everything he may say or do, whether right or wrong; but that, when they really believe him to be faithful, both to truth and duty, they should feel it their duty to stand by him, to shield him from the arrows of the wicked, and to encourage him as far as he obeys Christ. . . .

But when it is considered that those who bear the office in question are called upon, in their turn, to sit in the highest judicatories of the Church, and there to take their part in deliberating and deciding on the most momentous questions which can arise in conducting ecclesiastical affairs; and when we reflect that they are called to deliberate and decide on the conformity of doctrines to the word of God—to assist, as judges, in the trial of heretics, and every class of offenders against the purity of the gospel, and to take care in their respective spheres that all the ordinances of Christ's house be preserved pure and entire—when, in a word, we recollect that they are ordained for the express purpose of overseeing and guarding the most precious concerns of the Church on earth (concerns which have a bearing not merely on the welfare of a single individual or congregation, but on the great interests of orthodoxy and piety among millions); we may surely conclude, without hesitation, that the office which they sustain is one, the importance of which can scarcely be over-rated; and that the estimate which is commonly made of its nature, duties, and responsibility is far, very far, from being adequate. . . .

Were the foregoing views of the nature and duties of the Elder's office generally adopted, duly appreciated, and faithfully carried out into practice, what a mighty change would be effected in our Zion! With what a different estimate of the obligations and responsibilities which rest upon them would the candidates for this office enter on their sacred work! And with what different feelings would the mass of the people, and especially all who love the cause of Christ, regard these spiritual counsellors and guides in their daily walks, and particularly in their friendly and official visits! This is a change most devoutly to be desired. The interests of the Church are more involved in the prevalence of just opinions and practice in reference to this office, than almost any other that can be named. Were every congregation, besides a wise, pious and faithful Pastor, furnished with eight or ten Elders, to cooperate with him in all his parochial labors, on the plan which has been sketched: men of wisdom, faith, prayer, and Christian activity; men willing to deny and exert themselves for the welfare of Zion; men alive to the importance of everything that relates to the orthodoxy, purity, order and spirituality of the Church, and ever on the watch for opportunities of doing good; men, in a word, willing to 'take the oversight' of the flock in the Lord, and to labor without ceasing for the promotion of its best interests. Were every Church furnished with a body of SUCH ELDERS, can anyone doubt that knowledge, order, piety, and growth in grace, as well as in numbers, would be as common in our Churches as the reverse is now the prevailing state of things, in consequence of the want of fidelity on the part of those who are nominally the overseers and guides of the flock?

QUALIFICATIONS FOR THE OFFICE OF AN ELDER

The account which has been given of the nature and duties of the office of Ruling Elder is adapted to reflect much on the qualifications by which he who bears it ought to be distinguished. Those who are called to such extensive, interesting and highly important spiritual duties—duties which enter so deeply into the comfort and edification of the Church of God—it surely requires no formal argument to show, ought to possess a character in some degree corresponding with the sphere in which they are appointed to move. There cannot be a plainer dictate of common sense. Yet to attempt a brief sketch of the more important of the qualifications demanded for this office may not be altogether unprofitable. . . .

The design of appointing persons to the office of Ruling Elder is not to pay them a compliment; not to give them an opportunity of figuring as speakers in judicatories; not to create the pageants of ecclesiastical ceremony; but to secure able, faithful and truly devoted counsellors and rulers of the Church—to obtain wise and efficient guides, who shall not only go along with the flock in their journey heavenward, but GO BEFORE THEM in everything that pertains to Christian duty.

It cannot be doubted, indeed, that every member of the Christian Church is bound to exhibit a holy, devout and exemplary life; to have his mind well stored with religious knowledge. . . . As they occupy a place of more honor and authority than the other members of the Church, so they occupy a station of greater responsibility. The eyes of hundreds will be upon them as Elders, which were not upon them as private Christians. Their brethren and sisters over whom they are placed in the Lord will naturally look up to them for advice, for instruction, for aid in the spiritual life, and for a shining example. The expectation is reasonable and ought not to be disappointed. The qualifications of Elders, therefore, ought, in some measure, to correspond with it.

1. An Elder, then, ought, first of all, to be A MAN OF UNFEIGNED AND APPROVED PIETY. It is to be regretted when the piety of any member of the Church is doubtful or evidently feeble and wavering. It is deplorable when any who name the name of Christ manifest so much indecision in their profession; so much timidity and unsteadiness in their resistance to error and sin; so much conformity to the world; and so little of that undaunted, ardent, and thorough adherence to their professed principles—as to leave it dubious with many whether they are 'on the Lord's side' or not. But how much more deplorable when anything of this kind appears in those who are appointed to watch, to preside, and to exert an extensive

influence over a portion of the family of Christ! What is to be expected when the 'watchmen on the walls of Zion'—for such Ruling Elders are undoubtedly to be regarded—appear as beacons to warn private Christians of what ought to be avoided, rather than a models to guide, to attract, and to cheer them on to all that is spiritual, and holy, and becoming the gospel?

Can he who is either destitute of piety, or who has but a small portion of it, engage in the arduous and deeply spiritual duties of the Ruling Elder, with comfort to himself, or with any reasonable hope of success? It cannot be supposed. To fit ecclesiastical rulers for acting in their appropriate character, and for performing the work which pertains to it with cordial diligence, faithfulness and perseverance, will require cordial and decisive attachment to the service of the Church; minds intent upon the work; hearts filled with love to Jesus, and to the souls of men, and 'preferring Jerusalem above their chief joy.' Unless they are animated with this affectionate interest in their work; unless they're habitually impelled by an enlightened and cordial attachment to the great cause in which they are engaged; they will soon become weary of their arduous and self-denying labors; they will find waiting on the flock, visiting and praying with the sick, instructing the serious and inquiring, correcting the disorderly, watching over the spiritual interests of all, and attending the various judicatories of the Church an irksome task.

But with such a zeal as has been described, they will be ready to contend for the truth, to engage in the most self-denying duties, nay, to 'spend and be spent' for Christ. To promote the best interests of Zion will be their 'meat and drink.' No labors, no trials, no difficulties will move them; neither will they 'count their lives dear unto themselves,' so that they may 'finish their course with joy, and accomplish the work which they have received of the Lord Jesus.' A few such Elders in every Church would, with divine blessing, do more to silence infidelity—to strike even the scorner dumb—to promote the triumph of gospel truth, and to rouse, sustain and bear forward the cause of vital piety, than hundreds of those Ministers and Elders who act as if they supposed that supplying the little details of ecclesiastical formality was the whole purpose of their official appointment. And, in truth, we have no reason to expect, in general, that the piety of the mass of members in any Church will rise much higher than that of their rulers and guides. Where the latter are either lifeless formalists or, at best, but 'babes in Christ,' we shall rarely find many under their care of more vitality or of superior stature.

2.   Next to piety, it is important that a Ruling Elder be possessed of GOOD SENSE AND SOUND JUDGMENT. Without this he will be wholly unfit to act in the various difficult and delicate cases which may arise in the discharge of his duty. A man of a weak and childish mind, however fervent his piety, is by no means adapted to the station of an ecclesiastical ruler, counsellor and guide. He who bears the office in question is called to have intercourse with all classes of people, to engage in the most arduous and trying duties, and to deliberate and decide on some of the most perplexing questions that can come before the human mind. Can it be doubted that good sense and solid judgment are indispensable to the due discharge of such official work as this? How would a judge on the bench, or a magistrate in his office, be likely to get along without this qualification? Much more important is it, if possible, that the ecclesiastical ruler be enlightened and judicious: because he deliberates and decides on more momentous subjects, and because he has no other than moral power with which to enforce his decisions. Moses, therefore, spoke the language of good sense, as well as of inspired wisdom,

when he said to the people of Israel (Deut. 1:13): 'Take ye WISE MEN, AND UNDERSTANDING, and known among your tribes, and I will make them rulers over you.' This point, indeed, it would seem, can scarcely be made more plain than common sense makes it; and might, therefore, be considered as foreclosing all illustration, did not some Churches appear disposed to make the experiment, how far infinite wisdom is to be believed when it pronounces, by the Prophet, a woe against those who make choice of 'babes to rule over them.'

3. A Ruling Elder ought to be SOUND IN THE FAITH AND WELL INFORMED IN RELATION TO GOSPEL TRUTH. The Elder who is not orthodox in his creed, instead of contributing, as he ought, to build up the Church in the knowledge and love of the truth, will, of course, be the means of scattering error as far as his influence extends. And he who is not well informed on the subject of Christian doctrine will not know whether he is promoting the one or the other. Accordingly, when this class of Officers is ordained in our Church, we call upon them to do what we do not require from the private members of the Church, viz., solemnly and publicly to adopt the Confession of Faith 'as containing the system of doctrine taught in the Holy Scriptures.' When this is considered; and also that they are expected to be, to a certain extent, instructors and guides in divine things to many of those committed to their oversight; and, above all, that they will be often called to deliberate on charges of heresy, as well as immorality; and to sit in judgment on the doctrinal belief not only of candidates for admission into the Church as private members, but also on cases of alleged aberration from the truth in ministers of the gospel; the necessity of their being 'sound in the faith,' and of their having enlightened and clear views of the system of revealed truth is too plain to need argument for its support.

The truth is, the Ruling Elder who is active, zealous and faithful, will have occasion almost every day to discriminate between truth and error; to act as a guardian of the Church's orthodoxy; to pass his judgment, either privately or judicially, on real or supposed departures from it; and to instruct the inexperienced and the doubting in the great doctrines of our holy religion. And although all Elders are not expected to be profound theologians (any more than all Ministers), yet that the former, as well as the latter, should have a general and accurate acquaintance with the gospel system, and to be ready to defend its leading doctrines by a ready, pertinent, and conclusive reference to scriptural testimony, and thus able to 'separate between the precious and the vile' (in theory as well as in practice), is surely as little as can possibly be demanded of those who are placed as leaders and guides in the house of God.

4. Again, an Elder ought to be a man of EMINENT PRUDENCE. By prudence here is, of course, not meant that spurious characteristic which calls itself by this name, but which ought rather to be called timidity or a criminal shrinking from duty, on the plea that 'there is a lion in the way.' Yet, while we condemn this as unworthy of a Christian, and especially unworthy of a Christian counsellor and ruler, there is a prudence which is genuine and greatly to be coveted. This is no other than practical Christian wisdom, which not only discerns what is right, but also adopts the best mode of doing it—which is not at all inconsistent with firmness and the highest moral courage, but which regulates and directs it.

It has been often observed that there is a right and a wrong way of doing the best things. The thing done may be excellent in itself, but may be done in a manner, at a time, and attended with circumstances which will be likely to disgust and repel, and thus prevent all benefit. Hence a man who is characteristically eccentric, undignified, rash, precipitate, or indiscreetly talkative, ought by no means to be selected as an ecclesiastical ruler. He will probably do more mischief than good, will generally create more divisions than he heals, and will rather generate offenses than remove them. Perhaps there is no situation in human society which more imperiously calls for delicacy, caution, reserve, and the most vigilant discretion, than that of an ecclesiastical ruler. If popular rumor begins to charge a Church member with some delinquency, either in faith or practice, let one of the Elders—under the notion of being faithful—implicitly credit the story, go about making inquiries respecting its truth, winking and insinuating, and thus contributing to extend its circulation; and however pure his motive, he may, before he is aware, implicate himself in the charge of slander and become so situated in respect to the supposed culprit, as to render it altogether improper that he should sit in judgment on his case. The maxim of the wise man—'be swift to hear, slow to speak, slow to wrath'—applies to every human being, especially to every professing Christian, but above all to everyone who is appointed to maintain truth, order, purity, peace and love in the Church of God.

It requires much prudence to judge when it is proper to commence the exercise of discipline against a supposed offender. Discipline is an important, nay, a vital matter in the Christian Church. But it may be commenced indiscreetly, vexatiously, when that which is alleged cannot be shown to be an offense against the divine law—or when, though really a censurable offense, there is no probability that it can be proved. To attempt the exercise of discipline in such cases is to disgrace it—to convert it from one of the most important means of grace to an instrument of rashness, petulance, and childish precipitancy. Often, very often, has the very name of discipline been rendered odious, the peace of families and neighborhoods grievously disturbed, the influence of ecclesiastical judicatories destroyed, and the cause of religion deeply wounded, by judicial proceedings which ought either never to have been commenced, or to which the smallest measure of prudence would have given a very different direction.

The importance of the subject constrains me to add that prudence, much prudence, is also imperiously demanded in the exercise of dignified and cautious reserve while ecclesiastical process is pending. One great reason why it is thought better by Presbyterians to exercise discipline by a bench of wise and pious ecclesiastical Senators, than by a vote of the whole body of Church members, is that the public discussion and decision of many things concerning personal character—which the exercise of discipline necessarily discloses respecting others (as well as the culprit)—is adapted in many cases to do more harm than good, especially before the process is closed. To guard against this evil, it is very important that the Elders carefully avoid all unseasonable disclosures in respect to the business, which may be at any time before the Session. Until they have done what shall be deemed proper in a delicate case, it is surely unwise, by thoughtless blabbing, to throw obstacles in their own way, and perhaps to defeat the whole purpose which they have in view. Yet how often, by one imprudent violation of this plain rule, has the discipline of the Church been discarded or frustrated, and the character of those who administered it exposed to ridicule?

These, and similar considerations, serve clearly to show that no degree of piety can supercede the necessity of prudence in ecclesiastical rulers, and that, of all characters in a congregation, an indiscreet, meddling, garrulous, gossiping, tattling Elder is one of the most pestiferous. . . .

The qualification of which we speak has been in all ages, and from the nature of the case must ever be, of inestimable importance in every ruler and guide of the Church. But we may venture to pronounce that it never was so important to the Church that she should have such rulers as it is at the present day. Now that she is awaking from her slumber, and arousing to a sense of her long forgotten obligations; now that she is, as we hope, arising from the dust, and 'putting on her beautiful garments,' and looking abroad in the length and breadth of all those conquests which have been promised her by her Almighty Head; now that all her resources, physical and moral, are called for in every direction, with an emphasis and a solemnity never before equaled; is it not manifest that all who, in such a stage of her course, undertake to be her counsellors and guides, ought to be neither drones nor cowards—neither parsimonious of labor and sacrifice, nor disposed to sit down contented with small acquisitions?

Ruling Elders at the present day have, perhaps, an opportunity of serving the Church more extensively and effectually than every before. How desirable and important, then, that they have a heart in some measure commensurate with the calls and opportunities of the day in which their lot is cast! How desirable that they cherish those enlarged and liberal views, both of duty and of effort, which become those who are called to act a conspicuous and interesting part in a cause which is dear to all holy beings! So important is this, that it is probable we shall generally find that in liberality of contribution to various objects of Christian effort, and in enlargement of mind to desire and seek the extension of the Redeemer's kingdom, the mass of the members of any Church may commonly be graduated by the character of their Elders. If the leaders and guides of the Church are destitute of public spirit—and are not found taking the lead in large plans, labors and sacrifices for extending the reign of knowledge, truth and righteousness—it will be strange indeed if a more enlarged spirit is found prevailing among the generality of their fellow members.

7. The last qualification on which I shall dwell, as important in the office before us, is ARDENT ZEAL AND A SPIRIT OF IMPORTUNATE PRAYER. Large views and liberal plans and donations will not answer without this. The truth is, the Church of God has the most serious and unceasing obstacles to encounter in every step of her progress. As long as she is faithful, her course is never smooth or unobstructed. In maintaining truth, in guarding the claims of gospel holiness, and in sustaining discipline, the enmity of the human heart will not fail to manifest itself, and to offer more or less resistance to that which is good. The worldly and profane will ever be found in the ranks of determined opposition. And alas! that some who bear the name of Christ are not infrequently found in the same ranks—thus grieving the hearts and trying the patience of those who are called to act as the representatives and leaders of the Church. To meet and overcome difficulties of this kind requires all the fixedness of purpose, and all the zeal in the service of Christ, which his most devoted servants can bring to their work.

Besides all this, there is much in the daily duties of the Ruling Elder which puts to a very serious test all his devotedness to the cause of his Master. He is called to live like a Minister of the gospel, in the very atmosphere of prayer and religious conversation. In the chamber of the sick and dying; in conversing with the anxious inquirer, and the perplexed or desponding believer; in the private circle, and in the social meeting for prayer; abroad and at home, in the house and by the way; it must be 'his meat and drink' to be found ministering to the best interests of his fellow men. So that if he has but little zeal, but little taste or prayer, but little anxiety for the welfare of immortal souls, he will not—he cannot—enter with proper feeling into his appropriate employments. But if he is animated with a proper spirit, he will find it pleasant to be thus employed. Instead of shunning scenes and opportunities of usefulness, he will diligently seek them. And instead of finding them wearisome, he will feel no happiness more pure and rich than that which he experiences in such occupations as these.

It is evident, then, not only that the ecclesiastical ruler ought to have unfeigned piety, but that his piety ought to be of that decisive character, and accompanied with that fervent zeal, which bears its possessor forward without weariness in the discharge of self-denying duties. The higher the degree in which he possesses this characteristic—provided it is accompanied with wisdom, prudence and a knowledge of human nature—the greater will probably be his usefulness in the Church which he serves; and the greater, assuredly, will be his own personal enjoyment in rendering that service.

It is more than possible that this view of the qualifications proper for the office which we are considering, may cause some, when solicited to undertake it, to draw back, under the conscientious impression that they have not the characteristics which are essential to the faithful discharge of its duties. And it would be wrong to say that there are not some cases in which such an impression ought to be admitted. There can be no doubt that there are those who bear this office who ought never to have accepted it. To this class, unquestionably, belong all those who have no taste for the appropriate duties of the office, and who do not resolve sedulously and faithfully to perform them.

But let no humble devoted follower of Jesus Christ, who truly desires to serve and glorify him, and who is willing, from the heart, to do all that God shall enable him for the promotion of the Redeemer's kingdom—let not him be deterred, by the representation which has been given, from accepting the office, if called to it by his Christian brethren. The deeper his sense of his own unfitness, the more likely will he be to apply unceasingly and importunately for heavenly aid; and the nearer he lives to the throne of grace, the more largely will he partake of that wisdom and strength which he needs. There are, no doubt, some (as we have said) who are really unqualified for this office; but in general, it may be maintained that those who have the deepest impression of the importance and arduousness of its duties, and of their own want of adequate qualifications, are far better prepared for those duties than such as advance to the discharge of them with unwavering confidence and self-complacency.

****

Practical Assessments:

Several practical questions are now appropriate. Most of these below are taken (with some slight modifications; used with permission) from the *Officer Training Manual* of the First Presbyterian Church, Jackson, Mississippi (Session Three, p. 10). Several areas of spiritual life are probed.

1.   *In the Area of Personal Faith*
     a.   Do you believe in the necessity of regeneration? Have you been born anew?
     b.   Do you know God? Is your trust in Christ alone? Is your life God-centered?
     c.   Do you use the means of growth such as prayer and Bible study on your own regularly?

2. *In the Area of Support of the Program of the Church*
   a. Will you attend Sunday School?
   b. Will you attend the regular worship services of the Church?
   c. Will you attend the regular meetings for your office?
3. *In the Area of Stewardship*
   a. Do you believe in tithing and make a sincere effort to do so?
   b. Will you support the church budget as a priority of your giving?
   c. Will you give of your time as needed to serve and lead the church?
4. *In the Area of Cooperation*
   a. Are you in good relations with the church and its members?
   b. Are you in good relations with the other Officers?
   c. Are you in good relations with the Pastor?
5. *In the Area of Seeking the Purity, Peace, and Unity of the Church*
   a. Will you try to put down murmurings and complainings? Can you face them frankly, deal with them fairly, and then stand on principle with your fellow Officers?
   b. Will you lovingly follow Christ's commands to disciple and discipline members?
   c. Can you honestly answer the ordinations vows (BCO 24-5) in the affirmative?
6. *In the Area of Family Life*
   a. Do you have domestic troubles that could bring disrepute to the church?
   b. Have you ever been divorced or abusive in marriage? Please explain.
   c. Do you and your wife know how to hold your tongue against needlessly spreading gossip or talking critically about others?
   d. Are you involved in financial difficulties that might embarrass the church?
   e. Do you make an effort at having family devotions?
   f. Do you control your own household as specified in 1 Tim. 3:4-5?
7. *In the Area of Social Life*
   a. Do others think you drink to excess?
   b. Have you seriously considered the danger of being a stumbling block, and are you committed to providing exemplary conduct in keeping with your office?
   c. To the best of your ability, will you keep the Lord's Day?

Of course, each examining Session may wish to probe other questions, but these should lead to fruitful discussions and mutual sharing.

Preview: Different Forms of Church Government

Our understanding of the offices of Elder and Deacon are further clarified as we briefly compare the different forms of church government. There are three major forms of government, and in each the role for Officers is different. More will be said on this when we study the *Book of Church Order*, but for now let two things suffice: (1) an introduction to the different options of ecclesiastical government; and (2) a hypothesis that the office of Elder is the same as that of overseer.

The main forms of government in different denominations are:
   (1) **Episcopal (hierarchical).** All of these have a triangular-shaped management pyramid, with the higher office distinct and superior to the lower. Typical of this are:

      a. Roman Catholic
      b. Anglican
      c. Methodist
(2) Presbyterian (mediating).
(3) **Congregational (lowerarchical).** Typical of this are:
      a. Baptist
      b. Congregational
      c. Independent/non-denominational
      d. Pentecostal

The Civil Analogue for each of these may be charted as follows:

Episcopal	Monarchical
Presbyterian	Republican (federalist, representative, aristocratic)
Congregational	Democratic

Homework Assignment:
1. Make a summary list of duties and attitudes that belong to your office. How do you fit? What should you be attending to in order to grow in these areas?
2. What areas of character or relationship do you need to attend to in order to prepare yourself to assume office?
3. Read the WCF and make two lists:
    a. Points where you definitely do not agree at present (think of these as 'blood pressure' points that may evoke a strong reaction from you).
    b. Points that are new or that you are not sure that you agree with.

Next: An Introduction to our Doctrinal Standards.

Other resources: A reliable and fine exposition of our faith, complete with study questions and scripture references is: G. I. Williamson, *The Westminster Confession of Faith for Study Classes (P&R, 1964).*

For More Study: The following books are thorough, and eager candidates may wish to consult them, especially in view of how serious and long-lasting is the call to Office.

- *The Ruling Elder* by Samuel Miller (orig. 1832, reprinted by Presbyterian Heritage Publications, P. O. Box 180922, Dallas, TX 75218); an excerpt of this appears in my *Paradigms in Polity* (available from The Covenant Foundation, 648 Goldenwood Court, Powder Springs, GA 30127; pp 422-435).

- *The Elder and his Work* by David Dickson (orig. 1883, reprinted by Presbyterian Heritage Publications, P. O. Box 180922, Dallas, TX 75218).

- *The Elders of the Church* by Lawrence R. Eyres (Philadelphia, PA: Presbyterian and Reformed, 1975).

- *The Elders Handbook: A Practical Guide for Church Leaders* by Gerard Berghoef and Lester De Koster (Grand Rapids, MI: Christian's Library Press, 1979).

- *Elders as Shepherds of the Church of God* by Mark E. Ross (an excellent, short pamphlet that is available from First Presbyterian Church, 1324 Marion Street, Columbia, SC 29201; fax = 803-799-9172).
- *The Role of the Deacons in the Overall Mission of the Church* by Mark E. Ross (an excellent, short pamphlet available from First Presbyterian Church, 1324 Marion Street, Columbia, SC 29201; fax = 803-799-9172).
- *Jus Divinum*, David W. Hall, ed. (Dallas, TX: Naphtali Press, 1994; available from The Covenant Foundation, 648 Goldenwood Court, Powder Springs, GA 30127)

Note: Other fine articles, including a fuller one by Mark Ross on the Ruling Elder, are included in an issue *Faith and Practice*, vol. 3, no. 1 (Spring 1997). This issue is available from the editor at 2711-C Pinedale Rd., Greensboro, NC 27408 (Phone = 910-545-8606).

Session #1a: Holding Fast to Truth

Over the next several sessions, we will explore and discuss various topics addressed by the WCF. Prior to that, however, it may help to have some introduction into the necessity of confessing in general and the background of our particular confessional statement.

The Necessity and Propriety of Doctrine and Confessions

A first consideration is the necessity of confessing or publicly agreeing (the NT word for "confess" mean to say the same words) to fixed doctrine. Although it has become commonplace to hear well-meaning Christians announce that they hold to "No creed but Christ, no book but the Bible," that is virtually impossible to practice. The reality is that all Christians hold to certain doctrinal sets; the only question is which are more or less in keeping with the Scriptures. Holding to doctrine is not bad, unless the doctrine itself is unbiblical.

Indeed, we can witness doctrine as a mainstay of the ancient and early church. That doctrine is not a bad word may be seen from 1 Timothy 4:16, where Paul wrote to a church leader, urging him to watch his life and doctrine closely. He promised that hearers would be saved if that were done; one certainly would not, therefore, wish to do something adversarial to the salvation of hearers. Later in Titus 1:9 Paul also stipulated that the Elder should hold firmly to sound doctrine and be able to refute those who did not. Some public recognition of sound doctrine was already presupposed in the early church prior to 65 AD. That maturity and ability is also set forth as a qualification for an Elder in 1 Timothy 3:9. Officers of Christ's church must know scriptural doctrine, be able to point church members to short, previous codifications of it, and be trained in correcting unsound doctrine. That cannot happen if doctrine is not fixed, set, and recognized. Church members should also realize that the original word for doctrine is "teaching."

As the New Testament (henceforth NT) unfolds, it is not one faith among many, or "a faith," or whatever people sincerely hold to that is defended. Instead, it is "the faith." The following passages make it clear that "the faith" was a set of revealed truth:

- 1 Timothy 1:19
- 1 Timothy 4:1
- 1 Timothy 4:6
- 1 Timothy 4:16
- Jude 3, which speaks of "the faith, which was handed down once and for all to all the saints."

These verses make it clear that "the faith" is not evolving, changing, and in need of constant revision. God, in his mercy, has not founded the church on an imperfect platform that needs serial upgrades. One of our strengths to people looking for lasting institutions is to be able to point them to a church that has worked through doctrine, and that doctrine will not change between grandparents and their great-grandchildren. Few churches can offer that strength.

Doctrine is a strength, as long as it is biblical. And the WCF is one of the most biblical confessions ever crafted. It is revered, not for its own authority or insightfulness, but precisely because it so closely follows biblical formulation and, in many cases, actual biblical phraseology.

Furthermore, both testaments of Scripture evidence the use of creedal summaries. The well-known *Shema* in Deuteronomy 6:4-5 was used as a repetitive, summary of truth. Israel was to rehearse the nature of God as one and worthy of all our focus. Jesus himself asked the disciples to make confessions, and Peter responded, on one particular occasion, with uncommon perception. In Matthew 16, Peter confessed that Christ was the Son of God, and Jesus blessed him for that correct confession. Romans 10:9 commends confessing with our mouths, after we have believed in our hearts, that Jesus Christ is Lord. Later, 1 Corinthians 12:3 exhibits what may be the briefest NT confessional summary: "Jesus is Lord." That phrase is alluded to in Philippians 2:5-11, which refers to every knee bowing and every tongue confessing that "Jesus Christ is Lord." Apparently, fixed articles of belief were recognized and employed as standards of truth by the middle of the first century. One particularly full summary of Christian truth is exhibited in 1 Timothy 3:16. That short, creedal summary focuses on the life of Christ and his subsequent resurrection and ascension. With short clauses, much like the later Apostles' Creed, that verse summarizes the life and significance of Christ for all time. Moreover, Paul's customary use of the term, "the faithful sayings" (see 1 Tim. 4:9; 2 Tim. 2:11-13) further underscores that certain matters of truth were considered settled and fixed for all believers in all place and all times. That same attitude was present in the authors who gathered to study and express the faith finally handed down in the WCF.

Dr. George W. Knight commented in an article as follows:

> The statement of scriptural truths in confessional form has been commonly practiced in the Christian Church from a very early date, as if evidenced by the quite ancient Apostles' Creed. But the practice of having a summary of scriptural truths to which confession is made or to which Officers are to hold fast finds its origin in the pages of the New Testament itself. [He then lists Romans 10:9, 1 Corinthians 12:3 and 1 Timothy 3:16 as examples.] Also in the pages of the New Testament we see an insistence that the leaders of the church must embrace these statements of the church setting forth the teaching of the Scripture. Just as Paul has commended the previously mentioned "faithful words" or "sayings" so also he urges the Elder/bishop to hold "fast the faithful word which is in accordance with this teaching" (Titus 1:9). . . . This phenomenon of having statements setting forth the teaching of Scripture has become commonplace among the churches of the Reformation. The practice of requiring a prospective Officer to adopt the confessional standards as his own to demonstrate to the church his understanding of and commitment to the doctrines taught by Scripture arose as a method of protecting the Faith.

Far from being forbidden, then, holding to fixed confessions is little more than following the NT pattern. And the WCF never confuses its insights with scriptural inspiration. In its maiden chapter, it humbly confesses the limitation to creeds (WCF 1:10; see also WCF 31:3-4) and urges its readers to hold to *sola scriptura*.

Background of the Westminster Assembly

Throughout its history, the church developed a habit of confessing its faith, particularly in times of persecution and challenge. The church quickly codified the patterns of holding to fixed doctrinal formularies, as can be seen by the continuation of the Apostles' Creed, the Nicene Creed, the Athanasian Creed, and others (These are contained in Terry L. Johnson's, *Leading in Worship*—which may be ordered from: www.ipcsav.org—along with other creeds that are useful for public worship). Still, the church normally has crafted more creeds when under duress than at times of peace.

It should not be surprising that many creeds and confessions were adopted at and following the Reformation. Approximately one hundred years lapsed between Calvin's ministry in Geneva (he first arrived in 1536) and the convening of the Westminster Assembly (1643). During that century, all Protestant groups (and various Catholic orders, too) drafted up-to-date confessions, creeds, or catechisms to clarify and reinforce their biblical convictions. Calvinists on the Continent led the way, and English (including the Scots in the north) Puritans—some of whom later became the founders of America—added and clarified their faith as well. More Protestant creeds were written during that century than any other. The reason was because the faith was advancing (actually, returning to the true plumb-line of Scripture), and error (chiefly Roman Catholicism but also Anabaptist excesses) had to be denounced.

The immediate English context will also help students understand aspects of the WCF.[4] Charles I was the king, and by the late 1630s, he found himself surrounded by near-revolt. After the Reformation faith came to England, it began to root and spread. It nearly—one historian estimated that England was within an eyelash of becoming a Presbyterian (instead of Anglican) establishment—took over one of the most dominant and free nations in the world at the time. Most of Charles' opponents in Parliament shared Puritan, or at least anti-monarchical, sentiments. England was on the verge of a civil war in the early 1640s. Both opposing parties, the King and Parliament, hoped to use the church to bring some measure of peace or stability to the nation. In fact, one of the reasons (see below) that the Westminster Assembly was convened was the hope that the biblical religion could unite citizens in England, Scotland, and Ireland. Parliament, as one might infer, was very supportive of this idea. Indeed, as early as 1640, bills passed Parliament calling for a convening of 'divines' to attempt at least to settle the religious quarreling (See *To Glorify and Enjoy God*, pp 267-299; for more details on the Parliamentary legislation prior to the meeting of the Westminster Assembly).

After much wrangling and many broken promises (Charles vetoed bills to convene an assembly at least twice in 1641 and 1642), finally the Parliament prevailed, and on June 12, 1643 the Assembly was formally approved; Charles was quick to denounce it within 10 days.

The chronological table below sets forth some of the more important dates of the Assembly by the year. A select bibliography follows.

---

4 Portions of this discussion are taken from my *Windows on Westminster*, Copyright © 1993, Great Commission Publications, Suwanee, Georgia; used with permission.

Westminster Assembly Chronology of Important Dates

June 12, 1643	Ordinance by Parliament to call the Assembly
June 22, 1643	Proclamation by King prohibiting meeting for the stated purposes
July 1, 1643	Convening of Assembly by Parliament
July 12 - Oct. 12	Committees work on Re-drafting first fifteen of *Thirty-Nine Articles*
Aug. 17, 1643	Assembly approved in principle the Solemn League and Covenant
Sept. 15, 1643	Scottish Commissioners arrive
Sept. 25, 1643	Pledge to keep Solemn League and Covenant by Commons
Oct. 12, 1643	Parliament directs Assembly to work on government; cessation of revision of *Thirty-Nine Articles.*
Oct. 15, 1643	House of Lords adopts Solemn League and Covenant
April 22, 1644	Directory for Ordination presented to Parliament
May 24, 1644	Debate begun on Directory for Public Worship
Aug. 20, 1644	Appointment of Committee for Confession of Faith
Nov. 8, 1644	Form of Government sent to Parliament
Dec. 27, 1644	Directory for Public Worship presented to Parliament.
Jan. 3, 1645	Directory for Public Worship approved by Commons
Jan. 23, 1645	Resolution passed Commons, supporting presbyterianism in substance
Feb. 7, 1645	Catechism Committee Augmented
May 12, 1645	Report by Confession Committee
July 7, 1645	Assembly refers Directory For Church Government
Sept. 12, 1645	Rous's Psalms approved by Assembly
April 30, 1646	Committee from Commons proposes governmental queries
July 19, 1646	Death of Twisse; new moderator is Herle
Dec. 4, 1646	Confession of Faith (absent of Scripture proofs) presented to Commons (Dec. 3rd, according to Hetherington)
April 15, 1647	Debate begun on Larger Catechism
April 29, 1647	Confession of Faith (with Scriptures) presented to Commons
May 11, 1647	Confession sent to printer, after having been reviewed by other main committees.
Aug. 5, 1647	Debate begun on Shorter Catechism
Oct. 15, 1647	Larger Catechism completed and submitted to Parliament
Nov. 25, 1647	Shorter Catechism presented to Commons
March 22, 1648	House of Commons approved Confession
April 14, 1648	Catechisms (with Scriptures) presented to Parliament.
June 20, 1648	House of Lords approved Confession
July 24, 1648	Larger Catechism approved by House of Commons (never approved by Lords)
Sept. 25, 1648	Parliament approves Shorter Catechism
Feb. 7, 1649	Both Catechisms ratified by Scottish Estates of Parliament (after having been approved by the Scottish General Assembly, earlier in the summer of 1648)
Feb. 22, 1649	Last numbered Session; Adjournment
Mar. 25, 1652	Last sitting of Assembly Committee for Examining Ministers.

****

Select Bibliography

- Beveridge, William, *A Short History of the Westminster Assembly* (Edinburgh: T and T Clark, 1904 [reprinted by A Press [Greenville, SC], 1991).

- Carruthers, Samuel, *The Everyday Work of the Westminster Assembly* (London: Presbyterian Historical Society, 1943).

- Carson, John L. and David W. Hall, *To Glorify and Enjoy God: A Commemoration of the Westminster Assembly* (Edinburgh: Banner of Truth Trust, 1994).

- Gillespie, George, *The Works of George Gillespie* (Vol. II), (Edmonton, AB: Still Waters Revival Books, 1991).

- Hall, Peter, ed. *The Harmony of Protestant Confessions* (Edmonton, AB: Still Waters Revival Books, 1992).

- Hetherington, William M., *History of the Westminster Assembly of Divines* (Edmonton, AB: Still Waters Revival Books, 1991).

- Holley, Larry, *The Divines of the Westminster Assembly: A Study of Puritanism and Parliament* (New Haven, CT: Yale University Press, 1979).

- Mitchell, Alexander F., *The Westminster Assembly: Its History and Standards* (Edmonton, AB: Still Waters Revival Books, 1992).

- Mitchell, Alexander F. and Struthers, John, *Minutes of the Sessions of the Westminster Assembly of Divines* (Edinburgh: William Blackwood and Sons, 1874).

- Mitchell, A. W., *A History of the Westminster Assembly of Divines* (Philadelphia: Presbyterian Board of Publication, 1841).

- Patton, Francis, *The Genesis of the Westminster Assembly* (Richmond, VA: Presbyterian Committee of Publication, 1889).

- Paul, Robert F., *The Assembly of the Lord* (Edinburgh: T and T Clark, 1985).

- Reid, James, *The Memoirs of the Westminster Divines* (Edinburgh: Banner of Truth Trust, reprinted 1982 {Orig. in 1811}).

- Roberts, William Henry, ed., *Addresses at the Celebration of the Two-Hundred and Fiftieth Anniversary of the Westminster Assembly* (Philadelphia: Presbyterian Board of Publication, 1898).

- Shedd, William G. T., *Calvinism: Pure and Mixed* (Edinburgh: Banner of Truth, 1986).

- Smith, J. Henry, ed., *Memorial Volume of the Westminster Assembly, 1647-1897* (Richmond, VA: The Presbyterian Committee of Publication, 1897).

- Smyth, Thomas, "History of the Westminster Assembly" in *The Works of Thomas Smyth* (Columbia, SC: Bryan Publishing, 1908).

- Symington, William, "Historical Sketch of the Westminster Assembly of Divines" in *Commemoration of the Bicentenary of the Westminster Divines* (Glasgow, 1843).

- Warfield, Benjamin B., *The Westminster Assembly and Its Work* (Edmonton, AB: Still Waters Revival Books, 1991).

FYI Study *A Brief Political, Social, and Religious History of the Beginning of the Westminster Assembly* (optional; if the reader does not desire this much information on this

---

5 Portions of this discussion are taken from my *Windows on Westminster*, Copyright © 1993, Great Commission Publications, Suwanee, Georgia; used with permission.

particular subject, he may skip down to "The Importance and Relevance of the Westminster Confession" by John Murray)

Great events never arise in a vacuum.5 Most of us learn that it is quite an unsophisticated view of any epoch of history to think of it as arising out of nowhere, as if people and events have no preludes. Likewise, the Westminster Assembly did not merely begin on July 1, 1643. It had a considerable pre-history and a historic development, which in many ways shaped its outcomes.

The Westminster Assembly met in a day, which was much different from our own. Only recently had North America been colonized. A century and a half before the United States Constitution, what is now America was more of a wilderness, brimming with unconquered territories. Prior to the modern age of rights, there had been few advances in liberty, and the temper of the times was much closer to medieval chivalry, than to our modern rights-oriented societies. Although only three hundred and fifty years separate us, in many ways these Assembly-men ('divines' as they were called in their day because they studied divinity or theology) were closer in mindset to biblical times than they are to us today. So some effort to understand their ways and background is necessary.

The Westminster Assembly's origination, as noted above, finds its roots extending back as far as the Reformation. A millennium and a half after our Lord's resurrection, his visible church had become quite corrupt. Over the centuries, the church had taken increasingly large steps away from biblical teaching. God would raise up a few Reformers to help call the church back to her center-line. Even before Martin Luther's notorious posting of *The Ninety-Five Theses* (1517), other lesser known Reformers sought to return the church to the straight and narrow, many even losing their lives having been branded as heretics.

Of course the leading reformers were Luther in Germany, John Calvin (1509-1564) and William Farel in Switzerland, and John Knox in Scotland. These first generation Reformers paved the way for later developments, refinements, and doctrinal statements, as they arrived at non-Romanist forms of Christian belief. While most of the core theological truths were agreed upon, a Reformed consensus was not found on all other practical questions. Despite attempts to unify this Reformed-Protestant movement, various leaders of the Reformation had determinative influence over the varieties of Protestantism in different countries. Hence the Reformed churches in France, Holland, Hungary, England, and Scotland were each a little unique.

John Knox—who is often associated with the refinement of Presbyterian government—upon exile from Scotland, found Calvin's Geneva to be one of the most perfect embodiments of Christian teaching anywhere. He took those Reformation truths back to Scotland in the early 1560s. England, too, had its own strand of Reformation practice. After King Henry VIII broke with the Roman church in 1543, a native English Reformed church was formed. In the early days of this Anglican Church, under the favor of Edward VI, several doctrinal formulations were adopted, which would prove to be quite similar to the conclusions of the Westminster Confession of Faith. Both the *Forty-Two Articles* and the *Thirty-Nine Articles* (English doctrinal statements) were in some ways, grandparents of the Westminster Assembly's doctrine. Other confessions, particularly the *Irish Articles* of 1615, are also too similar to ignore the family resemblance.

In England, with the Crown officially supporting the state-church, it was difficult to follow through on reform impulses. The Anglican Church, although Reformed in doctrine, retained many worship and governmental practices of the Roman Catholic Church. Nevertheless, as the Scriptures were taught and translated, sincere Christians in England began to yearn to continue their reforms, just as Christians in Europe already had. Opposition to this continuing reform arose between the founding of the Anglican Church (1543) and the 1643 meeting at Westminster.

Those who did not agree with the worship or hierarchical practices of the Anglican Church, were called non-Conformists, Dissenters, or Puritans. Most of the participants at the Westminster Assembly were from this dissenting (non-state-church) group of Puritans. The late sixteenth century saw the Reformation theology take the English Universities by storm. Many of the greatest teachers and preachers in this age were early Presbyterians.

The first presbytery in England was erected under the leadership of the Father of English Presbyterianism, Thomas Cartwright (1535-1603), in 1572 in Wandsworth with as many as 500 ministers, some of whom were outstanding leaders in the land. Presbyterianism was rising on a steep slope of popularity at the turn of the seventeenth century. Although this was rapidly becoming the people's faith, it was perceived as a dangerous threat to the Bishop and the King.

However, as much as it was trampled under by the Monarch, still the resilient biblical faith kept arising and growing. It seemed as if the greater the opposition from the Crown, the greater Presbyterianism grew. Despite the opposition of the likes of King James, who clearly saw the connected threat, and reasoned "No Bishop, no King," nonetheless the groundswell of Reformed believers in the British Isles nearly demanded an Assembly. As historian Phillip Schaff observed, prior to the call for the Assembly, "the excesses of despotism . . . intolerance, and cruelty exhausted the patience of a noble, freedom-loving people, and kindled the blazing war-torch which burnt to the ground the throne and the temple." (For more on these quotations or for exact citation reference, please refer to the intended companion volume for this course, *Windows on Westminster*)

By the early 1640s, there was significant strife in England over the impact of the Reformation faith. Not only were there church-state conflicts (in this case between the Reformed churches and the King of England), but there were confusions within the Protestant-Reformation churches. The unity of England was at stake, and the need for Reformed Christians in the British Isles to unite and work together harmoniously was never greater. Most Reformation Christians had a healthy esteem for other provincial sectors of the Reformed movement. Rather than the independent-mindedness that is often prevalent among us today, there was admiration for what other Christians were doing, which led Reformed Christians in the British Isles to desire to counsel with one another.

The British Long Parliament began to meet on Nov. 3, 1640, and remained in continuous session until dismissed in 1652. In 1640, prior to the meeting of this Long Parliament, the oppression by the hierarchical church reached its zenith, as it called on all clergy to take what came to be known as the "et cetera oath," which was so named, by the Parliament's call for each clergyman to foreswear to never consent to "alter the government of this Church by archbishops, bishops, deans, and archDeacons, *etc.*, as it stands now established, and as by right it ought to stand," an obvious effort to prevent Presbyterianism spreading to England from the borders of Scotland. However, this would not last long nor pre-empt such ecclesiastical expansion, even if not long-lived.

In London, as early as 1641, the local ministers, smarting under the tyranny of the episcopacy, petitioned Parliament to convene a "free synod, to take into consideration and remove the grievances of the Church." Politics and partisanship were ever present in the struggle to even constitute the Assembly. King Charles, hoping to appease the moderate Protestants, allowed a 'Religion Committee' to serve Parliament in March 1641. Many of the men who would later become participants in the Westminster Assembly took part in these and other convocations, with Twisse, Featley, Burgess, White, Marshall, Calamy, and Hill meeting earlier with the Conference of the Lords' Committee in the very chamber where the Westminster Assembly would later be housed.

In May 1641, the Root and Branch Petition (calling for the elimination—Root and Branch—of a Bishop-ruled church) was submitted, drawing the King's ire once again. Later, in November of 1641, the Grand Remonstrance, which contained some 204 clauses, with clause #185 specifically calling for a synod of pious, learned, and judicious divines to meet and to deliberate on which measures would be most helpful for the "peace and good government of the church," was presented to the King, who promptly rejected it by Nov. 25, 1641. This Grand Remonstrance was re-submitted on December 1st, then later on December 20th, each time being vetoed by the King. Various preachers to Parliament, who would later serve as commissioners at the Westminster Assembly, such as Edmund Calamy (12/20/1641), Cornelius Burgess (3/30/1642) and Simeon Ashe (3/30/1642), also called for such a synod to be convened in their sermons before Parliament.

By May 25th, 1642, Parliament had done all necessary for convening the Assembly, even having appointed 102 divines; yet still the King stalled. The Assembly was originally scheduled to meet on July 1, 1642, but due to the King's opposition did not until a year later. In July 1642 Commons called for the Assembly to meet, even though delayed, and in August 1642 Charles renewed his threats against any who attended. October 10, 1642, saw yet another new bill calling for the Assembly, but still Charles used a pocket veto. The bill lapsed, and the King refused to give his assent to a total of six of these similar bills, finally being over-ridden in 1643. Had the King not been so recalcitrant, the Assembly could have met a year earlier, as far as Parliament was concerned.

In March (15th) of 1643, when the bill rose again, finally Parliament took matters into their own hands and, defying the King, such bill was finally approved on June 12, 1643, with the King (as would be expected as the Head of the Church of England) condemning any such synod on June 22, 1643. These Assembly-men who would write the WCF counted the costs and knew the opposition prior to their meeting. All that was left was for a Committee of Commons to prepare "lodgings" for those who would serve, which committee was appointed on June 26, 1643.

The original ordinance was clear in its aims, and the modern reader might benefit from a fairly full recounting of the actual wording:

Whereas, amongst the infinite blessings of Almighty God upon this nation, none is nor can be more dear unto us than the purity of our religion; and for that, as yet, many things remain in the liturgy, discipline, and government of the church, which do necessarily require a further and more perfect reformation, than as yet hath been obtained; and whereas, it hath been declared and resolved by the Lords and Commons assembled in Parliament, that the present church government, by archbishops, bishops, their chancellors, commissars, deans, and chapters, arch-Deacons, and other ecclesiastical Officers, depending upon the hierarchy, is evil, and justly offensive and burdensome to the kingdom, a great impediment to reformation and growth of religion, and very prejudicial to the state and government of this kingdom; and, therefore, they are resolved, that the same shall be taken away, and that such a government shall be settled in the church, as may be most agreeable to God's holy word, and most apt to procure and preserve the peace of the church at home, and nearer agreement with the church of Scotland, and other reformed churches abroad; and for the better effecting hereof, and for the vindicating and clearing of the doctrine of the church of England from all false calumnies and aspersions, it is thought fit and necessary, to call an assembly of learned, godly, and judicious divines, who, together with some members of both houses of Parliament, are to consult and advise of such matters and things, touching the premises, as shall be proposed unto them, by both or either of the houses of Parliament, and to give their advice and counsel therein, to both or either of the said houses, when, and as often, as they shall be thereunto required.

The ordinance directed that the divines meet in King Henry VII's chapel at Westminster beginning July 1, 1643, with both a positive task and a negative one: to (1) set down the biblical patterns of the Reformation faith in the areas of liturgy [worship form] and polity [church government], and (2) defend such Reformation distinctives from false aspersions, miscon-structions, and attack. These were latter-day Nehemiahs, armed with trowels in one hand to rebuild the temple and bearing swords in the other to defend from attack.

Beginning Organization

The Assembly opened on Saturday July 1, 1643, in the Abbey Church in Westminster, with Dr. William Twisse, the Parliament-appointed moderator (called the "prolocutor" in the 1640s), preaching from John 14:18 on the text of "I will not leave you comfortless." This Assembly recognized from its outset the importance of preaching and their need to have the Holy Spirit's guidance. Immediately following the sermon, the divines adjourned to King Henry VII's Chapel, where between 60 and 70 delegates answered the roll call to begin the convocation. Later, as many as twenty-one commissioners were added as replacements or substitutes. Of course, many who sympathized with the monarchy, never attended.

Thereafter, the Assembly would work by committees, as good Presbyterians often do. And they did not work in the ornate quarters of the Westminster sanctuary or chapel; they met in a smaller room in the cloister, the Jerusalem Chamber (see below).

This Assembly was frequently reminded of its potential significance. At the end of the first week, in a sermon before Parliament and the divines, Matthew Newcomen declared that, with the eyes of the world upon them, it was especially incumbent on the members to:

keep no silence, give the Lord no rest until He establish the house . . . except the Lord build the house, reform the Church, it is to no purpose to go about to reform it . . . . I need not tell you how many eyes and expectations there are upon this Assembly. . . . [W]hat you pray for, contend for . . . as you pray that God would establish his Church in peace, so labor to work out the Church's peace. And lastly, as you pray that God would make the Church a praise, so endeavor that also; endeavoring . . . that all her ways may be ordered according to the rule of God's Word: that the Gospel may run and be glorified: that those two great illuminating ordinances of Preaching and Catechizing, which are as the greater and lesser lights of heaven, may have such liberty, encouragement, maintenance, that all the earth may be filled with the knowledge of the Lord.

One of the earliest adopted procedures exhibited the highest regard for Scripture as the only infallible source for the final products of the Assembly. One week after the opening sermon by Twisse, each Commissioner was asked to subscribe to the following:

I, _____ do seriously and solemnly protest, in the presence of Almighty God, that in this Assembly, whereof I am a member, I will not maintain anything in matters of doctrine, but what I think in my conscience to be truth; or, in point of discipline, but what I shall conceive to conduce most to the glory of God, and the good and peace of his church.

Hence, this was an intentionally biblical group, who desired to be guided by the Reformation motto: *sola scriptura* (by Scripture alone). Moreover, this vow was renewed frequently to remind the participants of their original obligation to be nothing but scriptural. Some of the wording for this vow was likely from the suggestion of Herbert Palmer, who in a sermon before the House of Commons on June 28, 1643, a mere three days prior to the convening of the Assembly, reassured Parliament that, "You need not fear us, who can conclude nothing. . . . [W]e do mean nothing, and shall speak nothing but faithfully, I humbly wish a profession, or promise, or vow . . . to be made by all Ministers . . . that we shall propound nothing, nor consent, nor oppose, but what we are persuaded is most agreeable to the Word of God; and will renounce any preconceived Opinion, if we shall be convinced that the Word of God is otherwise. So shall we all seek Christ, and not ourselves, nor . . . victory or glory to ourselves."

Finding it necessary to recess for some organization prior to proceeding, the Assembly reconvened on Thursday July 6th. Most likely a committee on rules from Parliament issued a set of procedural rules to guide the Assembly. When the Assembly reconvened on July 6th, this set of rules (or By-laws; see below) was adopted.

The first order of business was to divide the membership into committees. Although many of our experiences with committees lead us to mock such as often being more cumbersome than helpful, these godly men believed that if members were working together for the Lord's glory, the whole would be greater than the sum of its parts. Acting as a Committee of the Whole would get the body nowhere. Hence the Assembly was divided into three committees, with the initial purpose being to revise the *Thirty Nine Articles*, the doctrinal standard of the Church of England. The First Committee, chaired by the Rev. Dr. Anthony Burgess, was to consider revisions to Articles I-IV and met in Henry VII's Chapel. The Second Committee, chaired by Dr. Edmund Stanton [Staunton], met in "the room used by the lower house of Convocation" and was assigned the revision of Articles V-VII, while the Third Committee, led by John

Gibbon, meeting in the Jerusalem Chamber, the Dean's lodging, was assigned Articles VII-X. The first meetings of these respective committees was Monday July 10th, at one o'clock PM. According to one historian of the Assembly (A. F. Mitchell), it is helpful to realize that these committees were patterned after the earlier Synod of Dort (1619). Later, other committees were erected to prepare the Confession and the Catechisms. The design of all these layers of committees and discussions, which might not be appreciated by the impatient, was to insure that biblical opinions served as iron-sharpening-iron (Prov. 27:17). The proverb, namely, "There is wisdom in many counselors" (Prov. 15:22), was well-heeded in this case. The result would be a document that the church could trust, and one that was freer from the bias, partisanship, and imbalance of many subsequent statements, which do not have the benefit of mature scrutiny and brotherly correction.

The ambiance of the meetings was also steeped in history. Whereas many think of a large hall for the meeting room, it was actually in rather close quarters (less than a thousand square feet, ca. 20 by 40 ft.) that the divines did most of their work. Surrounded by rich paneling, at the head of the room sat the Moderator's chair; behind him were large windows, which served as the primary source of light. In front of the Moderator's Chair, on the ground were the chairs for the 2 vice-moderators ("assessors"), Doctors Cornelius Burgess of Watford and John White of Dorchester. Running the length of the room was a long, narrow table at the head of which sat the clerks, Adoniram Byfield and Henry Roborough. Maximum seating was under 100 (about 80), with the room all lit by firelight. An eyewitness (Baillie) could best describe the room.

At the upper end of the room, there is a chair set on a frame, a foot from the earth, for the prolocutor, Dr. Twisse. Before it, on the ground, stand two chairs, for the two Mr. assessors, Dr. Burgess, and Dr. White. Before these two chairs, through the length of the room, stands a table, at which sit the two scribes, Mr. Byfield and Mr. Roborough. The house is all well hung, and has a good fire, which is some dainties [a commodity] at London. Foreanent the table, upon the prolocutor's right hand, there are three or four ranks of forms. On the lowest one five do sit. Upon the other, at our backs, the members of Parliament deputed to the Assembly. On the forms foreanent us, on the prolocutor's left hand, going from the upper end of the house to the chimney, and at the other end of the house, and backside of the table till it came to our seats, are four or five stages of forms, whereupon their divines sit as they please; albeit, commonly they keep the same place. From the chimney to the door there are no seats, but a void for a passage. The Lords of Parliament used to sit on chairs in that void, about the fire. We meet every day of the week, except Saturday. We sit commonly from noon to two or three in the afternoon. The prolocutor, at the beginning and end, has a short prayer.

Another preliminary matter should be noted. In light of the desire of the participants for the outcome to be as ecumenical as possible, shortly after convening, the Assembly sent a delegation to Scotland seeking to secure the cooperation of the Scottish leaders. A distinguished company of Lords, along with select divines (Marshall and Nye), were sent to Scotland bearing a letter from the English Parliament, lamenting that they were "ready to be swallowed up by Satan and his instrument." The Parliament then implored the Scottish church to send some delegates to help "serve God with one consent, and stand up against antichrist, as one man. These English ambassadors were cordially received by the Scottish Convention of Estates on August 2, 1643 (less than one month after the earliest committee work). The Scots approved the spirit of the request, although the delegates ultimately thought it wiser to sit as advisers *cum voce* (with voice but not vote) in the Assembly. Some of the finest Scottish theological minds ever were sent.

The proposed framework of agreement was the Solemn League and Covenant, which the Scottish church had previously adopted. In turn, to further uniformity, the Scottish leaders asked the English Parliament to approve the same Covenant as a condition for sending the theological advisers. So anxious was the English Parliament to have the advice of the Scots that they summarily agreed to these terms two weeks later on August 17, 1643. The significance of adopting this—taken with upheld hands, foreswearing a covenantal oath—is hard to overestimate. So strong was this event that it is recorded as being met with applause, "bursting into tears of a deep, full, and sacred joy" and estimated by one participant to be a "new period and crisis of the most great affair which these hundred years has exercised. One historian may have over-estimated, but nevertheless evaluated, "it was indeed the commencement of a new period in the history of the Christian Church, though that period has not yet run its full round, nor reached its crisis—a crisis which will shake and new-mold the world."

Some of the commitments spelled out in the Solemn League and Covenant are predictive of how the Assembly itself would conclude certain major issues. For example, the signers of this document subscribed to work for the "preservation of the reformed religion . . . doctrine, worship, discipline, and government, according to the word of God, and the example of the best reformed churches." This was no Assembly of broad belief; specifically the Reformed faith was sought. Moreover, they pledged themselves to the "extirpation of Popery, Prelacy, superstition, heresy, schism, profaneness, and whatsoever shall be found to be contrary to sound doctrine."

A little over a month later, after the English Parliament had adopted the Solemn League, it was referred to the Westminster Assembly itself. Meeting in St. Margaret's Church on September 25, 1643, the divines heard support for adopting this, and swiftly moved to do so. The Assembly eventually subscribed their names to the Solemn League and Covenant, as did the members of the House of Commons.

The **purposes** of the Assembly may be summarized as follows:
1. To revise the *Thirty-Nine Articles;*
2. To establish common doctrine and government between the "three nations" (England, Scotland, and Ireland);
3. To clarify and promote church government as taught be Scripture or *jure divino* (at the time called "divine-rule") Presbyterianism—as opposed to polity invented by tradition or human management forms;
4. To state nothing but what the Bible taught; thus, in England, the WCF came before, and was not designed to prop up, a pre-existing Presbyterian denomination.

The initial assignment had been to merely *revise* the *Thirty-Nine Articles*. Shortly after proceeding, however, these theologians set aside these articles and began to formulate what would become the Westminster Confession of Faith (Hereafter, WCF). Some ten weeks had been occupied in proposing revisions to the *Thirty-Nine Articles*. Being directed by Parliament on October 12, 1643, to proceed directly to attend to the Directory for Public Worship, and with the arrival of the Scottish Commissioners, the Assembly set aside the *Thirty-Nine Articles*, never again to return to them.

Parties, Procedures, and Politics

Most historians agree that the major types of church government were represented at the Assembly. It was by no means a homogenous group on every question. Although the Presbyterians were the most numerous, there were also Independents, Erastians, and Episcopalians (until the King ordered them to not participate) invited. It is important to remember that most of these divines had been ordained by episcopal ordination; moreover, some were satisfied, in the beginning, to pursue only modifications to episcopacy instead of the full-blown Presbyterian revolution.

Most of the public only considers the end-products of the Assembly and tends to think of this as a meeting of unanimous minds. That, however, is not the case. There were strong debates, disagreements (with one esteemed member, even suspended for a time because of his outburst), political maneuvering, and procedural hurdles. All of these gave opportunity for those human intrigues, which shape outcomes, and also show how times have not changed.

The various sides, including Parliament, each had their strategies and agenda. This Assembly was peopled by real human beings, who desired the reform of the church. Yet they did not always agree on method and a few other particulars. A better and more realistic understanding of the background of this important Assembly may be gained from some acquaintance with the rival parties.

Parties

Briefly the major participating parties were the Presbyterians, the Independents and the Erastians. Of these three, the smallest was the Erastian sector. In time, a rather complete system of ecclesiastical government developed, adopting a medical doctor, Thomas Erastus (1524-1583), as their patron saint. Even though not a perfect replica of Erastus' belief, this system came to be recognized as one which gave final authority only to the state (even in church matters) and stripped most authority—except by way of voluntary submission—away from the church. In Erastus' 1568 treatise of this, he "maintained that the pastoral office was properly and only persuasive, and that the minister had not in virtue of his office any right to exercise ecclesiastical discipline, or to refuse admission to the most sacred ordinances . . . He might set forth the character and qualifications of worthy communicants, counsel, warn, and entreat those he deemed unworthy, but might not restrain or exclude them. That and all other disciplinary and coercive acts belongs not properly to the minister but to the magistrate in virtue of his office."

At the time of the Assembly, Erastians believed that church power was only suasive (advisory and never coercive), lacking the power of the keys (Mt. 18:19-20). It deferred any punishment to the civil magistrate, who, according to their view, was the rightful possessor of this church power. The chief exemplars of this view at the Assembly were Selden, Lightfoot, Coleman, and Whitaker, all formidable exponents, but very much in the minority. According to one historian, the chief principle of Erastianism was the "all-supremacy of the State. The Church was a mere department of the State; the pastoral office was simply persuasive; ministers had no power to excommunicate or punish." To respond to this position, several London ministers in *The Divine Law of Church Government* (1646) and Gillespie in his 1646 *Aaron's Rod Blossoming* provided thorough rebuttals of this position. Erastianism never enjoyed much support in post-Westminster Presbyterianism. The predominant Erastian churches in our time are in Europe or Asia (such as the state churches of Sweden, Germany, or Russia), with little sympathy for this form of government in the USA.

In the debate against the esteemed and brilliant Selden, youthful George Gillespie saw the issue clearly, and assessed the pathology of Erastianism, for all to understand:

Erastianism . . . has not the honor of being descended from honest parents. The father of it is the old serpent; its mother is the enmity of our nature against the kingdom of our Lord Jesus Christ; and the midwife, who brought this unhappy brood into the light of the world, was Thomas Erastus. . . . The Erastian error being born, the breasts which gave it suck were profaneness and self-interest; its strong food, when advance in growth, was arbitrary government; and its careful tutor was Arminianism.

The second group, slightly larger than the Erastians but still vastly outnumbered, was the Independents. Posturing themselves as not as extreme as the Brownists (named after Robert Browne), nonetheless these Independents, who set forth their own principles in their *Apologeticall Narration . . .* held "That every particular congregation of Christians has an entire and complete power of jurisdiction over its members to be exercised by the Elders thereof within itself." These Independents, of course, still have their modern day representatives.

The Independents were responsible for the most challenging and time-consuming debate. Although they were Reformed in their theological sentiments, this group did not affirm the strong connectionalism advocated by the Presbyterians. Independents and Presbyterians, both anti-Romanist and anti-prelatic (anti-bishop), would be united in a great many aspects of faith and life. But on important governmental points, they disagreed.

The Independents were strong minded, frequently trying the patience of the Assembly. Said the participant Baillie, the Independents "truly speak much and very well," and he also wrote of "the Independents, our great retarders." Moreover, he alleged that the Independents were obstructionists who "debated all things too prolixie which came within twenty miles of their quarters." Later Baillie (and others) would strongly disapprove of the teaching and the tactics of the Independents in releasing their defense (*The Apologeticall Narration*) to the public prior to full debate in the Assembly.

What is amazing is the degree of rhetorical persuasion accomplished by Presbyterians in the 100 years prior to 1643. They clearly won the debate over church government, and that without having an advantage in the beginning. Prior to 1543 the only extant church in the British Isles was the Roman Catholic Church, with its episcopal form of hierarchical government. With the breach by King Henry VIII, in 1543 the Church of England commenced with its doctrine Reformed but its government still largely hierarchical. Thus well into the sixteenth century, all England knew was hierarchicalism of one degree or another, either papacy or prelacy. But

Presbyterian government, or rule by representative Elders, was scarcely extant until the second half of the sixteenth century.

With the rise of the puritans at Cambridge in the late sixteenth century, some small elements of Presbyterianism began to appear in England. Still it was officially repudiated. Yet a mere half century after the first Elizabethan subversive attempt (the publishing of Thomas Cartwright's *Book of Discipline* in 1584), as the Westminster Assembly convened, it was filled with ardent and convinced Presbyterians. How could it be, that in a climate where such was officially forbidden, that this biblical revolution of government thrived? Evidently the teachers and pastors won the debate by faithfully interpreting Scripture. The only surprise is the extent to which Presbyterian teachers had won the day.

Mitchell suggested two reasons for the near total vindication of Presbyterianism at this Assembly. The *first* is the superiority of the Scottish commissioners on this subject. It was thought that young Gillespie (only in his 30s at this time) was "more than a match for all the learned Erastians and Independents in the Assembly." It is impossible to overestimate the sway and expertise that the Scottish commissioners brought to the Assembly. If one were inclined to suspect plots, such outcome, if predictable, might be a sufficient explanation for why the English leaders and Parliament were so desirous, even willing to sign the Solemn League and Covenant, to secure the participation of the Scots.

The *second* reason is more political and pragmatic. Knowing the commitment of the divines who believed in divine right Presbyterianism (that view that Presbyterianism is the revealed plan of organization for God's church, given as a divine mandate), it was also the case that no compromise could be achieved on this issue. So if the Assembly wished to move ahead, it would likely have to accept this Presbyterian form of government in principle.

That the Presbyterians had won a total victory in the governmental debates from 1543 to 1643 is evidenced by their superiority of conquest, exhibited in the end results of the Assembly. The final result is a clearly Presbyterian document, which in many respects became the mother of later Presbyterian polities in western society.

Moreover, the same is true in doctrine. Apparently, there were no anti-Calvinists, Arminians, Antinomians, Pelagians, or Unitarians at this Assembly, despite their growing proportions in other surrounding parts of Europe. It may be even more remarkable that such document found the favor of both houses of Parliament, which was composed of brilliant and respected leaders.

"They harangue long and very learnedly": The Debates and Procedures

As one might suspect, there were many interesting debates during these six years, a few even reaching the boiling point. Overall, these discussions were characterized by moderation and orientation toward content. At the Westminster Assembly there was little of the showmanship, sensationalism, and demagoguery that is so prevalent in our own debating forums. As to the caliber of debate, one historian noted,

No pygmies contended there. It was a battle of Titans. The High Church Presbyterians of the Cartwright School, backed by the Scotch Commissioners, argued with splendid ability and genius for the Presbyterian form of government and the divine rights of Presbytery. They resorted to no quibbles, or sophistries, or intrigues, inside or outside of the Chamber, to gain their ends. They drew their weapons from the Word of God, and wielded them with a skill and mastery which the opposition, with Parliament on their side, could not overcome.

If one only studied the finished products of the debates (e.g., the Confession or the Directory for Worship), that might lead to misleading caricatures. Some of the best appreciation for the Confession of Faith may come as we recall a few aspects of the debates. While substance was the target of these debates, the process to reach agreement on that substance should not be forgotten or minimized.

First, it should be recalled that early on in the Assembly, a set of parliamentary guidelines were adopted by Parliament for the Assembly's debates. Exhibiting the character of the Assembly and the Parliamentary protocol of the day, as an important glimpse into the expectations of the members, the following by-laws were presented and adopted on July 6, 1643, to guide the Assembly hereafter. The first official act of the Assembly, these guidelines for debates and protocol are summarized below.

1. Vice-Moderators were appointed from 'assessors' to fill the place of the Moderator upon absence or illness.
2. Two clerks, who were not members of the Assembly—to insure non-partisanship and objectivity—were to take minutes. Selected were Henry Roborough and Adoniram Byfield (not to be confused with one of the divines added later, Richard Byfield). Most of the minutes have been certified as being in Adoniram Byfield's handwriting.
3. Every member must take a solemn vow from the outset "not to maintain anything but what he believes to be the truth, in sincerity." Two days later, on Saturday, July 8th, each member did in fact subscribe to that formula (cf. the vow above). This was a self-consciously biblical group, who desired to be guided by scripturally-informed consciences seeking to please God. Moreover, this vow was read afresh at the beginning of each week, on Monday morning, to remind the participants that they had a continuing obligation to remain scriptural.
4. No proposal was to be discussed the first day it was introduced, requiring the mature reflection and deliberation, which is often lost to the haste of deadlines or other schedules. These experienced men realized the tendency to be railroaded into unwise action if not given proper time to reflect on weighty proposals. They valued truth even more than efficiency.
5. "What any man undertakes to prove as necessary, he shall make good out of Scripture."
6. Submission to the Moderator, unless supported by the majority of the Assembly.
7. The right and privilege to present a dissenting opinion with reasons, if any member strongly disagreed, along with such appeal being sent to both houses of Parliament for their consideration.
8. Upon reading the final version of the motion, if the majority agree, such shall be entered as the judgment of the Assembly.

This Assembly, then, looked like any parliamentary body, complete with rules, by-laws, and procedures for the orderly dispatch of business. Visit any Presbytery, Synod, or General Assembly today, and similar procedures will be noticed. Commented Baillie on the gentlemanly manner of debate: "No man contradicts another expressly by name, but most discreetly speaks to the prolocutor [moderator]; and at most, holds on the general, 'The reverend brother who laterly, or who last spoke, on this hand, or that side, above, or below," much like modern Senators observing the protocol of speaking of the "Distinguished Senator from" some state.

Baillie described the debates: "Every committee, as the Parliament gives order in writ to take any purpose to consideration, takes a portion, and in the afternoon meeting prepares matters for the Assembly; sets down their minds in distinct propositions, and backs their propositions with texts of Scripture. After the prayer, Mr. Byfield, the scribe, reads the proposition and Scriptures, whereupon the Assembly debates in a most grave and orderly way. No man is called up to speak but who stands up of his own accord. He speaks so long as he will without interruption. . . . They harangue long and very learnedly. They study the question well beforehand, and prepare their speeches; but withal, the men are exceeding prompt, and well spoken. I do marvel at the very accurate and extemporal replies that many of them usually make. When upon every proposition, and on every text of Scripture that is brought to confirm it, every man who will has said his whole mind, and the replies, and duplies, and triplies, are heard, then the most part calls to the question."

An early historian of the Assembly noted: "In general, the debates were deliberate and learned; and the speakers treated each other with great courtesy and deference; but sometimes they became not only warm, but hot, . . . and in one instance, the Assembly was thrown into hubbub and confusion, while Dr. Burgess was speaking." In another place Baillie indicates that at times the Assembly was bogged down, when he speaks of "these ten days of debates . . . We have been . . . in a pitiful labyrinth these twelve days about Ruling Elders." Participant Charles Herle remarked, "Much has been said about our long debates; I wish the debates were longer and the speeches shorter; a great deal of time is spent in inveighing against others, and in keeping up a debate till an advantage is gotten in the state of the question."

Yet their tactics in debate could be instructive, as they held to the noblest ideals of deliberative Assemblies, and "they furnish a worthy example for ecclesiastical and legislative bodies today. The fullest opportunity was given for debate. In various instances the majority refrained from bringing matters to a vote, even when it was sure of carrying its point, in order that the decisions might not be forced but rather be made as acceptable as possible to all . . . one is compelled to admire that spirit of conciliation and of confidence in the power of truth which determined the policy of the body as a whole."

The debates illuminated both the character and the process of this Assembly. So did some of the other work, which demanded the attention of the members. Often these other tasks are not acknowledged. However, as we see more of what the Assembly did, we have a better sense of appreciation for the balance of this convocation. Robert Paul describes some of the other tasks of the Assembly for us:

Indeed, it is remarkable that the members of the Assembly were able to accomplish as much work as they did, for during the three months following the arrival of the Scots Commissioners they had been constantly required to make decisions on practical matters of administration, they had been subject to all sorts of orders and communications from Parliament, and they listened to a sermon by a probationer almost every morning. The administrative chores included such matters as drawing up rules for the future examination of ministers; but beyond this they had been asked to consider steps to provide for students prevented from continuing studies in Oxford, answer a point of conscience for a minister in Hamburg, draft a letter to be sent to churches in Europe, investigate a schism in the French Church in London, and take a collection for their porter and doorkeepers.

Politics

This Assembly was no more free from politics than any Assembly. One wag has described the heart of Presbyterianism as "Wherever two are more are gathered, there also are politics." Modern readers can glimpse some of the political moves, such as attempts at the outset to recruit the Scottish commissioners to aid in the elimination of prelacy, the contest of wills between Parliament and the Assembly to define proper roles of authority, the efforts of the Independents to garner more public acceptance, and even the possible use of procedural delays in the most pious of forms. Politics played as prominent role in seventeenth-century Assemblies, as they do today.

It was not above Parliament to convene the Assembly to assist it in the overthrow of the King. According to Francis Patton, there were numerous members of Parliament who, although not believing in the reformation, nonetheless wanted change in political administrations. In this party, "there was little piety, and they were swayed by political motives more than by religious convictions. They knew that the great body of the people were at heart more favorable to the old faith than the new . . . [so] they advocated no changes but such as were essential to the Protestant faith. They were willing to leave the outward frame of the Church as it was, and make as few changes in the rites and ceremonies as the interests of Protestantism might tolerate." Political motives were present even before the Assembly was convened.

Parliament quickly allied itself with the divines—not the monarchy and its handmaiden, the episcopacy. As Charles I summed up accurately, "King and prelate on the one side, against Parliament and Puritan on the other." As these two parties began to draw the lines, the divines also realized that when they convened they put their livings, as well as their lives on the line.

Not only were the Presbyterians co-belligerents with Parliament against hierarchies—in church or state—but there was also a divide between the Independents and the Presbyterians. Francis Patton noted: "A jealousy sprung up between the army and the Parliament. Republican sentiments prevailed among the Puritan soldiers. The doctrine of the Independents suited their democratic proclivities. A growing jealousy of Scotland and estrangement from their Northern allies prejudiced them more and more against Presbyterianism, and deepened their partiality for Independence. Some rash measures of Parliament, adopted in haste to restrain the alarming increase of heresy and promote uniformity, gave rise to a loud clamor in favor of toleration and against imaginary persecution." The air was filled with political posturing, even intrigue, as the Assembly met. Their very meeting was tinged with revolutionary significance. They were not free from political consequence.

Another aspect of political reality was the role of the Scottish commissioners, and their bartering to have their Covenant adopted at the outset of the Assembly. The Scots' gaining a pre-commitment to abide by Solemn League and Covenant was a brilliant political stroke for Presbyterianism (perhaps largely attributable to Alexander Henderson). With the outbreak of the Civil War, by 1643, the Independents in Parliament realized they needed an ally. The Scots were the best and quickest hope. Hence, Sir Henry Vane went to Scotland as an emissary, and, as Lingle suggests, a political motive may have been close to the surface: "As we read the story it looks as if the Scotch did a little trading. They promised aid on condition that the Presbyterians of Scotland should have some representation in the Westminster Assembly and all members of Parliament would sign a solemn League and Covenant to be drawn up by the Scotch."

So, there were definitely political motives at work. Some (e.g., Robert Paul) have even theorized that the original assignment to amend the *Thirty-Nine Articles* was a delaying tactic from the outset, conceived disingenuously so as to allow time for the Scottish commissioners to arrive. Of course, we cannot be certain of some of these political motives.

On another front, after Parliament convened the Assembly and gave them a large measure of support in a relatively radical direction, the governors would also have a difficult time curbing the Assembly's power. Parliament wanted to be sure that the divines did the job assigned by Parliament, while at the same time not getting out of Parliament's control. It soon became apparent that Parliament would have a difficult time both feeding *and* taming this tiger. Parliament was displeased that the divines repeatedly spoke of government as by divine rule, rather than as being permitted by the civil government, in that this leached over into what Parliament perceived as their own turf. Protective of this turf, on one occasion, the Parliament modified the original advice of the divines on the subject of appeal to interpose a greater role for Parliament: "That an appeal shall be from every classis to the commissioners of Parliament, chosen in every province, and from them to the Parliament itself." Thus the politicians wanted each case to be directed to Parliament (civil magistracy), instead of referred to the church courts. Such were the politics of the Assembly.

The very constituency, with some non-clergy, was designed as John Selden (also a member of the House of Commons) saw it: "There must be some laymen in the Synod to overlook the Clergy, lest they spoil the Civil work; just as when the good woman puts a cat into the milk house to kill a mouse, she sends her maid to look after the cat, lest the cat eat up the cream."

Parliament was quick to rope off the scope of the Assembly, as not concerned with civil matters at all. Parliament reminded the divines of the wording of the original bill calling for the Assembly, that it was off limits to consider the civil sphere or "anything therein contained . . . nor shall they in this Assembly assume to exercise, any jurisdiction, power, or authority ecclesiastical whatsoever or any other power than is herein particularly expressed." Shortly after the earliest instances of conflict of interest, spokesman from Parliament met with some of the divines, and reminded the clergy that their task was "to advise the Houses in such points as they should lay before them, but not to dictate to those to whom they owed their being as an Assembly."

Parliament and Assembly were politically related. For a brief season, Presbyterian polity was even favored in England. While the Scottish presbyters desired even greater freedom from the state, even this mild form of Presbyterianism led to such an outcry, that the Parliament voted to burn what they deemed as the 'Scottish amendments' "by the hands of the common hangman." Yes, politics was as usual.

Several other incidences of political maneuvering are clear from the record. The Assembly diarist, Robert Baillie, was also a behind-the-scenes solicitor of foreign support for the Presbyterian platform. He frequently wrote other synods and national groups, pleading for them to make their views known to the Assembly, so as to sway it in favor of the international Calvinistic standards. These divines wanted these truths to prevail and labored for them with all means at their disposal. Baillie also was known for his diplomacy and skill in striking deals.

It is also hypothesized that at several occasions, the Independents in Parliament used Fasts for delaying tactics. In light of the ongoing civil war at the time, with battles raging in the west, it was not unusual for Parliament to try to leverage any advantage they could. It should also be noted that the Independents used the secular press, in the release of their *Apologeticall Narration* as one of the earliest examples of taking a case directly to the people, and by-passing the deliberative body. Politics may have had a larger role than many think.

A. F. Mitchell even raises the possibility that Parliament delayed final approval of the Westminster standards by remanding the Confession and Catechisms back to the Assembly to have scriptural proofs added. It is possible, as Mitchell suggests ("Their motives, however, were suspected, and the Order was complied with by the divines somewhat reluctantly"), but we are not able to finally decide. Still it is safe to acknowledge that there were certain intrigues and schemes, as with any Assembly.

The Sessions numbered 1,163 and the Assembly had met for five and a half years before adjourning on February 22, 1649. This historic Assembly would leave a lasting shadow over the whole of western civilization. Their final productions and posterity are a legacy worth remembering.

An earlier historian of the Assembly supported the plea for a reintroduction of these Westminster standards in our homes. Invariably, as others have sought an improvement of the old faith, "it has been found, that while under this pretext, one step of deviation from the old orthodoxy has been taken, no convenient stopping place has been found . . . No doubt, there are many 'hard sayings' in the Bible; many difficulties which no human ingenuity can entirely remove or solve. Sometimes by rejecting that part of the truth that appears most objectionable, it is hoped, that the difficulty will be removed, and the truth recommended to reasonable men. But in such departures from orthodoxy, the relief is only apparent; for although we may escape a more obvious and prominent difficulty, we are sure to find one more untractable, arising out of our new hypothesis."

And as if warning against a spirit which elevates open-ness to the level of ultimate value, much as in our own day, Mitchell continued (fully aware of the full-blown humanity of the divines), "and if to avoid this [objection], we reject something more of the orthodox doctrine, we only plunge deeper into the mire, until at last, we are obliged, for consistency sake, to give up the whole system, or retrace our steps, and return to the point of our first deviation from the straight line of truth." Thus does the work of the Westminster Assembly have much lasting validity for us today.

Much of this history is essential for understanding the historic faith contained in the Westminster Confession of Faith. Yet we should recall that it was not only in the post-Reformation times that leading Christians met together to resolve issues. In fact the earliest patterns of biblical government show Christians from a region meeting together to solve disputes. For example, in the Book of Acts (Chapter 15), amidst the missionary expansion of the gospel in the first century, the leaders of the church had to take time out to settle an important controversy. These leaders at Westminster saw themselves continuing the biblical practice of this and other Scriptures. It might help each of us to re-study such passages to appreciate the value of submitting to one another, under the inspired Word of God, to find application for our own day.

According to Scripture, God has made us so that we can learn from Christians who have gone before us. Most of the 11th chapter of Hebrews reviews the faithfulness of the OT saints. Stephen, in Acts 7, does the same thing in a sermon amidst fierce opposition. At times it is beneficial to review what has gone before to see where we should be headed.

Romans 15:4 teaches that the past has great value for present and future Christian living. In fact, all of the inerrant Word of God, which is certainly prior to any of our lives, should be remembered, "For everything that was written in the past was written to teach us [today], so that through endurance and the encouragement of the Scriptures we might have hope." Thus, the remembering of God's past, contains promise to engender endurance, encouragement, and hope—graces we very much need today.

1 Corinthians 10 contains a famous memory verse, the one which promises believers that no temptation is unique, nor beyond that which we can bear (1 Cor. 10:13). Still however, as widely memorized as it is, its context is frequently ignored. As the first five verses of that chapter speak of the believers in Moses' time as sharing the same spiritual dynamics as we today, verse 6 states, "Now these things [in the past] occurred as examples to keep us from setting our hearts on evil things as they did." Note, the past is our kind instructor, providing examples "if we have ears to hear" to assist us in avoiding evil. But often we are too present-minded, or current information-infatuated to benefit from the past.

Verse 11 continues to inform: "These things happened to them as examples and were written down as warnings for us, on whom the fulfillment of the ages has come. So, if you think you are standing firm, be careful that you do not fall!" Then, with that context in mind, with the value of historical example underscored, we are comforted (as we remember the past and God's faithfulness) that indeed, "No temptation has seized you except what is common to man [Note: human experience in earlier generations, too]. And God is faithful; he will not let you be tempted beyond what you can bear. But when you are tempted, he will also provide a way out so that you can stand up under it" (1 Cor. 10:13).

The Westminster Assembly concluded finally in 1649. The next years would be years of upheaval in England. The Westminster standards were widely embraced and disseminated for another decade following the conclusion of the historic Assembly. After years of civil strife, by 1661 the Anglicans were firmly re-entrenched and made efforts to secure their establishment again. By 1662, over 2,000 Puritans were ejected from their pulpits taking their Westminsterian

Calvinism with them. However, England would lose this lampstand of truth, but the faith would spread elsewhere.

Not surprisingly, the Westminster standards, which had already been lodged in Scottish law and consciousness, were prominent in Scotland and Ulster. From those places, and through additional Puritan emigration to the New World, this proven doctrinal norm would makes its way over to America and become a stalwart part of colonial culture and religion. The Westminster Shorter Catechism was used by many Christian parents—not only by Presbyterians, who did not organize in the United States until 1689—to instruct subsequent generations. New England congregationalists even adopted a version of the WCF, with only the slightest alterations, primarily in the area of church government. In short, the WCF served as *the* basic creed, even for non-Presbyterians, from the American founding period up to the American Revolution.

After the earliest formation of Presbyterian congregations, presbyteries, and Synods, the American Presbyterian Church adopted the WCF as its own doctrinal statement in 1729. The Adopting Act (discussed below; see Session 7) reflected the respect, loyalty, and sincere identity of American Presbyterians, rooted in Scripture as expressed by a time-tested confession. Even comparatively small disruptions in the 1740s did not dispute the importance and accuracy of the WCF as a biblical summary; most divisions prior to 1800 in American Presbyterianism were over matters of ministerial method and evangelistic approach.

Both Northern and Southern Presbyterianism held officially to the WCF until 1861 and beyond. Following the Civil War, the Southern Presbyterian Church—the immediate parent of the PCA—had a strong tradition and rationale for holding to its original confession. In 1843 and again in 1897-1898, the esteem of the PCUS for the WCF is observed from their respective 200th and 250th denomination-wide commemorations of the Westminster Assembly. However, the 20th century would witness a laxity toward confessional matters, first in the North and later in the South. By 1973, the PCA was formed to continue the old Southern Presbyterian patterns of worship, mission, government, and doctrine. Certain explicit declarations, regardless of latter-day commentaries, make it clear that the PCA admired, respected, and desired to cling to the teachings of the WCF.

Other denominations would also work out slightly differing cultures of confessional adherence. Several other Reformed denominations were confessional and offered helpful approaches, but by far the main feeder traditions of the PCA's confessional ethos were: Scottish and frontier. By that, I mean that the PCA has attempted to combine the best of insights about the WCF from its ancient European fathers and also from the forged experiences of American Presbyterianism.

HOMEWORK: Do a little research of your own on the Westminster Assembly or read the article below by John Murray.

FYI Study (optional): The Importance and Relevance of the Westminster Confession
John Murray6

---

6 Taken from John Murray, *Collected Writings of John Murray,* The Banner of Truth Trust, Edinburgh, Scotland, 1976, Vol. 1: *The Claims of Truth*, chapter 43, pp. 316-322; used with permission.

The Westminster Assembly was called by ordinance of both Houses of Parliament and met for the first time on July 1, 1643. Nearly all the sessions were held in the Jerusalem Chamber in Westminster Abbey.

The first work which the Assembly undertook was the revision of the Thirty-Nine Articles of the Church of England. On October 12, 1643, when the Assembly was engaged in the revision of the sixteenth Article, there came an order from both Houses of Parliament to treat of such discipline and government as would be most agreeable to God's Word, and most apt to procure and preserve the peace of the Church at home and nearer agreement with the Church of Scotland and other Reformed Churches abroad, and also to treat of a directory for worship. It was in pursuance of this order that the Assembly prepared what are known as "The Form of Presbyterial Church Government" and "The Directory for the Public Worship of God."

On August 20, 1644, a committee was appointed by the Assembly to prepare matter for a Confession of Faith. A great deal of the attention of the Assembly was devoted to this Confession during the years 1645 and 1646. It was not until December 4, 1646, that the text of the Confession was completed and presented to both Houses of Parliament as the "humble advice" of the divines. This did not, however, include the proof texts. These were not presented to the Houses until April 29, 1647.

The amount of work and time expended on the Confession of Faith will stagger us in these days of haste and alleged activism. But the influence exerted all over the world by the Confession can only be understood in the light of the diligent care and prayerful devotion exercised in its composition.

The Westminster Confession is the last of the great Reformation creeds. We should expect, therefore, that it would exhibit distinctive features. The Westminster Assembly had the advantage of more than a century of Protestant creedal formulation. Reformed theology had by the 1640s attained to a maturity that could not be expected a hundred or even seventy-five years earlier. Controversies had developed in the interval between the death of Calvin, for example, and the Westminster Assembly, that compelled theologians to give to Reformed doctrine fuller and more precise definition. In many circles today there is the tendency to depreciate, if not deplore, the finesse of theological definition which the Confession exemplifies. This is an attitude to be deprecated. A growing faith grounded in the perfection and finality of Scripture requires increasing particularity and cannot consist with the generalities that make room for error. No creed of the Christian Church is comparable to that of Westminster in respect of the skill with which the fruits of fifteen centuries of Christian thought have been preserved, and at the same time examined anew and clarified in the light of that fuller understanding of God's Word which the Holy Spirit has imparted.

The Westminster Confession was the work of devoted men and the fruit of painstaking, consecrated labour. But it was still the work of fallible men. For that reason it must not be esteemed as sacrosanct and placed in the same category as the Bible. The latter is the only infallible rule of faith and life. The framers of the Confession were careful to remind us of this. "All synods or councils, since the Apostles' times, whether general or particular, may err; and many have erred. Therefore they are not to be made the rule of faith, or practice; but to be used as a help in both" (31:4). It is not superfluous to take note of this reminder. We are still under the necessity of avoiding the Romish error. One of the most eloquent statements of the Confession is that of 1:6: "The whole counsel of God concerning all things necessary for his own glory, man's salvation, faith and life, is either expressly set down in Scripture, or by good and necessary consequence may be deduced from Scripture: unto which nothing at any time is to be added, whether by new revelations of the Spirit, or traditions of men."

In the category to which the Confession belongs, it has no peer. No chapter in the Confession evinces this assessment more than that which the framers chose for good and obvious reasons to place at the beginning—"Of the Holy Scripture." In the whole field of formulation respecting the doctrine of Scripture nothing is comparable to that which we find in these ten sections. With the most recent deviations from biblical doctrine in mind, it is as if this chapter had been drown up but yesterday in order to controvert them. Section I, for example, is so carefully constructed that, if chronology were forgotten, we might think that what is being guarded is the doctrine that Scripture itself is the revelatory Word of God in opposition to the present-day dialectical theology which regards it as merely the witness to revelation. When the Confession says, "Therefore it pleased the Lord . . . to commit the same wholly unto writing," what is in view as committed wholly to writing is *God's self-revelation* and *the declaration of his will unto his church.* And so in the next section we find that Holy Scripture is stated to be synonymous with, or defined in terms of "the Word of God written."

Again, the distinction drawn so clearly between the ground upon which the *authority* of Scripture rests (section iv) and the way by which this authority is attested to us (section v) is one exactly framed to meet a current error. Those influenced by this error who aver that the Confession teaches that the authority of Scripture is derived from the "inward work of the Holy Spirit bearing witness by and with the Word in our hearts" (section v) have failed to pay attention to what is elementary in the sequence of these two sections. The authority rests upon the fact that God is the author of Scripture; it is *our* full persuasion and assurance that is derived from the internal testimony of the Spirit. The Confession could not have been more explicit in setting forth this distinction. Thereby it has given direction for all proper thinking on the question of authority.

One of the most controversial chapters in the Confession is the third, "Of God's Eternal Decree." The development of this chapter and the finesse of formulation are masterful. There are three subjects dealt with, the decree of God in its cosmic dimensions, the decree of God as it respects men and angels, and the decree of God as it respects men. In connection with the first, the all-inclusiveness of the decree, embracing sin itself, is asserted, but with equal emphasis also that "God is not the author of sin, nor is violence offered to the will of the creatures" (section I). In connection with angels and men, the statement most offensive to critics is that some are "fore-ordained to everlasting death" (section iii). What is too frequently overlooked is that this statement, as it has respect to men, is explicated more fully in section vii. Here the doctrine, often called that of reprobation, is analyzed as to its elements in a way unsurpassed in the whole compass of theological literature. Nowhere else in so few words is this delicate topic handled with such meticulous care and discrimination. The concluding section (viii) places the "high mystery of predestination" in proper perspective in relation to human responsibility and the comfort to be derived from it for all those who sincerely obey the gospel. Sovereign election of grace is not alien to the gospel. It is a tenet of the gospel, and the fount from which the gospel flows, as well as the guarantee that the gospel will not fail of its purpose.

All true theology is realistic; it takes the data of revelation and the facts of life seriously. At no point does a theology governed by sentiment rather than by facts quibble with the teaching of Scripture more than on the subject of sin. The confession is not afraid to enunciate the doctrine of total depravity, and thus it says unequivocally that by original corruption "we are utterly indisposed, disabled, and made opposite to all good, and wholly inclined to all evil" (VI, iv). Less than this is not a true transcript of the biblical teaching that there is none that doeth good, no, not even one, that the imagination of the thought of man's heart is only evil continually, and that the carnal mind is enmity against God. The severity of the Scripture's indictment, reflected in the Confessional teaching, is complemental to the radical concept of grace which the Confession entertains. However necessary it is to be true to the data of Scripture and the facts of life on the doctrine of depravity, this would only seal despair, were it not that grace is as thorough as sin is total. Herein lies the grandeur of sovereign grace. "Those of mankind that are predestinated unto life, God, before the foundation of the world was laid, according to His eternal and immutable purpose, and the secret counsel and good pleasure of His will, hath chosen, in Christ, unto ever-lasting glory, out of his mere free grace and love" (III, v).

It is this theme of sovereign grace and love that the Confession pursues and unfolds in its various aspects. One of the most remarkable chapters for fullness of doctrine and condensation of expression is "Of Christ the Mediator" (VIII). The whole doctrine of the person of Christ, of his finished work and continued ministry is set forth. If we are thinking of Chalcedon and the doctrine then formulated, nothing is more adequate or succinct than "that two whole perfect, and distinct natures, the God head and the manhood, were inseparably joined together in one person, without conversion, composition, or confusion" (VIII, ii). If we are thinking of the atonement in both its nature and design what in so few words could be more inclusive than: "The Lord Jesus, by his perfect obedience, and sacrifice of himself, which he, through the eternal Spirit, once offered up unto God, hath fully satisfied the justice of his Father; and purchased, not only reconciliation, but an everlasting inheritance in the kingdom of heaven, for all those whom the Father hath given unto him"? (VIII, v).

When the Confession deals with the application of redemption, it is noteworthy how the various topics are arranged. It sets forth first the phases which are the actions of God-Calling, Justification, Adoption, Sanctification (X-XIII)—and then those which are concerned with human response—Faith, Repentance, Good Works, Perseverance, Assurance of Grace (XIV-XXIII). Undoubtedly, the consideration that salvation is of the Lord and that all saving response in men is the fruit of God's grace dictated this order. It is consonant with the pervasive emphasis upon the sovereignty of grace.

That the application should be regarded as having its inception in effectual calling should not be overlooked. This is where Scripture places it, and it is rightly conceived of as an efficacious translation out of a state of sin and death into one of grace and salvation by Jesus Christ. Calling is not to be defined in terms of human response. The latter is the *answer* to the call. This perspective in the Confession needs to be appreciated—effectual calling is an act of God and of God alone. There is, however, one shortcoming in the definition the Confession provides. Calling is specifically the action of God the Father and this accent does not appear in the Confession.

In the two Catechisms produced by the Westminster Assembly, it is striking to observe how large a proportion is devoted to the exposition of the ten commandments. This shows how jealous the divines were in the matter of the Christian life. A similar proportion is not devoted to the law of God in the Confession. But the emphasis is proportionate to what a Confession should incorporate. It is well to not what is said about good works (XVI), the law of God XIX), Christian liberty (XX), the Sabbath day (XXI), marriage and divorce (XXIV). Grace has often been turned into license. No creed guards against this distortion more than the Confession of the Westminster

Assembly. Grace pure and sovereign is the theme throughout. But grace is unto holiness, and it confirms and enhances human responsibility. "The moral law doth for ever bind all, as well justified persons as others, to the obedience thereof. . . Neither doth Christ, in the gospel, any way dissolve, but much strengthen this obligation" (XIX, v).

In days of increasing encroachment upon the liberties which are God-given, the charter of liberty needs again to be resounded: "God alone is Lord of the conscience, and hath left it free from the doctrines and commandments of men which are, in any thing, contrary to his Word, or beside it, in matters of faith or worship" (XX, ii). And when the church thinks that the modes of worship are a matter of human discretion, we need to be recalled to the regulative principle that "the acceptable way of worshipping the true God is instituted by himself, and so limited by his own revealed will, that he may not be worshipped according to the imaginations and devices of men, or the suggestions of Satan, under any visible representation, or any other way not prescribed in the holy Scripture" (XXI, I). Or, when the sacred ties of matrimony are lightly regarded and even desecrated, what could be more relevant than the principles and restrictions enunciated in chapter XXIV?

The flabby sentimentality so widespread is not hospitable to the rigour and vigour of a document like the Confession. Its system of truth and way of life do not comport with current patterns of thought and behaviour. This is the reason for the collapse of the religious and moral standards, which our Christian faith represents. It is folly to think that we can retain or reclaim Christian culture on any lower level than that which the Westminster Assembly defined. Christian thought may never be stagnant. When it ceases to be progressive, it declines. But we do not make progress by discarding our heritage. We build upon it or, more accurately, we grow from it.

Oftentimes it is pleaded that the Christian message must be adapted to the modern man. It is true that the message must be proclaimed to modern man, and to modern man in the context in which he lives and in language he can understand. But it is much more true and important to plead that modern man must be adapted to the gospel. It is not true that the doctrine of the Confession is irrelevant to the modern man. It is indeed meaningless to him until he listens to it. But when a man today becomes earnest about the Christian faith, when he given heed to Scripture as the Word of God, when he faces up to the challenge of unbelieving ways of thought and life and demands the answer which Christianity provides, he cannot rest with anything less than the consistency and vigour which the Confession exemplifies. Unbelief is potent and subtle, and the believer requires the truth of God in its fullest expression if he is to be furnished to faithful witness and confession.

Session #2: Westminster Doctrine

The following brief commentary should serve to introduce the Officer to the major themes and tension points of our Confession. We will not cover every detail of the Confession, but these main themes should be studied and agreed upon.

The Doctrine of Scripture: God's Word

Most confessional statements either assume an implicit authority from the outset, or later in the document, explicitly state that Scripture is their authority. Of course, some church confessions do not reserve the sole authority for Scripture, allowing either tradition, the voice of the church, reason, experience, or some combination of these to serve as co-authorities. However, all of the great Protestant confessions of the sixteenth and seventeenth centuries recognized Holy Scripture as authoritative and unrivalled by any other source—not merely superior by degree but in kind as well. Scripture, the participants at Westminster believed, was issued from God, and because of that divine origin, no other sources were on par with the Bible.

What is so unique about the WCF, however, is how refined and how explicit this base of authority is from the very beginning. Few confessions (if any) have Scripture more prominently or more extensively displayed. The divines at Westminster are unusual in their attempt to confess Scripture so clearly as first principle. The modern reader quickly infers from this the serious regard, which these fathers of the faith held for the Bible. Where most confessions would begin with a discussion God, or faith, or other basic matters, the WCF is distinguished from its other contemporaries by highlighting Scripture in its very first trumpet call. This is not to say that the Assembly elevated the Bible over God in importance; only to recognize that this Assembly was honestly attempting to communicate its very basis for all that would follow.

Furthermore, this statement about Scripture is equally one of the most thorough chapters in the entire WCF, as well as perhaps the most extensive post-Reformation confessional statement on Scripture. The reader will be hard pressed to find a fuller or sounder treatise of Scripture. Chapter 1 of the Confession became a hallmark of Presbyterianism for centuries to follow. Noted B. B. Warfield, "There is certainly in the whole mass of confessional literature no more nobly conceived or ably wrought-out statement of doctrine than [this] chapter . . . placed at the head of their Confession and laid at the foundation of their system of doctrine." Others too, have also ranked this chapter as among the greatest, with Philip Schaff reckoning it as "the best Protestant counterpart of the Roman Catholic doctrine of the rule of faith . . . No other Protestant symbol has such a clear, judicious, concise, and exhaustive statement of this fundamental article of Protestantism."

With such high praise in the beginning, it should also be noted that Schaff probably said more than we even realize when he described the first chapter of the WCF as one of the premier statements within all of Protestantism. This chapter is not only a grand statement of Scripture for Reformed Presbyterians, but many of the strongest bible-believers of all denominations could well fly their flags under this banner. It is a superb summary, not just of one tradition of Bible believers at the time, but moreover is a climactic summation of the recovered tradition of Bible belief. Few who know and believe the Bible will dispute the claims of this maiden chapter, and it has served as a mighty fortress for many believers, especially in times of assault on the very revelation of God.

Besides briefly introducing this great text, we also will want to supplement it with other statements by those who had a hand in writing the original.7 By this means, we will not only receive elaboration on the meaning of the individual sections, but also have confirmation as to its original intent, clarified by original authors. We could equally look into other similar Protestant expressions of the time and find a great chorus of believers who confessed the same thing about the Bible as did the divines.

Warfield suggests that this first chapter's discussion of the meaning and use of the Bible was in exact agreement with other summary statements of the day, in fact, likely even modeled from parts of the earlier *Irish Articles of Religion* (1615). That is likely true. However, there were also, no doubt, other contributors to this great set of beliefs. One could also compare a paragraph from the Scotsman George Gillespie to see how similar his very language is to WCF 1:5. Gillespie wrote: "The Scripture is known to be indeed the word of God by the beams of divine authority it hath in itself . . . such as the heavenliness of the matter; the majesty of the style; the irresistible power over the conscience; the general scope, to abase man and to exalt God; nothing driven at but God's glory and man's salvation . . . the supernatural mysteries revealed therein, which could never have entered the reason of men; the marvelous consent of all parts and passages (though written by divers and several penmen), even where there is some appearance of difference . . . these, and the like, are characters and marks which evidence the Scriptures to be the word of God."

This chapter, no doubt was a composite, contributed by many authors, ranging from the Scottish Gillespie to the Irish archbishop James Ussher. Yet the cardinal point is to see this as an authentic expression of true Protestantism, a collaborative effort by many Bible-believers from diverse backgrounds and traditions. In short, this was a definitive statement of what the Bible is, and how it is to be viewed, not just by an individual, or a few men, but as representative of the very best of international Protestant thinking. This was not an eccentric view of Scripture; rather the harmonious view of many believers. And as approved by the Assembly, after debating each paragraph, we have received an awesome statement of Scripture, which can either be used to help us greatly in our own times, or ignored if we seek to reinvent a critical wheel.

Attributes of Scripture

The first paragraph of the Confession teaches that the Scriptures are necessary, which is also a comment both on human ability, as well as nature around us. As the Confession teaches, humans are unable to truly know God unless he chooses to reveal himself. The divines apparently knew that the well-known passage in Deuteronomy 29:29 informing us that the "secret things belong to the Lord, but the things which He reveals belong to us and our children," indicated that there are some things about God which are knowable, while other things are unknowable.

People are unable to plumb the depths of those things, which God has not revealed. We can only know what he has chosen to make known through Scripture or natural revelation. As this first paragraph indicates, God does reveal some information through nature and creation. The Psalmist affirms that, "The heavens declare the glory of God, the skies show his handiwork . . . There is no speech or language where their voice is not heard" (Ps. 19:1,3). Romans 1:20 also testifies that the power and eternal godliness of our Lord may be known through that which is created. True

---

7 Portions of this discussion are taken from my *Windows on Westminster*, Copyright © 1993, Great Commission Publications, Suwanee, Georgia; used with permission.

knowledge is revealed by way of the created order, yet it is *insufficient* to lead us to ample truth. Some things may be deduced from the creation, but not enough to know Christ as our Savior.

The result is that all human beings are given enough through nature around them, so as to require them to seek this Creator. If they refuse to do this, they have enough revealed information to render them truly guilty before the Sovereign of the universe. However, this additional information is not available from the "light of nature" or "the works of creation and providence." In order to have additional information about salvation and godly living, we must turn to the holy Scriptures, which alone contain this information.

As one of the participants of the Assembly, Anthony Burgess, wrote in another place on this same topic: "As for that dangerous opinion, that makes God's calling of man to repentance by the Creatures, to be enough and sufficient, we reject, as that which cuts at the very root of free grace: A voice, indeed, we grant they have, but yet they make Paul's trumpet, an uncertain sound; men cannot by them [creational revelation] know the nature of God and his Worship, and wherein our Justification doth consist." Assembly-man, William Bridge stated, "Though Human Reason be a Beam of Divine Wisdom, yet if it be not enlightened with an higher Light of the Gospel, it cannot reach unto the things of God as it should. . . . For though reason be the Gift of God, yet it doth proceed from God as he is God, and General Ruler of the World."

By giving Scripture, God perfectly met our human desire to know more than what could be learned from the natural order. As an outgrowth of his good pleasure, God revealed himself in different modes at different times with several purposes in mind. The Confession is helpful to expound the purposes for which God gave Scripture. They were:

> (1) for the better, more sure, spreading of the truth,
>
> (2) for the sounder establishment of the church on the foundation of the unchanging Scriptures,
>> (3) for the comfort of Christians, when they were undergoing trials associated with the weakness of the flesh or the attack of Satan,
>> (4) for a perpetual record in writing, so as to settle disputes and give us guidance.

With these purposes in mind, God gave the Scriptures, which were "most necessary," in that God's former ways of revealing himself—through dreams, prophets, miraculous signs, and audible voice—were no longer his modes of revelation. These ceased with the age of the apostles and prophets (Eph. 2:20 and 3:5). Since then God has committed his sufficient will and mind in the canon of Holy Scripture.

The second paragraph of the Confession goes on to list the books of the canon (which means measuring rod or standard) of sacred Scripture. These 66 books (listed in the front of most modern translations of the Bible), and these alone, are recognized as "Holy Scripture, or the Word of God written" (WCF 1:2). In addition the Confession ascribes unique status and authority to these, "All which are given by inspiration of God, to be the rule of faith and life." No other written works were to be submitted to as "inspired," or breathed-by-God, except these. This sentiment follows the teaching of Paul, written long ago: "All Scripture is God-breathed (literally, inspired), and is profitable for doctrine, reproof, correction, and training in righteousness" (2 Tim. 3:16). Again the Confession sought only to say that which the Scripture itself said.

It is important to recall that this was in stark contrast to the Roman Catholic tradition of the time. Over the centuries the Roman Catholic Church, when it could not sufficiently document its new dogmas, had to resort to writings outside of Scripture. They, and many other medieval Christians, turned to the books that were known as the Apocrypha (a set of books containing fables, some history, and other writings usually to support one religious sect or other collected over the years). Such apocryphal books as *The Wisdom of Solomon, Baruch, Bel and the Dragon, I and II Esdras, I and II Maccabees* and *The Letter of Jeremiah* were not infallible, nor "immediately inspired" (WCF 1:8) of God. Westminster participant, and perhaps the leading linguist of the time, John Lightfoot, spoke of the apocrypha as "not the finger of God, but the work of some Jews . . . the wretched apocrypha . . . the yoke of superstition."

Unfortunately the medieval church allowed these books to be recognized as on the same level of authority as Scripture, and it was left to the reformers and Confessions like this one, to restore the original canon to the church. Those apocryphal books had *never* been a part of the original; they were added in later years. After much accrued abuse, this Confession, along with the other reformers, put this error to rest. The apocryphal books were not inspired (2 Tim. 3:16) as the biblical books were, and hence were to be of no other authority in the church, than any other human writings. Even the best of Christian books may have some very useful insight, and we should receive truth from whatever its source. However, a distinction must be made in our minds, as to whether these other writings are always infallible, or if only sometimes helpful. The difference is critical.

As to the value of this inspired, sufficient, and authoritative Word of God, Calamy attested,

> It is certain that all Scripture is of Divine inspiration, and that the holy men of God spake as they were guided by the Holy Ghost. . . . It transcribes the mind and heart of God. A true Saint loveth the Name, Authority, Power, Wisdom, and Goodness of God in every letter of it, and therefore cannot but take pleasure in it. It is an Epistle sent down to him from the God of heaven . . . The Word of God hath God for its Author, and therefore must needs be full of Infinite Wisdom and Eloquence, even the Wisdom and Eloquence of God. There is not a word in it, but breathes out God, and is breathed out by God. It is . . . an invariable rule of Faith, an *unerring* (emphasis added) and infallible guide to heaven.

From these and any actual study of the other writings of these original authors of the WCF, it can be seen, that their view of the Scripture was that it was inspired, infallible, inerrant, and authoritative in all that it taught. These grandfathers of the faith received the words of Scripture like the early Thessalonian disciples, who "received it as it really is, the word of God (1 Thess. 2:13). As one historian of the Confession observed, amidst the first (of which many are still continuing today) assault on the original intent of the Confession, those who seek to pervert the plain meanings of these paragraphs, must not only distort Scripture, but history itself, so abundant was the testimony of the original intent. Concludes Warfield, "If they [the divines] did not believe in these doctrines, human language is incapable of expressing belief in doctrines. Is it not a pity that men are not content with corrupting our doctrines, but must also corrupt our history?"

Authority, Perfection, and Clarity of Scripture

Warfield was helpful to speak of the "properties" or characteristics of Scripture. Paragraphs 4-7 of WCF 1 address the authority, perfection, and perspicuity (clearness) of Scripture. First consider the authority of Scripture. In this section we are told that the authoritative status of Scripture does not depend on merely the word of any individual, nor even collectively on the church. At the time, the standard Roman Catholic ground for the authority of the Scriptures was not "Because the Bible tells me so," but "Because the Church tells me so." If a church was corrupt, and the authority of Scripture depended on it, then Christians would be in trouble.

Thus the WCF desired to set out the proper basis for authority, not dependent on the intellect or ability of any person, nor even on the Church, but on the sole, unchanging and infallible basis: on God himself. Hence the WCF says that the authority for which Scripture should be believed and obeyed depends only on God (who is truth himself) as the author. Therefore it is to be received as authoritative in all matters because it comes directly from God "who cannot lie." The belief in the Scripture's authority is a by-product of our belief in God as infallibly truthful and incapable of lying. These authors tied the truthfulness of Scripture to the very character of God.

To further clarify, these sections also tell us that, even though certain "proofs" of the Bible may be helpful from time to time, they will not sufficiently prove the truthfulness and authority of Scripture. The first part of paragraph 5 in chapter 1 summarizes how we may have *partial regard* for Scriptures based on its own inherent value. Scripture is so perfect in itself, that as we read it (even a non-Christian), we may be profoundly moved and even come to a "high and reverent esteem of holy Scripture" by reading it. The reasons for this are numerous. Due to the sheer heavenliness of the matters considered, the effectiveness of the things taught to change lives in this world, the literary majesty of the style, the unified consistency of all its parts (even spanning over a thousand pages in most editions, without real internal contradiction), and the teaching about God's glory and our salvation, people may come to have great respect for the Bible. But respect and admiration is one thing; bowing to Scripture as our authority for living is another. The Bible does not present itself as a book to be respected, but as a revelation to be obeyed. It does have numerous "incomparable excellencies and entire perfection," but still those character traits are not the ones that lead us to submit to the Scriptures as the authority for our lives.

Even with all these internal excellencies, however, the person reading Scripture, even with these inherent excellencies will not come to a full persuasion of its truth until or unless the Holy Spirit is working with the Word as well. As the Confession says, "our full persuasion and assurance of the infallible truth, and divine authority . . . is from the inward work of the Holy Spirit, bearing witness by and with the word in our hearts" (WCF 1:5). So the work of persuading us of the authority of the Bible is properly the work of the Holy Spirit.

Many Christians want so desperately to communicate the excellencies of the Bible to their friends or family members that they occasionally fall into the trap of trying to reason someone into an acceptance of Scripture. We certainly should attempt to share the grand teachings of Scripture, but we must constantly be reminded that the unbeliever (Rom. 2:14-15, and 8:7) will not and cannot comprehend the things of the Lord, until he is born again and made new. Our reasoning ability will not convince any that they should obey Scripture. One much stronger than we must do that, and that is the Holy Spirit. It is not wrong to try to help a person understand Scripture's authority, but we must remember that this great work is up to the Holy Spirit.

Samuel Rutherford, a participant of the Assembly, who was also the author of *Lex Rex*, put it well: "The preaching of the word only, if alone without the Spirit, can no more make an hair white or black, or draw us to the Son, or work repentance in sinners, than the sword of the Magistrate can work repentance. . . . What can preaching of man or angel do without God, is it not God and God only who can open the heart?"

The next paragraph of the Confession continues this teaching, as it says, "Nevertheless, we acknowledge the inward illumination of the Spirit of God to be necessary for the saving understanding of such things as are revealed in the word." So the Confession not only depends on the Spirit to convince of authority, but the presence and work of the Holy Spirit is also necessary for the correct lighting up of the Word. Apparently these authors looked to the Holy Spirit for much and were not expecting that growth in the Word would come apart from his vital ministry. This statement is Trinitarian and fully dependent on the work of the Third person of the Godhead.

The sixth paragraph of the Confession also gives the ordinary believer some wonderful assurance. In it we are told that God's whole counsel (Acts 20:27) regarding our salvation and life is either explicitly set forth in the Bible, or else by properly researched implications, may be learned from Scripture. God did not give his Word to us to conceal but to reveal. It is not so difficult to understand that ordinary people fail to comprehend. In fact, compared to some literature (like assembly instructions for child's swing-set), it is much less technical. If you can assemble a child's toy, or download computer applications, you can figure out the Bible. It usually depends on our attitude and teachableness. Do you know anyone who would diligently concentrate on reading an instruction manual, or search for an extra deduction on IRS forms, only then to attend our churches and plead that Scripture is too inscrutable? God knows better. And so did the Westminster divines.

The things of God are so clear that any ordinary person may understand them. Certainly there are many particular things, which God has not revealed to us. Numerous matters of worship circumstance, church government (e.g., the number of Elders prescribed for each church), and other human groups may have to be determined by the use of sanctified common sense, according to the general principles revealed in God's Word. We do not have an exhaustive teaching on each and every circumstance in the Bible. Yet its principles are adequate to guide us in important decisions.

As the following section goes on to show, there are definitely some things in the Bible that are hard to understand. But the basics and the things we need to know are clearly enough revealed so that any interested person can comprehend. The Bible is not a book marked "For Theologians Only." We also are in good company in this respect. One of the greatest apostles, Peter, also admitted that he had difficulty understanding some of the teachings of Paul (2 Pet. 3:15). If Peter recognized the difficulty of interpreting some verses, then we too, should be patient with ourselves and others in difficult sections of Scripture.

The authors of the Confession—even with all their expertise—realized that all verses of Scripture would not be easy to interpret nor even agreed upon by all interpreters. Yet the fundamental things which God wants us to know, "those things which are necessary to be known, believed, and observed for salvation," are so clearly set forth in some section of Scripture, that it does not require a high level of education, for an interested person to gain an adequate understanding of these things. Theologians call this the "perspicuity" of Scripture, and one modern commentator (G. I. Williamson) has helpfully referred to this as the "see-through-ableness" of Scripture.

This is important to note, for Scripture does not place a pre-requisite of higher education on grace. It is not by works or by superior intellect that Scripture works. The Bible is not intended only for the super-intelligent. It is composed, under God's inspiration, so as to be understandable by the ordinary person. It is not, as the medieval Roman Catholics thought, a book that only the technically trained clergy could understand. With the "due use of the ordinary means," or the normal availing of oneself to study guides and widely available tools for Bible study, these ideas which are essential for salvation and Christian living are "open secrets," available to any believer who is interested in learning.

Paragraph 6 also includes an important qualifier, as it says that nothing at any time is to be added to the level of Scripture, either by professed new revelations or the accumulated traditions of people. This sufficiency of Scripture is an age-old teaching, and one that protects us against new innovations from the fertile minds of those who think they know God better than the original writers of Scripture. In the later twentieth century, some purported to bring revealed thoughts from God which were to be received as prophecy, as if from Isaiah, Jeremiah, or the Apostle Paul. There were also some in the 1640s who advocated the same thing, and the Westminster divines wisely set forth for us the dangers of that view. We are not to expect that the canon of Scripture will grow or be supplemented. As Revelation 22:18-19 indicates, nothing was to be added to that set of written teachings, and the age of revelation was over.

The eighth paragraph clarifies the real basis of the biblical faith. The Reformation had produced great zeal and enthusiasm for a return to the original fountains of learning. As a result there was a great revival of interest in the original Greek and Hebrew texts of the Bible. As WCF 1:8 teaches, it was the original manuscripts, the OT in Hebrew and the NT in Greek, which were "immediately inspired . . . and therefore authentical." It is not a particular Bible version that is inerrant, but the earliest Greek and Hebrew texts, which have been faithfully translated in our most modern English versions (e.g., the original NIV or the NASB or the NKJV). It was these original manuscripts which God kept pure and without corruption throughout all ages "by his singular care and providence." So, God by a special act of providence has preserved the biblical texts.

This being the case, if we wish to settle any controversy or point of interpretation, the final appeal is to the Scriptures, not the church, nor a learned individual, although these may be aids. Accordingly, it is God's will that these original languages be translated so that the Word of God can be read in the common language of the people. It is God's desire that his revelation be known to many, and contrary to an earlier impulse which kept the Scriptures in Latin, the Westminster teaching is that the Bible is far too valuable to be locked up only in the possession of the clergy.

God wants the Word translated so his people can have the word of God richly dwelling in them (cf. Col. 3:16), so that they may acceptably worship him, and "through patience and comfort of the Scriptures, may have hope" (WCF 1:8). Thus does God want his people to not only have the Word but also to know it and understand it.

The final two paragraphs of the first chapter stick together and also targeted existing errors of the day. The ninth paragraph teaches us not only about the unity of Scripture (that the sense of Scripture is to be interpreted with consistency, without internal contradictions) but also a very important rule of how to interpret the Scriptures. The authors of the Confession wanted the common person to have confidence that he, too, could interpret the Bible. These divines had already admitted that some passages would be difficult to interpret, and that any valid interpretation must rest on the original language version of the Bible. But in this next-to-last section of the first chapter, they also confessed that the unfailing manner of arriving at truthful interpretations of the Bible was to compare Scripture with Scripture. This "infallible rule of interpretation" is to seek the meaning for a difficult passage in the clarity of a more straightforward verse. Other places that speak more clearly are to clear up many of our difficulties. Thus the Westminster divines gave the people an interpretive secret, as well as affirmed the inner consistency of the biblical message.

For example, if we are reading in Romans 8:1 and come to "there is no *condemnation* for those who are in Christ Jesus," we may wonder what that means. In that verse, it is not immediately clear if that means no one will ever judge us to be bad, or if this refers to God's view of the believer. So we may turn to the Concordance in the back of our Bibles (or an individual volume) and look up other uses of the word "condemnation." From doing so, we see that it means, "to pronounce guilty in light of sin," and also that another verse in the same chapter uses this word. Down in v. 33 of Romans 8, we see that no charges against God's elect convince the Father, for it is "God who justifies" and Christ Jesus who died and was raised to life for our justification, which is the mirror opposite of condemnation. We now plug in that clarified meaning, which is interpreting Scripture with Scripture, as WCF 1:9 states.

The final paragraph makes clear, if not already, that the Bible and the Bible alone is authoritative in determining any questions about religion. Remember that prior to the Reformation, it was often given to clerical councils, or "doctors" of the church to decide what certain verses meant. This was not the case with the Reformation tradition. As this chapter teaches, Scripture is the "Supreme Judge," standing uniquely alone—over any pronouncements of councils, even the best of religious leaders' writings, doctrines contrived by others, or claims to private spiritual enlightenment. The Bible and the Bible alone is recognized as deserving this status. And when the Bible speaks, we are to examine all other thoughts by it (2 Cor. 10:5 speaks of taking every thought captive to obedience to the Word), and "we are to rest" in its teachings. And the real, underlying reason, is because the Holy Spirit speaks in the Scriptures. It is not a dead book, but alive and sharper than a two-edged sword, even able to dissect, as a surgeon's scalpel, very closely related matters (Heb. 4:12-13).

The Bible is one of the keys to Christian living. And it is set forth first in this document, which speaks volumes about what the authors thought was important. Jesus was of the opinion that the Scripture was so perfect, so inter-related that "the Scripture cannot be broken" (Jn. 10:35). Our Lord was also the one who affirmed the OT as being totally truthful; so much so, that sooner would heaven and earth pass away that the slightest stroke or dot of it would be incorrect (Mt. 5:18). Paul said to Timothy that *all* (not some) Scripture was God-breathed and profitable (2 Tim. 3:16), and the apostle Peter taught Scripture did not arise from the prophet's own interpretation . . . but men spoke from God as they were carried along by the Holy Spirit (2 Pet. 1:20-21). These were the same views as those held by the divines at Westminster.

Turn of the century scholar B. B. Warfield, who valiantly sought to resist new attacks on the Bible, concludes of this first Chapter in the WCF:

> If it be compared in its details with the teachings of Scripture, it will be found to be but the careful and well-guarded statement of what is delivered by Scripture concerning itself. If it be

tested in the cold light of scientific theology, it will commend itself as a reasoned statement, remarkable for the exactness of its definitions and the close [connection] of its parts. . . . Numerous divergences from it have been propounded of late years, even among those who profess the Westminster doctrine as their doctrine. But it has not yet been made apparent that any of these divergences can commend themselves to one who would fain hold a doctrine of Scripture which is at once Scriptural and reasonable, and a foundation upon which faith can safely build her house. In this case, the old still seems to be better.

This first chapter is an excellent beginning for this Confession. Furthermore, the following chapters of the WCF are equally faithful in their statement of scriptural teachings.

Session #2a: God and His Works: Election, Creation, and Providence

Following the clear sentiments of the WCF on the nature and use of Scripture, the next four chapters focus on God and his works. Chapter two of the WCF sets forth the attributes and Trinitarian character of God. Chapters 3 through 5 discuss the prominent works of God the Father: his eternal decree, creation, and then the sustaining of that decree and creation—his providence.

Election

The second chapter of the WCF attracts very little criticism; it is easily understood, straightforward, and eminently biblical. The first two paragraphs list a number of God's attributes, and the third paragraph contains a simple statement of the doctrine of the Trinity. It quickly becomes clear that these first two chapters are so biblical—and that should be recalled as we look at future sections—that one can hardly disagree with the content, unless he disagrees with Scripture itself. A wonderful, full definition of God is provided, and his attributes are clearly displayed.

About the only phrasing from WCF 2 that is routinely question is the second line of 2:1 that depicts God as "without body, parts, or passions." The authors obviously meant to deny that God had a *human* body, parts, or passions. He is not fickle, mutable, nor driven by sinful or whimsical passion. However, other verses make it clear that the Holy Spirit can be grieved and that God loves. So, a proper understanding of the context and intent of this clarifies that God is not blown by emotions; rather he is fixed in his decree.

The third chapter tackles a topic that is very controversial today but was not so provocative in the Assembly. Most other creeds stated similar sentiments. One might wish to consult an old Baptist creed, the *Thirty-Nine Articles* of the Church of England, or other post-Reformation confessions to see how wide the consensus was on this subject. It is only the more modern trends and theologies that have called this into question. From the study/handout below, the critical biblical data is gathered. This may help the student prior to discussing chapter 3. Our first question should not be "How does this make me feel?" or "What was I taught growing up on this subject?" or "Does this diminish the position of man?" or "Will this be popular or intuitive when evangelizing?" Instead, our first question should be: Does the WCF faithfully represent the scope of biblical teaching on this subject? The studies below should assist in answering that line of questioning.

Handout: The Bible on Pre-Destination and Election

I.   Biblical Terminology
   A. Hebrew – *yadaq* – to know (by choice of election) – Genesis 18:19; Amos 3:2; Hosea 13:5 – *bahar* – to choose (passim)
   B. Greek
      1. *Proginoskein* (same as *yadaq* above) Acts 2:23; 3:18, 20 Romans 8:29, 11:2; 1 Peter 1:2, 20
      2. *Pro-orizein* (Pre-ordered) Acts 4:28; Romans 8:29-30; 1 Corinthians 2:7; Ephesians 1:5, 11
      3. *Protithemi* (Pre-placed) Romans 8:28; Romans 9:11; Ephesians 1:11; 3:11; 2 Timothy 1:9

4. *Prohetoimazo* (Pre-prepared) Romans 9:23; Ephesians 2:10; 2 Peter 2:3

N. B. — also the consciousness of Pre-Destination in the numerous other "*Pro*" words and the Greek phrase—"it was necessary" (*dei*).

Election — eklegesthai or *ekloge* – Acts 1:24; 9:15; 15:7; Romans 9:11; 11:5, 7, 28; 1 Corinthians 1:27-28; Ephesians 1:4; Colossians 3:12; 1 Thessalonians 1:4; 2 Thessalonians 2:13; 1 Timothy 5:21; 2 Timothy 2:10; Titus 1:1; 1 Peter 1:7, 1:20, 2:4, 9; 2 Peter 1:10; Revelation 17:14

Others — Galatians 3:17; 1 Peter 1:11; Acts 17:26; Romans 3:25; Ephesians 1:9

II.   Biblical Evidence — Main Passages
   1. Jesus' teaching (see below)
   2. Acts speeches — 2:23; 3:18-20; 4:28; 13:48; 17:26
   3. Romans 8:28-39
   4. Romans 9:6-24 & 11:2
   5. Ephesians 1:3-14
   6. 1 Peter 1:2, 20
   7. 2 Timothy 1:9 & Jude 4
   8. Old Testament passages: Psalms 139:1-4; 1 Sam. 23:11-12; Hosea 2:23; Is. 25:1; 44:21

      *Case studies in Old Testament
      a. Joseph (cf. especially Genesis 45:5-9; 50:20) — Genesis 37-50
      b. Pharaoh — Exodus 7-11. Note: 3 times it says "Pharaoh hardened his heart" and 11 times "God hardened his heart"
      c. 1 Kings 22

III.   Jesus' Own Words

Pre-Destination Perspective	*Responsibility Perspective*
A. Matthew 22:14; 24:22; 24; 31	Passim
B. Mark 13:20, 22, 27	Passim
C. Luke 18:7; 23:35; 2:21	Passim
D. John 6:37*; 44; 64; 65; 8:47; 8:12	Jn 3:16; 5:24; 6:54; 7:17;
10:4, 6; 12:32; 13:18, 21; 38; 15:16; 19; 17:2, 9; 18:37	

   *Draw, drag (cf. John 12:32; 18:10; 21:6, 11; Acts 16:19; 21:30; James 2:6)

IV.   Biblical Perspective
   A. 2 Caveats
      1. Must be handled with care (WCF 3;8).
      2. Avoid extremes of rationalism (mechanistic) and humanism.
   B. Know the *intent* or *purpose* of the doctrine.
      1. To give God the credit in salvation — Doxological.
      2. To demonstrate the Sovereignty of God.
      3. To provide comfort, assurance to the believer.
   C. Summary Propositions — forming parameters

1. Pre-Destination is not mechanistic, it is dynamic.
2. God is not the author of evil.
3. God is never "out of control" or in the position of having been caught off guard and needing to form a contingency plan, i.e., Sovereignty is never thwarted.
4. God *lovingly* (Ephesians 1:4-5) executed Pre-Destination.
5. The ultimate cause of Pre-Destination is God's choice—not because we are good.
6. In Jesus' teaching, Pre-Destination and free offer of the gospels are not incompatible.
7. There are two types of statements, reflecting (1) the Divine perspective, which is primoridial, and (2) the human perspective. These are different in origin of perspective but not contradictory.
8. Paul and other New Testament writers have no problem affirming Pre-Destination as a glorious doctrine.
9. Pre-Destination seeks to be Theocentric above being Anthropocentric.
10. God takes the initiative in our salvation.

Do This Study Also

1.   In Revelation 13:8 who are "*all* whose names have not been written in the Book of Life belonging to the Lamb that was slain *before* the foundation of the world? (cf. also Ephesians 1:4-5 and 1 Peter 1:19-20 to this choosing in eternity past.)

2.   Who are "certain men whose condemnation was marked out long ago" in Jude 4?

3.   Who is spoken of in these words, "Their condemnation has long been hanging over them (RSV–"from of old') and their destruction has not been sleeping," (2 Peter 2:3)?

4.   Does 2 Timothy 1:9 allow us to assert that God saves us because he knows how we will be?

5.   Do Ephesians 1:4 (and 1 Thessalonians 1:4) teach that God elected these believers to salvation before they ever made a choice? And what about the disobedient in 1 Peter 2:8?

6.   Does Proverbs 16:4 mean that God even made the evil for his own purposes?

7.   Did God prepare Hell for the devil? (Matthew 25:41)

8.   In John 17:6, 9, 12 is Jesus speaking of a definite group of those given to him by God.

9.   How do you interpret Romans 9:18, 22, 23?

****

Now that it has been established from Scripture that God acts and chooses as he is revealed in the verses above, one may have a higher appreciation of the WCF.

Much of chapter three reads like constitutional law in that it is carefully drawn and full of disclaimers, which are not always weighed fully. The WCF denies that a proper understanding of this doctrine renders God as the agent of our sin, nor does it violate the creature's ability to make choices in keeping with his nature, nor does it remove the need for means to ends. Neither has God chosen people because he sees that they will be assets to his team. Some (including angels) are chosen to eternal life and some are chosen/passed over to eternal death. That number is fixed in God's decree and cannot be altered, since it flows from his perfect choice. Those who will be saved are brought to God through the saving work of Christ—and only those who are called, justified, adopted, and glorified are saved. God passed over the rest and ordains them to dishonor and wrath.

This exalted doctrine is not intended to confuse or deflate. Instead, a proper understanding of the Scriptures on this subject will do several things: (1) promote obedience; (2) provide assurance of our salvation based on God's choice and keeping power, not the ability of man; and (3) lead to humility, praise, and diligence. If we understand this correctly, we are humbled, blessed, and motivated—far from resting on our laurels. Officers should know instances of how this doctrine helps, not hinders, ministry.

Many of us have found the following sermon by Charles Spurgeon to be helpful and a sound statement of this doctrine. Coming from an earlier Baptist pastor, this sermon indicates how universal this (often out-of-favor now) teaching once was.

FYI Study (optional) ELECTION
A SERMON DELIVERED ON SABBATH MORNING, SEPTEMBER 2, 1855,
BY THE REV. C. H. SPURGEON,
AT NEW PARK STREET CHAPEL, SOUTHWARK. (NO. 41-42)

"But we are bound to give thanks always to God for you, brethren beloved of the Lord, because God hath from the beginning chosen you to salvation through sanctification of the Spirit and belief of the truth: Whereunto he called you by our gospel, to the obtaining of the glory of our Lord Jesus Christ." - 2 Thessalonians 2:13,14.

IF there were no other text in the sacred word except this one, I think we should all be bound to receive and acknowledge the truthfulness of the great and glorious doctrine of God's ancient choice of his family. But there seems to be an inveterate prejudice in the human mind against this doctrine; and although most other doctrines will be received by professing Christians, some with caution, others with pleasure, yet this one seems to be most frequently disregarded and discarded. In many of our pulpits it would be reckoned a high sin and treason to preach a sermon upon *election*, because they could not make it what they call a "practical" discourse. I believe they have erred from the truth therein. Whatever God has revealed, he has revealed for a purpose. There is nothing in Scripture which may not, under the influence of God's Spirit, be turned into a practical discourse: "for all Scripture is given by inspiration of God, and is profitable" for some purpose of spiritual usefulness. It is true, it may not be turned into a free-will discourse—that we know right well—but it can be turned into a practical free-grace discourse: and free-grace practice is the best practice, when the true doctrines of God's immutable love are brought to bear upon the hearts of saints and sinners. Now, I trust this morning some of you who are startled at the very sound of this word, will say, "I will give it a fair hearing; I will lay aside my prejudices, I will just hear what this man has to say." Do not shut your ears and say at once, "It is high doctrine." Who has authorized you to call it high or low? Why should you oppose yourself to God's doctrine? Remember what became of the children who found fault with God's prophet, and exclaimed "Go up, thou bald-head; go up, thou bald-head." Say nothing against God's doctrines, lest haply some evil beast should come out of the forest and devour you also. There are other woes beside the open judgment of heaven—take heed that these fall not on your head. Lay aside your prejudices: listen calmly, listen dispassionately: hear what Scripture says; and when you receive the truth, if God should be pleased to reveal and manifest it to your souls, do not be ashamed to confess it. To confess you were wrong yesterday is only to acknowledge that you are a little wiser to-day and instead of being a reflection on yourself, it is an honor to your judgment, and shows that you are improving in the knowledge of the truth. Do not be ashamed to learn, and to cast aside your old doctrines and views, but to take up that which you may more plainly see to be in the Word of God. But if you do not see it to be here in the Bible, whatever I may say, or whatever authorities I may plead, I beseech you, as you love your souls, reject it, and if from this pulpit you ever hear things contrary to this Sacred Word, remember that the Bible must be the first and God's minister must lie underneath it. We must not stand on the Bible to preach, but we must preach with the Bible above our heads. After all; ye have preached, we are well aware that the mountain of truth is higher than our eyes can discern; clouds and darkness are round about its summit, and we cannot discern its topmost pinnacle; yet we will try to preach it as well as we can. But since we are mortal, and liable to err, exercise your judgment; "Try the spirits, whether they are of God;" and if on mature reflection on your bended knees, you are led to disregard election—a thing which I consider to be utterly impossible—then forsake it; do not hear it preached, but believe and confess whatever you see to be God's Word. I can say no more than that by way of exordium.

Now, first. I shall speak a little concerning the *truthfulness* of this doctrine: "God hath from the beginning chosen you to salvation." Secondly, I shall try to prove that this election is *absolute*: "He hath from the beginning chosen you to salvation," not *for* sanctification, but "*through* sanctification of the Spirit and belief of the truth." Thirdly, this election is *eternal* because the text says, "God hath *from the beginning* chosen you." Fourthly, it is *personal*: "He hath chosen *you*." Then we will look at the *effects* of the doctrine—see what it does; and lastly, as God may enable us, we will try and look at its *tendencies*, and see whether it is indeed a terrible and licentious doctrine. We will take the flower, and like true beer, see whether there be any honey whatever in it; whether any good can come of it, or whether it is an unmixed, undiluted evil.

I. First, I must try and prove that the doctrine is TRUE. And let me begin with an *argumentum ad hominem*—; I will speak to you according to your different positions and stations. There are some of you who belong to the Church of England, and I am happy to see so many of you here. Though now and then I certainly say some very hard things about Church and State, yet I love the old Church, for she has in her communion many godly ministers and eminent saints. Now, I know you are great believers in what the Articles declare to be sound doctrine. I will give you a specimen of what they utter concerning *election*, so that if you believe them, you cannot avoid receiving election. I will read a portion of the 17th Article upon Predestination and Election:—"Predestination to life is the everlasting purpose of God, whereby (before the foundations of the world were laid) he hast continually decreed by his counsel secret to us, to deliver from curse and damnation those whom he hath chosen in Christ out of mankind, and to bring them by Christ to everlasting salvation, as vessels made to honor. Wherefore they which be endued with so excellent a benefit of God be called according to God's purpose by his Spirit working in due season: they through grace obey the calling: they be justified freely: they be made sons of God by adoption: they be made like the image of his only-begotten Son Jesus Christ: they walk religiously in good works, and at length, by God's mercy, they attain to everlasting felicity." Now, I think any churchman, if he be a sincere and honest believer in Mother Church, must be a thorough believer in election. True, if he turns to certain other portions of the Prayer Book, he will find things contrary to the doctrines of free-grace, and altogether apart from scriptural teaching; but if he looks at the Articles, he must see that God hath chosen his people unto eternal life. I am not so desperately enamoured, however, of that book as you may be; and I have only used this Article to show you that if you belong to the Establishment of England you should at least offer no objection to this doctrine of predestination.

Another human authority whereby I would confirm the doctrine of election, is the old Waldensian creed. If you read the creed of the old Waldenses, emanating from them in the midst of the burning heat of persecution, you will see that these renowned professors and confessors of the Christian faith did most firmly receive and embrace this doctrine, as being a portion of the truth of God. I have copied from an old book one of the Articles of their faith: —That God saves from corruption and damnation those whom he has chosen from, the foundations of the world, not for any disposition, faith, or holiness that before saw in them, but of his mere mercy in Christ Jesus his Son, passing by all the rest according to the irreprehensible reason of his own free-will and justice."

It is no novelty, then, that I am preaching; no new doctrine. I love to proclaim these strong old doctrines, which are called by nickname Calvinism, but which are surely and verily the revealed truth of God as it is in Christ Jesus. By this truth I make a pilgrimage into the past, and as I go, I see father after father, confessor after confessor, martyr after martyr, standing up to shake hands with me. Were I a Pelagian, or a believer in the doctrine of free-will, I should have to walk for centuries all alone. Here and there a heretic of no very honorable character might rise up and call me brother. But taking these things to be the standard of my faith, I see the land of the ancients peopled with my brethren—I behold multitudes who confess the same as I do, and acknowledge that this is the religion of God's own church.

I also give you an extract from the old Baptist Confession. We are Baptists in this congregation—the greater part of us at any rate—and we like to see what our own forefathers wrote. Some two hundred years ago the Baptists assembled together, and published their articles of faith, to put an end to certain reports against their orthodoxy which had gone forth to the world I turn to this old book—which I have just published Baptist Confession of Faith. Paper covers, — 4d. — Cloth, 8d. — Roan, gilt edges, ls. London: Alabaster & Passmore, Paternoster Row; and J. Paul, Chapter-House Court, St. Paul's.—and I find the following as the 3rd Article: "By the decree of God, for the manifestation of his glory, some men and angels are predestinated, or foreordained to eternal life through Jesus Christ to the praise of his glorious grace; others being left to act in their sin to their just condemnation, to the praise of his glorious justice. These angels and men thus predestinated and foreordained, are particularly and unchangeably designed, and their number so certain and definite, that it cannot be either increased or diminished. Those of mankind that are predestinated to life,

God, before the foundation of the world was laid, according to his eternal and immutable purpose, and the secret counsel and good pleasure of his will, hath chosen in Christ unto everlasting glory out of his mere free grace and love, without any other thing in the creature as condition or cause moving him "hereunto." As for these human authorities, I care not one rush for all three of them. I care not what they say, *pro* or *con*, as to this doctrine. I have only used them as a kind of confirmation to your faith, to show you that whilst I may be railed upon as a heretic and as a hyper-Calvinist, after all I am backed up by antiquity. All the past stands by me. I do not care for the present.

Give me the past and I will hope for the future. Let the present rise up in my teeth, I will not care. What though a host of the churches of London may have forsaken the great cardinal doctrines of God, it matters not. If a handful of us stand alone in an unflinching maintenance of the sovereignty of our God, if were are beset by enemies, ay, and even by our own brethren, who ought to be our friends and helpers, it matters not, if we can but count upon the past; the noble army of martyrs, the glorious host of confessors, are our friends; the witnesses of truth stand by us. With these for us, we will not say that we stand alone, but we may exclaim, "Lo, God hath reserved unto himself seven thousand that have not bowed the knee unto Baal." But the best of all is, God *is with us*. The great truth is always the Bible, and the Bible alone. My hearers, you do not believe in any other book than the Bible, do you? If I could prove this from all the books in Christendom; if I could fetch back the Alexandrian library, and prove it thence, you would not believe it any more; but you surely will believe what is in God's Word. I have selected a few texts to read to you. I love to give you a whole volley of texts when I am afraid you will distrust a truth, so that you may be too astonished to doubt, if you do not in reality believe. Just let me run through a catalogue of passages where the people of God are called elect. Of course if the people are called *elect*, there must be *election*. If Jesus Christ and his apostles were accustomed to style believers by the title of elect, we must certainly believe that they were so, otherwise the term does not mean anything. Jesus Christ says, "Except that the Lord had shortened those days, no flesh should be saved; but for the *elect's* sake, whom he hath chosen, he hath shortened the days." "False Christs and false prophets shall rise, and shall shew signs and wonders, to seduce, if it were possible, even the *elect*." "Then shall he send his angels, and shall gather together his elect from the four winds, from the uttermost parts of the earth to the uttermost part of heaven."—Mark 13:20, 22, 27, "Shall not God avenge his own *elect* who cry day and night unto him, though he bear long with them?"—Luke 18:7. Together with many other passages which might be selected, wherein either the word "elect," or "chosen," or "foreordained," or "appointed," is mentioned; or the phrase "my sheep," or some similar designation, showing that Christ's people are distinguished from the rest of mankind. But you have concordances, and I will not trouble you with texts.

Throughout the epistles, the saints are constantly called "the elect." In the Colossians we find Paul saying, "Put on therefore, as the *elect* of God, holy and beloved, bowels of mercies." When he writes to Titus, he calls himself, "Paul, a servant of God, and an apostle of Jesus Christ, according to the faith of God's *elect*." Peter says "*Elect* according to the foreknowledge of God the Father." Then if you turn to John, you will find he is very fond of the word. He says, "The Elder to the *elect* lady;" and he speaks of our "*elect* sister." And we know where it is written "The church that is at Babylon, *elected* together with you." They were not ashamed of the word in those days; they were not afraid to talk about it. Now-a-days the word has been dressed up with diversities of meaning, and persons have mutilated and marred the doctrine, so that they have made it a very doctrine of devils, I do confess; and many who calls themselves believers, have gone to rank Antinomianism. But not withstanding this, why should I be ashamed of it, if men do wrest it? We love God's truth on the rack, as well as when it is walking upright. If there were a martyr whom we loved before he came on the rack, we should love him more still when he was stretched there. When God's truth is stretched on the rack, we do not call it falsehood. We love not to see it racked but we love it even when racked, because we can discern what its proper proportions ought to have been if it had not been racked and tortured by the cruelty and inventions of men. If you will read many of the epistles of the ancient fathers, you will find them always writing to the people of God as the "elect." Indeed the common conversational term used among many of the churches by the primitive Christians to one another was that of the "elect." They would often use the term to one another, showing that it was generally believed that all God's people were manifestly "elect."

But now for the verses that will positively prove the doctrine. Open your Bibles and turn to John 15:16, and there you will see that Jesus Christ has chosen his people, for he says, "Ye have not chosen me, but I have chosen you, and ordained you, that ye should go and bring forth fruit, and that your fruit should remain: that whatsoever ye shall ask of the Father in my name, he may give it you." Then in the 19th verse, "If ye were of the world, the world would love its own but because ye are not of the world, but I have chosen you out of the world, therefore the world hateth you." Then in the 17th chapter and the 8th and 9th verses, "For I have given unto them the words which thou gavest me; and they have received them and have known surely that I came out from thee, and they have believed that thou didst send me. I pray for them: I pray not for the world, but for them which thou hast given me for they are thine." Turn to Acts 13:48: "And when the Gentiles heard this, they were glad, and glorified the word of the Lord; and as many as were ordained to eternal life believed." They may try to split that passage into hairs if they like; but it says, "ordained to eternal life" in the original as plainly as it possibly can; and we do not care about all the different commentaries thereupon. You scarcely need to be reminded of Romans 8, because I trust you are all well acquainted with that chapter and understand it by this time. In the 29th and following verses, it says, "For whom he did foreknow, he also did predestinate to be conformed to the image of his Son, that he might be the first-born among many brethren. Moreover, whom he did predestinate, them he also called: and whom he called, them he also justified and whom he justified, them he also glorified. What shall we then say to these things? If God be for us, who can be against us? He that spared not his own Son, but delivered him up for us all, how shall he not with him also freely give us all things? Who shall lay anything to the charge of God's elect?" It would also be unnecessary to repeat the whole of the 9th chapter of Romans. As long as that remains in the Bible, no man shall be able to prove Arminianism; so long as that is written there, not the most violent contortions of the passage will ever be able to exterminate the doctrine of election from the Scriptures. Let us read such verses as these— "For the children being not yet born, neither having done any good or evil, that the purpose of God according to election might stand, not of works, but of him that calleth; it was said unto her, The Elder shall serve the younger." Then read the 22nd verse, "What if God, willing to show his wrath, and to make his power known, endured with much long suffering the vessels of wrath fitted to destruction. And that he might make known the riches of his glory on the vessels of mercy, which he had afore prepared unto glory," Then go on to Romans

11:7—"What then? Israel hath not obtained that which he seeketh for; but the election hath obtained it, and the rest were blinded," In the 6th verse of the same chapter, we read—"Even so then at this present time also there is a remnant according to the election of grace." You, no doubt, all recollect the passage in 1 Corinthians 1:26-29: "For ye see your calling, brethren, how that not many wise men after the flesh, not many mighty, not many noble, are called: but God hath chosen the foolish things of the world to confound the wise; and God hath chosen the weak things of the world to confound the things which are mighty; and base things of the world, and things which are despised, hath God chosen, yea, and things which are not, to bring to nought things which are: that no flesh should glory in his presence." Again, remember the passage in 1 Thessalonians 5:9;—God hath not appointed *us* to wrath, but to obtain salvation by our Lord Jesus Christ;" and then you have my text, which methinks would be quite enough. But, if you need any more, you can find them at your leisure, if we have not quite removed your suspicions as to the doctrine not being true.

Methinks, my friends, that this overwhelming mass of Scripture testimony must stagger those who dare to laugh at this doctrine. What shall we say of those who have so often despised it, and denied its divinity; who have railed at its justice, and dared to defy God and call him an Almighty tyrant, when they have heard of his having elected so many to eternal life? Canst thou, O rejector! cast it out of the Bible? Canst thou take the penknife of Jehudi and cut it out of the Word of God?

Wouldst thou be like the women at the feet of Solomon, and have the child rent in halves, that thou mightest have thy half? Is it not here in Scripture? And is it not thy duty to bow before it, and meekly acknowledge what thou understandest not—to receive it as the truth even though thou couldst not understand its meaning? I will not attempt to prove the justice of God in having thus elected some and left others. It is not for me to vindicate my Master. He will speak for himself, and he does so: —"Nay, but, O man, who art thou that repliest against God? Shall the thing formed say to him that formed it, Why hast thou made me thus? Hath not the potter power over the clay of the same lump to make one vessel unto honor and another unto dishonor?" Who is he that shall say unto his father, 'What hast thou begotten?' or unto his mother, 'What hast thou brought forth?' "I am the Lord—I form the light and create darkness. I, the Lord, do all these things." Who art thou that repliest against God? Tremble and kiss his rod; bow down and submit to his scepter; impugn not his justice, and arraign not his acts before thy bar, O man!

But there are some who say, "It is hard for God to choose some and leave others." Now, I will ask you one question. Is there any of you here this morning who wishes to be holy, who wishes to be regenerate, to leave off sin and walk in holiness? "Yes, there is," says some one, "I do." Then God has elected you. But another says, "No; I don't want to be holy; I don't want to give up my lusts and my vices." Why should you grumble, then, that God has not elected you to it? For if you were elected you would not like it, according to your own confession. If God this morning had chosen you to holiness, you say you would not care for it. Do you not acknowledge that you prefer drunkenness to sobriety, dishonesty to honesty? You love this world's pleasures better than religion; then why should you grumble that God has not chosen you to religion? If you love religion, he *has* chosen you to it. If you desire it, he has chosen you to it. If you do not, what right have you to say that God ought to have given you what you do not wish for? Supposing I had in my hand something which you do not value, and I said I shall give it to such-and-such a person, you would have no right to grumble that I did not give to you. You could not be so foolish as to grumble that the other has got what you do not care about. According to your own confession, many of you do not want religion, do not want a new heart and a right spirit, do not want the forgiveness of sins, do not want sanctification; you do not want to be elected to these things: then why should you grumble? You count these things but as husks, and why should you complain of God who has given them to those whom he has chosen? If you believe them to be good and desire them, they are there for thee. God gives liberally to all those who desire; and first of all, he makes them desire, otherwise they never would. If you love these things, he has elected you to them, and you may have them; but if you do not, who are you that you should find fault with God, when it is your own desperate will that keeps you from loving these things—your own simple self that makes you hate them? Suppose a man in the street should say, "What a shame it is I cannot have a seat in the chapel to hear what this man has to say." And suppose he says, "I hate the preacher; I can't bear his doctrine; but still it's a shame I have not a seat." Would you expect a man to say so? No: you would at once say, "That man does not care for it. Why should he trouble himself about other people having what they value and he despises?" You do not like holiness, you do not like righteousness; if God has elected me to these things, has he hurt you by it?

"Ah! but," say some, "I thought it meant that God elected some to heaven and some to hell." That is every different matter from the gospel doctrine. He has elected men to holiness and to righteousness and through that to heaven. You must not say that he has elected these simply to heaven, and others only to hell. He has elected you to holiness, if you love holiness. If any of you love to be saved by Jesus Christ, Jesus Christ elected you to be saved. If any of you desire to have salvation, you are elected to have it, if you desire it sincerely and earnestly. But, if you don't desire it, why on earth should you be so preposterously foolish as to grumble because God gives that which you do not like to other people?

II. Thus I have tried to say something with regard to the truth of the doctrine of election. And now, briefly, let me say that election is ABSOLUTE: that is, it does not depend upon what we are. The text says, "God hath from the beginning chosen us unto salvation;" but our opponents say that God chooses people because they are good, that he chooses them on account of sundry works which they have done. Now, we ask in reply to this, what works are those on account of which God elects his people? Are they what we commonly call "works of law,"—works of obedience which the creature can render? If so, we reply to you—If men cannot be justified by the works of the law, it seems to us pretty clear that they cannot be elected by the works of the law: if they cannot be justified by their good deeds, they cannot be saved by them. Then the decree of election could not have been formed upon good works. "But," say others, "God elected them on the foresight of their faith." Now, God gives faith, therefore he could not have elected them on account of faith, which he foresaw. There shall be twenty beggars in the street, and I determine to give one of them a shilling; but will any one say that I determined to give that one a shilling, that I elected him to have the shilling, because I foresaw that he would have it? That would be talking nonsense. In like manner to say that God elected men because he foresaw they would have faith, which is salvation in the germ, would be too absurd for us to listen to for a moment. Faith is the gift of God. Every virtue comes from him.

Therefore it cannot have caused him to elect men, because it is his gift. Election, we are sure, is absolute, and altogether apart from the virtues which the saints have afterwards. What though a saint should be as holy and devout as Paul, what though he should be as bold as Peter, or as loving as John, yet he would claim nothing from his Maker. I never knew a saint yet of any denomination, who thought that God saved him because he foresaw that he would have these virtues and merits. Now, my brethren, the best jewels that the saint ever wears, if they be jewels of trio own fashioning, are not of the first water. There is something of earth mixed with them. The highest grace we ever possess has something of earthliness about it. We feel this when we are most refined, when we are most sanctified, and our language must always be—

"I the chief of sinners am;
Jesus died for me."

Our only hope, our only plea, still hangs on grace as exhibited in the person of Jesus Christ. And I am sure we must utterly reject and disregard all thought that our graces, which are gifts of our Lord, which are his right-hand planting, could have ever caused his love. And we ever must sing—

"What was there in us that could merit esteem
Or give the Creator delight?"
"Twas even so Father we ever must sing,
Because it seemed good in thy sight."

"He will have mercy on whom he will have mercy:" he saves because he will save. And if you ask me why he saves me, I can only say, because he would do it. Is there anything in me that should recommend me to God?

No; I lay aside everything, I had nothing to recommend me. When God saved me I was the most abject, lost, and ruined of the race. I lay before him as an infant in my blood. Verily, I had no power to help myself. O how wretched did I feel and know myself to be! If you had something to recommend you to God, I never had. I will be content to be saved by *grace*, unalloyed, pure grace. I can boast of no merits. If you can do so, I cannot. I must sing—

"Free grace alone from the first to the last
Hath won my affection and held my soul fast."

III. Then, thirdly, this election is ETERNAL. "God hath from the beginning chose you unto eternal life. Can any man tell me when the beginning was?

Years ago we thought the beginning of this world was when Adam came upon it; but we have discovered that thousands of years before that God was preparing chaotic matter to make it a fit abode for man, putting races of creatures upon it, who might die and leave behind the marks of his handiwork and marvelous skill, before he tried his hand on man. But that was not the beginning, for revelation points us to a period long ere this world was fashioned, to the days when the morning stars were begotten when, like drops of dew, from the fingers of the morning, stars and constellations fell trickling from the hand of God; when, by his own lips, he launched forth ponderous orbs; when with his own hand he sent comets, like thunderbolts, wandering through the sky, to find one day their proper sphere. We go back to years gone by, when worlds were made and systems fashioned, but we have not even approached the beginning yet. Until we go to the time when all the universe slept in the mind of God as yet unborn, until we enter the eternity where God the Creator lived alone, everything sleeping within him, all creation resting in his mighty gigantic thought, we have not guessed the beginning. We may go back, back, back, ages upon ages. We may go back, if we might use such strange words, whole eternities, and yet never arrive at the beginning. Our wing might be tired, our imagination would die away; could it outstrip the lightnings flashing in majesty, power, and rapidity, it would soon weary itself ere it could get to the beginning. But God from the beginning chose his people; when the unnavigated ether was yet unfanned by the wing of a single angel, when space was shoreless, or else unborn when universal silence reigned, and not a voice or whisper shocked the solemnity of silence, when there was no being and no motion, no time, and nought but God himself, alone in his eternity; when without the song of an angel, without the attendance of even the cherubim, long ere the living creatures were born, or the wheels of the chariot of Jehovah were fashioned, even then, "in the beginning was the Word," and in the beginning God's people were one with the Word, and "in the beginning he chose them into eternal life." Our election then is eternal. I will not stop to prove it, I only just run over these thoughts for the benefit of young beginners, that they may understand what we mean by eternal, absolute election.

IV. And, next, the election is PERSONAL. Here again, our opponents have tried to overthrow election by telling us that it is an election of nations; and not of people. But here the Apostle says, "God hath from the beginning chosen *you*." It is the most miserable shift on earth to make out that God hath not chosen persons but nations, because the very same objection that lies against the choice of persons, lies against the choice of a nation. If it were not just to choose a person, it would be far more unjust to choose a nation, since nations are but the union of multitudes of persons, and to choose a nation seems to be a more gigantic crime—if election be a crime—than to choose one person. Surely to choose ten thousand would be reckoned to be worse than choosing one; to distinguish a whole nation from the rest of mankind, does seem to be a greater extravaganza in the acts; divine sovereignty than the election of one poor mortal and leaving out another. But what are nations but men? What are whole peoples but combinations of different units? A nation is made up of that individual, and that, and that. And if you tell me that God chose the Jews, I say then, he chose that Jew, and that Jew, and that Jew. And if you say he chooses Britain, then I say he chooses that British man, and that British man, and that British man. So that is the same thing after all. Election then is personal: it must be so. Every one who reads this text, and others like it, will see that Scripture continually speaks of God's people one by one and speaks of them as having been the special subjects of election.

"Sons we are through God's election,
Who in Jesus Christ believe;
By eternal destination
Sovereign grace we here receive."

We know it is personal election.

V. The other thought is—for my time flies too swiftly to enable me to dwell at length upon these points—that election produces GOOD RESULTS, "He hath from the beginning chosen you unto sanctification of the spirit, and belief of the truth." How many men mistake the doctrine of election altogether! and how my soul burns and boils at the recollection of the terrible evils that have accrued from the spoiling and the wresting of that glorious portion of God's glorious truth! How many are there who have said to themselves, "I am elect," and have sat down in sloth, and worse than that! They have said, "I am the elect of God," and with both hands they have done wickedness. They have swiftly run to every unclean thing, because they have said, "I am the chosen child of God, irrespective of my works, therefore I may live as I list, and do what I like." O, beloved! let me solemnly warn every one of you not to carry the truth too far; or, rather not to turn the truth into error, for we cannot carry it too far. We may overstep the truth; we can make that which was meant to be sweet for our comfort, a terrible mixture for our destruction. I tell you there have been thousands of men who have been ruined by misunderstanding election; who have said, "God has elected me to heaven, and to eternal life," but they have forgotten that it is written, God has elected them "through sanctification of the Spirit and belief of the truth." This is God's election—election to sanctification and to faith. God chooses his people to be holy, and to be believers. How many of you here then are believers? How many of my congregation can put their hands upon their hearts and say, "I trust in God that I am sanctified?" Is there one of you who says, "I am elect" —I remind that you swore last week. One of you says, "I trust I am elect"—but I jog your memory about some vicious act that you committed during the last six days. Another of you says, "I am elect"—but I would look you in the face and say, "*Elect!* thou art a most cursed hypocritical and that is all thou art." Others would say, "I am elect"—but I would remind them that they neglect the mercy-seat and do not pray. Oh, beloved! never think you are elect unless you are holy. You may come to Christ as a sinner, but you may not come to Christ as an elect person until you can see your holiness. Do not misconstrue what I say—do not say "I am elect," and yet think you can be living in sin. That is impossible. The elect of God are holy. They are not pure, they are not perfect, they are not spotless; but, taking their life as a whole, they are holy persons. They are marked, and distinct from others: and no man has a right to conclude himself elect except in his holiness. He may be elect, and yet lying in darkness, but he has no right to believe it; no one can see it, there is no evidence of it. The man may live one day, but he is dead at present. If you are walking in the fear of God, trying to please him, and to obey his commandments, doubt not that your name has been written in the Lamb's book of life from before the foundation of the world. And, lest this should be too high for yon, note the other mark of election, which is faith, "belief of the truth." Whoever believes God's truth, and believes on Jesus Christ, is elect. I frequently meet with poor souls, who are fretting and worrying themselves about this thought—"How, if I should not be elect!" "Oh, sir," they say, "I know I put my trust in Jesus; I know I believe in his name and trust in his blood; but how if I should not be elect?" Poor dear creature! you do not know much about the gospel, or you would never talk so, for *he that believes is elect.* Those who are elect, are elect unto sanctification and unto faith; and if you have faith you are one of God's elect; you may know it and ought to know it, for it is an absolute certainty. If you, as a sinner, look to Jesus Christ this morning, and say—

"Nothing in my hands I bring,
Simply to thy cross I cling,"

you are elect. I am not afraid of election frightening poor saints or sinners. There are many divines who tell the enquirer "election has nothing to do with you." That is very bad, because the poor soul is not to be silenced like that. If you could silence him so, it might be well, but he will think of it, he can't help it. Say to him then, if you believe on the Lord Jesus Christ you are elect. If you will cast yourself on Jesus, you are elect. I tell you—the chief of sinners—this morning, I tell you in his name, if you will come to God without any works of your own, cast yourself on the blood and righteousness of Jesus Christ; if you will come now and trust in him, you are elect—you were loved of God from before the foundation of the world, for you could not do that unless God had given you the power, and had chosen you to do it. Now you are safe and secure if you do but come and cast yourself on Jesus Christ, and wish to be saved and to be loved by him.

But think not that any man will be saved without faith and without holiness. Do not conceive, my hearers, that some decree, passed in the dark ages of eternity, will save your souls, unless you believe in Christ. Do not sit down and fancy that you are to be saved without faith and holiness. That is a most abominable and accursed heresy, and has ruined thousands. Lay not election as a pillow for you to sleep on, or you may be ruined. God forbid that I should be sewing pillows under armholes that you may rest comfortably in your sins. Sinner! there is nothing in the Bible to palliate your sins. But if thou art condemned O man! if thou art lost O woman! thou wilt not find in this Bible one drop to cool thy tongue, or one doctrine to palliate thy guilt; your damnation will be entirely your own fault, and your sin will richly merit it, because ye believe not ye are condemned. "Ye believe not because ye are not of my sheep." Ye wilt not come to me that ye might have life." Do not fancy that election excuses sin—do not dream of it—do not rock yourself in sweet complacency in the thought of your irresponsibility. You are responsible. We must give you both things. We must have divine sovereignty, and we must have man's responsibility. We must have election, but we must ply your hearts, we must send God's truth at you; we must speak to you, and remind you of this, that while it is written, "In me is thy help," yet it is also written, "O Israel, thou hast destroyed thyself."

VI. Now, lastly, what are the true and legitimate tendencies of right conceptions concerning the doctrine of election. First, I will tell you what the doctrine of election will make saints do under the blessing of God; and, secondly what it will do for sinners if God blesses it to them. "First, I think election, to a saint, is one of the most *stripping* doctrines in all the world—to take away all trust in the flesh, or all reliance upon anything except Jesus Christ. How often do we wrap ourselves up in our own righteousness, and array ourselves with the false pearls and gems of our own works and doings. We begin to say "Now I shall be saved, because I have this and that evidence." Instead of that, it is naked faith that saves; that faith and that alone unites to the Lamb irrespective of works, although it is productive of them. How often do we lean on some work, other than that of our own Beloved, and trust in some might, other than that which comes from on high. Now if we would have this might taken from us, we must consider election. Pause my soul, and consider this. God loved thee before thou hadst a being. He loved thee when thou wast dead in trespasses and sins, and sent his Son to die for thee. He purchased thee with his precious blood ere thou couldst lisp his name. Canst thou then be proud?

I know nothing, nothing again, that is more *humbling* for us than this doctrine of election. I have sometimes fallen prostrate before it, when endeavoring to understand it. I have stretched my wings, and, eagle-like, I have soared towards the sun. Steady has been my eye, and true my wing, for a season; but, when I came near it, and the one thought possessed me, —"God hath from the beginning chosen you unto salvation," I was lost in its lustre, I was staggered with the mighty thought; and from the dizzy elevation down came my soul, prostrate and broken, saying, "Lord, I am nothing, I am less than nothing. Why me? Why me?" Friends, if you want to be humbled, study election, for it will make you humble under the influence of God's Spirit. He who is proud of his election is not elect; and he who is humbled under a sense of it may believe that he is. He has every reason to believe that he is, for it is one of the most blessed effects of election that it helps us to humble ourselves before God. Once again. Election in the Christian should make him very *fearless* and very *bold*. No man will be so bold as he who believes that he is elect of God. What cares he for man if he is chosen of his Maker? What will he care for the pitiful chirpings of some tiny sparrows when he knoweth that he is an eagle of a royal race? Will he care when the beggar pointeth at him, when the blood royal of heaven runs in his veins? Will he fear if all the world stand against him? If earth be all in arms abroad, he dwells in perfect peace, for he is in the secret place of the tabernacle of the Most High, in the great pavillion of the Almighty. "I am God's," says he, "I am distinct from other men. They are of an inferior race. Am not I noble? Am not I one of the aristocrats of heaven? Is not my name written in God's book?" Does he care for the world? Nay: like the lion that careth not for the barking of the dog, he smileth at all his enemies; and when they come too near him, he moveth himself and dasheth them to pieces. What careth he for them? He walks about them like a colossus; while little men walk under him and understand him not. His brow is made of iron, his heart is of flint—what doth he care for man? Nay; if one universal hiss came up from the wide world, he would smile at it, for he would say,—

"He that hath made his refuge God,
Shall find a most secure abode."

"I am one of his elect. I am chosen of God and precious; and though the world cast me out, I fear not. Ah! ye time-serving professors, some of you ear bend like the willows. There are few oaken-Christians now-a-days, that can stand the storm; and I will tell you the reason. It is because you do not believe yourselves to be elect. The man who knows he is elect will be too proud to sin; he will not humble himself to commit the acts of common people. The believer in this truth will say "*I* compromise my principles? *I* change my doctrines? *I* lay aside my views? *I* hide what I believe to be true? 'No.' Since I know I am one of God's elect, in the very teeth of all men, I shall speak God's truth, whatever man may say." Nothing makes a man so truly bold as to feel that he is God's elect. He shall not quiver, he shall not shake, who knows that God has chosen him.

Moreover, election will make us *holy*. Nothing under the gracious influence of the Holy Spirit can make a Christian more holy than the thought that he is chosen. "Shall I sin," he says, "after God hath chosen me? Shall I transgress after such love? Shall I go astray after so much loving kindness and tender mercy? Nay, my God; since thou hast chosen me, I will love thee; I will live to thee—

'Since thou, the everlasting God,
My Father art become;'
"I will give myself to thee to be thine for ever, by election and by redemption, casting myself on thee, and solemnly consecrating myself to thy service."

And now, lastly, to the ungodly. What says election to you? First, ye ungodly ones, I will excuse you for a moment. There are many of you who do not like election, and I cannot blame you for it, for I have heard those preach election, who have sat down, and said, "I have not one word to say to the sinner." Now, I say you *ought* to dislike such preaching as that, and I do not blame you for it. But. I say, take courage, take hope, O thou sinner, that there is election. So far from dispiriting and discouraging thee, it is a very hopeful and joyous thing that there is an election. What if I told thee perhaps none can be saved, none are ordained to eternal life; wouldst thou not tremble and fold thy hands in hopelessness, and say, "Then how can I be saved, since none are elect?" But, I say, there is a multitude elect, beyond all counting—a host that no mortal can number. Therefore, take heart, thou poor sinner! Cast away thy despondency—mayest thou not be elect as well as any other?—for there is a host innumerable chosen. There is joy and comfort for thee! Then, not only take heart, but go and try the Master. Remember, if you were not elect, you would lose nothing by it. What did the four Syrians say? "Let us fall unto the host of the Syrians, for if we stay here we must die, and if we go to them we can but die." O sinner! come to the throne of electing mercy, Thou mayest die where thou art. Go to God; and, even supposing he should spurn thee, suppose his uplifted hand should drive thee away—a thing impossible—yet thou wilt not lose anything; thou wilt not be more damned for that. Besides, supposing thou be damned, thou wouldst have the satisfaction at least of being able to lift up thine eyes in hell, and say, "God, I asked mercy of thee and thou wouldst not grant it; I sought it, but thou didst refuse it." That thou never shalt say, O sinner! If thou goest to him, and askest him, thou shalt receive; for he never has spurned one yet! Is not that hope for you? What though there is an allotted number, yet it is true that all who seek belong to that number. Go thou and seek; and if thou shouldst be the first one to go to hell, tell the devils that thou didst perish thus—tell the demons that thou art a castaway, after having come as a guilty sinner to Jesus. I tell thee it would disgrace the Eternal—with reverence to his name—and he would not allow such a thing. He is jealous of his honor, and he could not allow a sinner to say that.

But ah, poor soul! not only think thus, that thou canst not lose anything by coming; there is yet one more thought-dost thou love the thought of election this morning? Art thou willing to admit its justice? Dost thou say, "I feel that I am lost I deserve it, and that if my brother is saved I cannot murmur. If God destroy me, I deserve it, but if he saves the person sitting beside me, he has a right to do what he will with his own; and I have lost nothing by it." Can you say that honestly from your heart? If so, then the doctrine of election has had its right effect on your spirit, and you are not far from the kingdom of heaven. You are brought where you ought to be, where the Spirit wants you to be; and being do this morning, depart in peace; God has forgiven your sins. You would not feel that if you were not pardoned, you would not feel that if the Spirit of God were not working in you. Rejoice, then, in this. Let your hope rest on the cross of Christ. Think not on election, but on Christ Jesus. Rest on Jesus—Jesus first, midst, and without end.

FYI Study: More Discussion of WCF 3("Election")

[T]he cardinal principle of the alone Headship of Jesus Christ . . . colored all their discussions and directed them to all their conclusions. As the sovereignty of God was the formative principle in their theology, so the sovereignty of God, the Son, was the shaping principle in their system of government and worship. The key in each case was the same. When they passed from doctrine to polity, or from polity to doctrine, or from both to worship, there was no break in the harmony.

It helps to have some of the opposition in mind, to better understand some of the truths in the Westminster standards.8 It is often pointed out that few doctrines are formulated neutrally or without reaction to some error or event. That is no doubt true in regard to these teachings. It might be helpful to understand these teachings on the Sovereignty of God as exact opposites of the sovereignty of man or more particularly as opposites of the sovereignty of a particular man—the King or the Pope.

This doctrine is in some respects very political, at least revolutionary in terms of its rejection of the monarch's authority. Upholding the sole sovereignty of God was an act of political subversion in the 1640s. The attempt to undermine the sovereignty of the King or the Pope, and in turn replacing that with only the Sovereignty of God, was biblical, radical, and, in effect, political. If we can grasp that, it may help us appreciate some things, especially since this Confession will inevitably cut against our grain in some places.

Arminians (those who believe that man—on his own—chooses God or determines his own destiny) were evidently not present at the Assembly. Although most of the clergy had previously received Episcopal ordination, these divines were not of the Arminian persuasion, as compared to many of the state-sponsored Anglicans, who had begun the descent toward a more man-centered approach. One commentator said that if there was an Arminian present he didn't make a peep, and T. Dwight Witherspoon (1897) noted: "If there was an Arminian in all the body he did not have courage to lift his head. Nor should this surprise us, for the Church of England . . . was, in its best elements, as intensely Calvinistic as the Church of Scotland, or that of Holland." In fact, Witherspoon went so far as to characterize the adversary of the Westminster beliefs, Arminianism, in this way: "Men may play with Arminianism in times of peace, but in the great crises of spiritual conflict there is nothing but the solid bedrock of eternal sovereignty of God on which the foot can rest with any sense of security; and in times like these, churches, as well as individuals, unconsciously become Calvinists."

The purpose of this study is to explore and contrast the differences between the Westminster Assembly participants' view on the critical doctrine of God's sovereignty and its rivals. The differences were, and are, profound, political, and worth our attention, challenging though these may be.

---

8 Portions of this discussion are taken from my *Windows on Westminster*, Copyright © 1993, Great Commission Publications, Suwanee, Georgia; used with permission.

There are few parts of the Confession of Faith, which are more contested than this particular set of ideas. Let me say from the outset, however, that none of the other alternatives are near as compatible with scriptural teaching as this Westminster doctrine. As we consider God's sovereignty let us first of all begin with a working definition. In the mid-seventeenth century when the Westminster Assembly met, the notion of sovereignty was clearly understood, perhaps better than we understand in our own times. A 'sovereign' was one who had authoritative rule and decision-making power. Although a number of other evangelical Christians did (and do) confess that they believe in the "sovereignty" of God, frequently their very idea of sovereignty is different from the one contained in the minds of the divines. Sovereignty, by definition, is a pretty absolute term, which does not admit shared authority. A little sovereignty is like semi-pregnancy; either one is or isn't. As we look into this concept it will be necessary to understand this idea of absolute sovereignty at the outset.

As we study and compare these ideas with Scripture, we will find that the Westminster Assembly authors were as faithful in representing Scripture on this particular topic as they were on others. That is a primary and challenging issue to every reader of the WCF. As people who have been brought up in an age which believes strongly in freedom of choice, desires referenda on various political issues, and frequently votes to determine our own future destiny, often we find it difficult to accept the fact that the Scriptures teach that God is our true sovereign who reveals and who also has authoritative working power. The question that should be asked as we study these parts of the Confession is: Does the Confession represent true biblical teaching? Or is it a fabrication of human thought? As we pursue those questions readers should put aside various backgrounds and consider the Word of God first by hearing these authors' confession of it.

To properly appreciate the WCF teaching on the sovereignty of God we should review chapter 2, where the foundation for God's sovereignty is laid in his very attributes. The WCF, immediately following its discussion of the Holy Scripture, sets forth the attributes of God as the Trinitarian God. As we see, from a scriptural study of this topic, those attributes are not only the foundation but also the ultimate reasons why God does certain things. If we correctly understand *who* God is, then we have a better grasp on *what* he does according to scriptural teaching. Hence the WCF is wise to depict the attributes of God as the foundation of his works and activity. With a keen eye toward scriptural representation there are very few of those attributes that anyone should question. And if God's very character is as described in chapter 2 of the Confession of Faith, then we will find that his working in chapter 3 is similar.

Many a Christian will start reading the first paragraph of chapter 3 of the WCF and become offended by its bold statement. Sometimes it is helpful to acquaint people with these doctrines by first pointing their attention to the purpose of such doctrine as the Confession explains it in 3:8. In that section the WCF says, "The doctrine of this high mystery of predestination is to be handled with special prudence and care, that men, attending the will of God revealed in His Word, and yielding obedience thereunto, may, from the certainty of their effectual vocation, be assured of their eternal election. So shall this doctrine afford matter of praise, reverence, and admiration of God; and of humility, diligence, and abundant consolation to all that sincerely obey the Gospel."

The Confession wants to make it clear that there is great value in this teaching, but that it is a "high mystery" and to be handled with "special prudence and care." The goal of this scriptural teaching is to help persons, as they consider it, both to yield obedience and also to glean the certainty of their effectual calling. In 2 Peter 1:10, Peter too, urged his hearers "to give diligence to make their calling and election sure." To do so is to obey God and seek the mind of God in our own case. Moreover, the Confession of Faith teaches that this doctrine, if properly understood, leads to a number of practical benefits. It should also be said at this point that, if a person does not see this teaching as beneficial, it is likely that he has a misunderstanding of the essence of the doctrine. So if we find ourselves averse to the high mystery of predestination, or if it causes us great anxiety or vexation of spirit, then we need to return to the Scriptures and understand its purpose as it was meant to be. The divines said that its purpose was to bring about benefits such as praise, reverence, and admiration of God, as well as humility, diligence and great consolation to believers.

Earlier confessional statements stated things in the same manner. The *Thirty-Nine Articles* speak of predestination and election as "so excellent a benefit of God" (Article 17), which is "full of sweet, pleasant, and unspeakable comfort to godly persons, and such as feel in themselves the working of the Spirit of Christ, mortifying the works of the flesh and their earthly members, and drawing up their mind to high and heavenly things." The Anglican *Thirty-Nine Articles* also recognize that the doctrine of predestination could have great benefit to believers, but also could result in great consternation among unbelievers. Ultimately we always are to keep before us the fact that we are to act on and obey those things, which are expressly declared to us in the Word of God, understanding that there are some secret things (Deut. 29:29) that the Lord does not reveal to us. Hence we are to act on that which is clearly revealed.

The earlier *Articles of Faith for the Church of Ireland* (from which some of the chapters in the WCF are derived) also spoke of predestination as having a confirming and encouraging effect for believers, although possibly incomprehensible to unbelievers. Earlier in the century, the Synod of Dort (Article 12) had confessed: "Out of the sense and certainty of this election, the children of God daily draw more and more manner of humbling themselves before God, of adoring the depth of his mercies, of purifying themselves, and of loving him fervently who first loved them so much: so far is this doctrine of election, and the meditation thereof, from making them carnally secure, or backward in observing God's commandments. Which abuse, by God's just judgment, is wont to befall those, who either rashly presume, or vainly and malapertly prate of the grace of election, refusing withal to walk in the ways of the elect." In the seventeenth century there was wide agreement among biblical people on this topic.

It is seen from these confessions prior the Westminster Assembly that the doctrine of predestination had an effect of daily drawing Christians to be more and more humble, and to assist us in adoring the depths of God's mercy and to exalt in his Name. Still it was counseled that this doctrine should be propounded with discretion. Thus we see that the other confessional statements share the same spirit of the Westminster Assembly in cautioning against the misuse of predestination, but also in encouraging the excellent use. In sum, if we will first understand the intent or purpose of the doctrine we will have a better opportunity to see its scripturalness. In summation there are three primary purposes of the teaching of WCF Chapter 3:

1) To give God the credit in salvation,
2) To demonstrate his sovereignty as Scripture teaches, and
3) To provide comfort or assurance to the believer.

Now with this understanding of the purpose and intent as our guideline—such that if we come to conclusions other than within that purpose we will only receive them as caution signs telling us to go back and re-study Scripture—let us return to the very first paragraph of Chapter 3. Now it may be seen that the first paragraph of the Confession is itself very scriptural in its assertion that God's decree (his plan for working out salvation and other events in history) was established not by other events outside of him but instead by his own eternal, wise, and holy consideration of his own plan. He began this plan in eternity past. The phrasing "God from all eternity did" is taken from the scriptural phrase used a number of times in Scripture, which speaks of God establishing his plan "before the foundation of the earth" (Consider, for example, Mt. 25:34, Rev. 13:8, Eph. 1:4, and Jn. 17:5, 24.). Hence, before creation ever occurred, before there was ever an external universe, God had a plan for salvation in history, and it is rooted not in external events—for there were none at that time—rather it is rooted only in his own holy and wise counsel which he determined to bring about freely and unchangeably. Yet the WCF is also equally scriptural and balanced to assert that neither is God the author of sin, nor is violation given to the will of the creature, nor are their acts as secondary causes taken away but rather validated.

It is helpful to remember that the language of the Westminster Confession was written as a constitutional-legal document. In this first paragraph, the first statement gives us the positive teaching, while the second part of the paragraph states three disclaimers, i.e., that (1) God is not himself the one who produces sin (James 1:13), and (2) that neither does God absolutely take away the willfulness or responsibility of human creatures, or (3) neither are the in-between acts and causes taken away. There are a number of causes in our world. God of course is the ultimate one. However, in between his ultimate will and actual human events, many other actors and causes arise. These are secondary causes, which are also ordained by God.

It will be very important for us to comprehend the Westminster teaching if we understand what the authors were trying to distance themselves from, or what they avoided in these areas. Other theologians might place more emphasis on free will and human ability, and one can frequently hear others suggest that God only established things from the past in keeping with what human beings would do, so as to never violate or infringe upon their will. That statement is but a restatement of an ancient heresy (Pelagianism), which was condemned by the church as being an erroneous sense of scriptural teaching as early as the fifth century. Hence the Westminster Assembly authors were seeking to be merely scriptural, and many of the very phrases in the first paragraph are taken from actual verses in Scripture. It would be a constructive study for anyone to find the number of scriptural illustrations in that first paragraph.

It should be remembered that the divines were at pains to make sure that God's sovereignty had full sway. Their most important consideration was to prevent any restraints from being put on God's freedom. As early as chapter 2 in the WCF, the divines confessed God as being most holy and most free. Chapter 3 therefore, could be understood as an attempt to protect God's own freedom, even if it meant restricting others' freedom. We might also recall that those drawing up the wording on "God's Decree" were conscious that there was a British sovereign who, from time to time, sought to usurp God's various prerogatives. The second paragraph of WCF 3 states that indeed God does decree whatever can come to pass on any supposed conditions. Moreover, the basis of his plan of salvation is not because he simply foresaw it as happening in future history or that somehow it would come about because of certain conditions. If that were the case, God would not be sovereign; instead, blind human history would be sovereign. It is not the case that God merely peers down the tunnel of human history to see what will happen, say in the year 2000, and then stamps his approval or disapproval on what is going to happen anyway, as if that were his plan. If that were the case, then, God would not be in control, but human beings and human history would be. Rather, these Divines had a strong belief that God was in control and that human history would conform itself to God's plan—not vice versa.

This truth—that God is the sole sovereign—is taught in many places in Scripture. It can be seen most clearly, for example, in Romans 9 where God speaks of determining certain things even to the extent of differentiating between those who are identical in their birth, according to his own will (Romans 9:11). Romans 9:18 says that God will have mercy on whom he will and will harden whom he will, thus indicating that God is sovereign. Jesus himself taught that not even a sparrow can fall to the ground without our Father knowing it (Mt. 10:29) and that the very hairs of our head are numbered. The New Testament church believed this strongly too, as Peter preaches in Acts 4 that God's hand determined Jesus' own death (Acts 4:27-28). Several times in the Book of Acts it is affirmed that God foreordained or pre-ordered certain events (for example, Acts 2:23, 3:18-20, 4:28, 13:48, 17:26).

It might be helpful for anyone to pause at this point and take out a simple Concordance to look up the number of times that election or predestation are used in the Bible. It has been said in more cases than we can imagine, and also by those who should know better, that predestation is a man-made doctrine. However, as one sees that the Scriptures teach this—and not only teach it in a few cases but by many references—one can call predestation a man-made doctrine only based on unfamiliarity with Scripture. Again, the challenging question to us in our own times is to ascertain whether or not the WCF has asserted unscriptural teachings. If they are scriptural in their teachings, then we should receive them with admiration and respect, and we should have our lives benefit as this chapter teaches. However, if they have invented or presented unscriptural teachings, then indeed these are worthy of rejection.

The next two paragraphs also clarify certain parts of God's decree of election and predestination. WCF 3:3 states that God, for the manifestation of his own glory, predestined some men and angels to life and others are foreordained to everlasting death. It is crucial to note that both men and angels are included here in this summary statement, noting that even the Fall and the fallen angels come under God's decree of predestination. The careful reader will also note that there is a word change in that paragraph, i.e., that some men and angels are *predestined to life* while others are *foreordained to everlasting death*. There is some scriptural difference in the usage of these words. However, the meaning and application as to whether or not God has the final determination as sovereign is no different by any meaning of those words. The divines obviously did not want to indicate that there was a degree of difference in God's determination of some to life and others to death. Rather, they were seeking to be as close to scriptural language as possible; hence the difference in those words.

These men and angels, the next paragraph goes on to tell us, are so predestined and designed that even their very number cannot be changed, that is, they cannot be either increased or diminished. This statement is not so much seeking to tell us that no one has an opportunity to enter the Kingdom of Heaven, as it is assuring us that God is truly sovereign as he says and that our eternal destiny rests in his hand so much so that the end result is unchangeable even by our own acts or by historical accidents. Thus the number is exactly what God wishes it to be. God's work of predestination and salvation is perfect, and he executes and completes it with all the perfection of who he is and in keeping with the beginning of his decree.

Some Bible-believers take strong exception to chapter 3 in the WCF. Many evangelicals, in fact, who seek to advance true and proper human responsibility align themselves more closely with those who are of an anti-Westminster persuasion. They argue that those who end up in heaven or hell will do so based upon their own determination or their own freely chosen acts. Both men and angels are included in this teaching that the free will of human beings is more determinative for salvation than is the sovereignty of God. As modern as these anti-Westminster people sound, and as emphatic as they are on human rights and ability, when we compare these ideas to Scripture, we find that in all cases the sovereign will of God is more important and more elevated than the choice or free decisions of human beings. These biblical students valued God's will, ability, and freedom over man's. It is important to note that none are saved by God's eternal predestination because of their goodness, nor should they have a haughtiness as if they have some ability that others don't. In fact, the Synod of Dort (I, 7) states clearly that when Christ chose a certain number of human beings he did not do so because they were "better, more worthy than others, but lying in the common misery with others."

After the statement of these general principles in paragraphs 1-4, in paragraphs 5-7 the WCF then applies this to two different classes of men: believers and unbelievers. Paragraph 5 speaks only of believers. Those out of the mass of humanity who have been pre-chosen by God before the foundation of the earth have been chosen in Christ to everlasting glory. One could turn in Scripture to Ephesians 1:4 to see this doctrine taught very plainly: "For he chose us in him before the creation of the world to be holy and blameless in his sight and in love he predestined us to be adopted as his sons" (Eph. 1:4-5). That verse tells us that God did choose us as Christians before the creation of the world to be predestined. Furthermore, this predestination is spoken of as having been formed in love, not in hatred or with a petty motivation of excluding others. Moreover, the statement in Ephesians 1:3-14 begins with a doxology—"Praise (Not Cursed!) be to God"—for doing this, while verse 6 speaks of our praise being given to his glorious grace through which he has freely chosen us. The mystery of this choosing according to his good pleasure is one that again leads us to be "For the praise of his glory" (Eph. 1:12). That's pretty positive!

Thus Christians have been chosen out of God's free grace and love, not according to nor depending on some pre-knowledge of God as to their faith, perseverance, or any other good in them. It is important to note that the Confession has an eye toward humility in reminding us that it is not because of our inherent goodness, perseverance, or any utility within the kingdom of God, which is the reason for God's choosing us. Rather, we are chosen and undeserving of his grace the whole time (cf. Rom. 9). The next paragraph speaks of the decree of God or his plan as it is actually worked out in the life of the elect. The sixth paragraph tells us that God has not only appointed the elect unto eternal glory, but that along with that, he also has ordained the various secondary roles for people, using the "means" toward that end. "Means" refers to things as common as other believers witnessing to a person who becomes a Christian, or an unconverted person reading a Christian book which stimulates spiritual interest leading to rebirth, or a number of other events—perhaps even including tragedy or difficulty that bring us to our knees. All of these are secondary causes or means ordained unto the end.

In addition this paragraph teaches that all of those who are in fact in Christ, having been fallen in Adam, once they are redeemed are also effectually called, justified, adopted, and sanctified as Romans 8:29-32 teaches. All of those who are God's children are not only incapable of earning their way to salvation, but throughout the whole of our life it is a work of grace stemming from God's eternal election. And neither according to this paragraph (and according to Scripture) are any other people justified and adopted, and sanctified, but the elect only.

Once again the challenge to the student of Scripture is to compare these teachings with the Bible. As one does so, it is likely that he will come to the same beliefs that the authors of the Confession did. The seventh paragraph treats the painful and controversial subject of why unbelievers are not in heaven or what happens to them. The Confession says that those not given God's special election (or the remaining part of mankind), God passes over and ordains them to dishonor and wrath for their sin, which also is to the praise of his glorious justice. Again the basis for this is found within God's sovereign power over his creatures and his own good pleasure.

Many other biblical Christians throughout history (see Spurgeon above), beginning with the great leaders in the New Testament on up through St. Augustine and down through medieval times, agreed with what was rediscovered by the Reformers and clearly stated in the Confessions of Ireland (1615), the Synod of Dort (1618-1619), and climatically in the Westminster Assembly in the 1640s. The teaching of Scripture is clearly set out in these doctrines. Consequently, if one holds the contrary of these positions, he has to undo or speak against these teachings; but the scriptural testimony is strong and clear. The plain scriptural teaching cannot be discounted. In fact the authors of the Assembly were so convinced of these teachings that they set them out with clear vigor and confidence. A study of other contemporaneous confessions would be a helpful confirmation that the Assembly was not creating doctrine but instead was simply putting forth that which was merely scriptural. It is helpful to recall the vow taken by the members of the Westminster Assembly to remember that they were not seeking to innovate doctrine but only to repeat that which was in scripture (cf. the vow above, which they took).

Of the importance and distinguishing mark of this teaching, twentieth century theologian John Murray noted:

> On this crucial issue, therefore, Calvin, Dordt, and Westminster are at one. The terms of expression differ, as we might expect, and the Westminster Confession with inimitable finesse and brevity has given to it the most classic formulation. But the doctrine is the same and this fact demonstrates the undissenting unity of thought on a tenet of faith that is a distinguishing mark of our Reformed heritage and without which the witness to the sovereignty of God and to his revealed counsel suffers eclipse at the point where it must jealously be maintained. For the glory of God is the issue at stake.

A word is in order about the proper role of human responsibility. The Scriptures certainly teach that we are responsible for our actions and that Christians (and even unbelievers) do take actions, which are products of their own will. Moreover, there are statements in the Bible that seem on the surface to indicate that any person may come to God, or that "whosoever will may come." It is important as we interpret those scriptures to neither minimize the truthfulness of those, nor to fail to harmonize those with the rest of Scripture's teaching. Scripture consistently has statements, which have various points of view. At times we are provided the divine perspective and, at other times, the human perspective. Each perspective is different in its origin, but they are in no way contradictory. Hence, the Scripture teaches *both* that God has a sovereign will and that people have a human and reasonable responsibility. The important thing is to understand that in both Old and New Testaments the authors of Scripture affirm and praise God's sovereignty as a glorious doctrine. It is not one that is hidden, nor is it one that is a cause of embarrassment to the church. The WCF authors saw this in this light' moreover, they saw that predestination was a grand attempt to be God-centered instead of being man-centered. At all times the authors of the Confession wanted to defend God (who lovingly executed predestination) as taking the initiative in our salvation. Yet he was never out of control or in the position of having been caught off guard or somehow as needing to form a contingency plan. God's sovereignty was never thwarted. In comparison or contrast to the earthly king's authority, which could be thwarted and could be fallible, God's sovereign rule was infallible, unchangeable, and unable of being resisted.

Lest one think that the Westminster divines lightly adopted these wordings, which admittedly caused greater stumbling block than any other single aspect of the Westminster teaching, the process by which they took these stands should be remembered. The consideration of these words went through several layers of committee deliberations, with both large committees and small committees originally drafting wording. After such wording was drafted, an expert committee of theologians (consisting of seven divines along with the four Scottish commissioners) refined the work and with closer scrutiny examined the teaching before presenting this back to the Assembly as a whole. Then with one of the other major committees finally re-examining the language, it was presented to the Assembly as a whole for consideration.

Warfield says that this particular topic was discussed in excess of twenty times, even though most of the work was originated and thoroughly critiqued in committee. This can certify to us that, "it was not passed by the Assembly without the most careful scrutiny or without many adjustments and alterations, so that as passed it represents clearly the deliberate and reasoned judgment of the Assembly as a whole." In addition, Baillie commented on the thoroughness of the debate on this topic: "We had long and tough debates about the decrees of election; yet thanks to God that all has gone right according to our mind." Warfield gives a strong plea in his conclusion:

> We have here no hasty draft, rushed through the body at breakneck speed and adopted at the end on the credit of the Committee that had drafted it. The third chapter . . . is distinctly the work of the Assembly itself, and comes to us as the well-pondered and thoroughly adjusted expression of the living belief of that whole body. The differences that existed between the members were not smoothed over in ambiguous language. They were fully ventilated. Room was made for them when they were considered unimportant . . . We cannot say that this or that clause represents this or that party in the Assembly. There were parties in the Assembly, and they were all fully heard and what they said was carefully weighed. But no merely party opinion was allowed a place in the document. When it came to voting the statements there to be set down, the Assembly as such spoke; and in speaking it showed itself capable of speaking its own mind. It is doing only mere justice to it, therefore, to read the document as the solemn and carefully framed expression of its reasoned faith.

Before the Westminster teaching is ever objected to, one should first consider its opposite as held in some of the other systems. It is strongly believed that if one compares this human Confession with the words of Scripture, then one will see that this Assembly's authors sought to put forward what was mere Christianity. As we hear their testimony we find that this has great value for our lives and churches today.

As one historian summarized this teaching, the divines "conceived that their business was not to adjust the Bible to man, nor to cut and clip the Book to fit human prejudice and accommodate human conceit, but to faithfully adjust man to the Bible."

Creation

Many recent studies have helped us understand certain aspects of the Westminster divines' thought on the subject of creation. Unfortunately, some of their sentiments on this subject were not always well-researched before conclusions were drawn. Indeed, most of us in the twentieth century were taught that the earlier divines left much ambiguity on this subject. They were, however, actually quite clear—in contrast to theologians of the past two centuries.

Although not all Presbyterians have had access to primary sources that indicate the original intent of the divines on certain matters, recent research has made certain things clear that were once thought to be foggy. How those truths are applied, of course, is up to the courts of original jurisdiction, subject to the review of the higher courts. What is clear, though, is that the Westminster divines were quite forthright and biblical in their brief chapter on creation.

In simple and unambiguous language in chapter 4 of the WCF, they taught that creation began with the pleasure of the Triune God. The created order manifests some attributes of God; and this creative work of God is ultimately for his own glory. Several other specifics are included in WCF 4:1. First, God created *ex nihilo* or out of nothing; this proven theological maxim assured that nothing is superior to or prior to God. He sparked all of his very good creation. Second, his creation extends to all realms, whether visible or invisible. God not only created external, physical reality but also the realm of the unseen. Third, he did it with little effort and without the aid of natural processes. God created in the space of six days. Obviously, the WCF could have omitted this phrase or made it ambiguous (e.g., as does the Nicene Creed with its wording, "all things visible and invisible"). These biblical authors, living long before the rise of modern science, did not indicate—either in the explicit wording contained in these standards or in their own published writings and sermons—that they affirmed creation over a long period of time. It was not merely "in six days" but specifically "*in the space* of six days" to accomplish two things: (1) to repudiate Augustine's (and his few remaining disciples') view that creation happened in an instant and that the six days were poetic representations for the mind of man to latch on to; and (2) to affirm the only other extant view, namely, that creation actually happened in days as we know them now. In his study guide for the WCF, G. I. Williamson concluded, long before it was more defensible, that there was "no good reason to doubt that God did create the world in six twenty-four hour days."

Although some fine Reformed Presbyterians have not seen this as an essential, and although the PCA has allowed exceptions within a small range (chiefly as long as human evolution is ruled out and Adam and Eve are viewed as historic individuals), the teaching of the WCF is rather clear on this subject. For years, even its hostile critics have sensed as much. We also need to remember that all of creation was unstained by sin and was "all very good."

For more reference, see; "The Westminster Divines" in *Holding Fast to Creation* (2011; available as Kindle e-book), pp. 71-111. Several other relevant studies are available in this e-book edition.

FYI Study (optional) See also many of the earlier studies on this, along with primary source material in *Holding Fast to Creation* (Kindle e-book at Amazon.com).

The second paragraph in WCF 4 discusses the creation of humans. This crown of God's creation is made in God's image, with two distinct genders possessing immortal souls. Man, as distinguished from other parts of God's creation, had knowledge, moral capacity, and true holiness. As originally created, man was perfect, having both the righteous standards of God engraved on his heart and the power to keep that law. He had an unbiased liberty of will that is not present after the Fall, but this original liberty was subject to change. As long as Adam and Eve kept God's law, they were holy and happy. Sin and death entered after their fall.

Needless to say, if we take seriously the witness of these Westminster ancestors, Adam and Eve were singular and historic human beings—just as real, in fact, as Jesus. They made effective decisions for all their covenantal posterity, as Jesus did, and they were not the products of evolution or a lengthy creational development; instead, they were created as full-blown persons on the 6th day of God's creation—and they were, like all the rest of God's creation, "very good."

Providence

Chapters 3-5 of the WCF delineate the major works of God the Father. In our previous session, we summarized the range of topics covered. However, no Officer of a Reformed church should be expected to uphold doctrinal summaries merely because a set of articles confesses such. Instead, the truths that we hope to pass on and the adherences we have for public office must be founded firmly on Scripture.

The handout above (at the beginning of Session 2a) has provided part of the necessary scriptural testimony to the truths affirmed in WCF 3. The first section of that study exhibits numerous scriptural verses where these concepts occur in Scripture. The Hebrew and Greek words are provided to save the student time, but most industrious Officer candidates could find all these and more by simple access to a good Concordance. These terms originate in the Bible, and there are more references to this subject than to the Virgin Birth, the Deity of the Holy Spirit, references to the mode of baptism, and many other popular end-time ideas, such as the millennium, a secret rapture, etc. The sheer amount of references to these powerful concepts may surprise some, and it is not uncommon in uninstructed fellowships to hear someone utter, "the word predestination is not even in the Bible." Few things could be further from the truth.

The initial conclusion we wish to elicit, therefore, is a simple but wide-ranging one. It is that the concepts of divine election, predestination, and foreknowledge are abundantly biblical. These are not traditions of man, nor are they manufactured as implications to save a weak theological system.

The second part of that study identifies major passages that contain concentrated discussions of this topic. As we attempt to harmonize this teaching with the "whosoever will" passages in the gospels, one should, thirdly, take notice of how Jesus himself refers to elect and divine choosing. Our Lord refers to these concepts in the red lettered verses more than many people have noted. Reconciling his statements may, at times, be difficult, but that should not dissuade us from affirming what the Bible does say.

Then, it is important to understand a little about the purpose and misuses of this doctrine. Following that, I sought to put down 10 propositions that seem to be undeniably biblical. Those 10 propositions may provide a fresh or creative approach, which may even clear some of the mental logjams we (or some theological tradition) have created for ourselves.

Often, people will follow a type of progression to adopt the conclusions of the WCF, which goes something like this. *First*, we may react in anger or repudiation because this truth flies squarely in the face of our democratic processes and civil notions of equal opportunity. However, once we see how replete the Bible is with references to this topic, it becomes difficult to dismiss the teaching about election as a Calvinistic myth. *Next*, many folks—having seen how often this thread pops us—begin the task of reconciliation. *Eventually*, most believers come to rest in some form of co-existence between God's sovereignty and human responsibility. Still, the Officer of the church needs to mature a little beyond that, even; he needs to be able to endorse all of Scripture's teaching and champion even the notions, which go against the grain of popular culture, no matter how pervasive. *Finally*, God leads some to embrace election as Paul did, as a glorious doctrine as exhibited in Ephesians 1:3-4. Let that be the goal of our study.

In the end, the WCF has done a remarkably fine job of culling the biblical truths on this subject, admittedly contrary to the willfulness of the modern West.

Chapter 5 resumes many of these themes under the rubric of providence. After God's divine choice in salvation and after his creation, he certainly does not retire from nurturing or governing the universe he has planned and created. The chapter on providence states that God upholds, directs, disposes, and governs all aspects of his creation. The extent of this, as Jesus taught, spans to the smallest sparrow and the hairs on our heads. He exercises his providence according to his infallible wisdom, in keeping with his free and unchanging decree. Although providence fits with God's foreknowledge, he does not provide in reaction to human events, but, as the first cause, he brings things about infallibly. All the while, God uses secondary causes or normal means to the end—like humans to serve as the agents to share the gospel or godly parents to rear covenant children—to work out his providence. Obviously, since he is free, he also may suspend that ordinary providence and miraculously or directly work above and beyond his normal means.

This providence even comprehends the Fall of Adam and angels—and that not merely as an acquiescence to a greater historic power. In all this, God is never the direct agent who causes sin—only humans are responsible for that. God also allows providence to chastise his children, to correct many things, and to bring us into a closer state of dependency on him. Unbelievers are also subject to providence, and this can often produce a callousness that further hardens them. God also dispenses a special providence to care for and guide his church.

Session #3: Man and Sin

The Doctrine of Man

WCF 4:2 charted the positive anthropology of the Westminster divines. Chapter 6, then, continues to describe the Fall and the subsequent nature of man thereafter. Since this election and providence apply to the Fall of man, the WCF next devotes its attention to the nature of Adam's sin. Chapter 6 contains our confession's doctrine of total depravity. As this chapter intimates, this depravity extends to all members and faculties of the human person. There is not an area or ability that is unaffected by this. Thankfully, the restraining grace of God and the law limit an ultimate outbreak of depravity.

All our sin has its origin in the fall of our first parents. They sinned, and all their descendants received that bias. From that original sin flows all actual, freely chosen sins. As a result, we are wholly defiled in all our parts and "utterly indisposed, disabled . . . and opposite to all good, and wholly inclined to evil." One could easily compare WCF 6:4 with Genesis 6:5, which speaks of every inclination of the heart of man as only evil all the time.

This doctrine of human depravity has many implications. From it we learn:
- That man cannot claw his way to eternal life;
- That man cannot comprehend the ways of God apart from a work of grace in his heart;
- That man cannot put himself aright with God;
- That men should not be trusted with unchecked power, either in church or state;
- That men need strong restraints lest they oppress others;
- That men need the strongest plan of salvation, including the atonement by One who can actually make them right with God.

So, what is to be done in light of those truths? That condition is what preoccupied Martin Luther during much of his life. Once Luther understood things as he wrote in *The Bondage of the Will*, he knew that the justification of sinful man by the holy God would require a great work. Luther's appreciation of sin and its bondage is what led him to such an appreciation of divine justification (see comments below for more on the WCF doctrine of justification). Luther's starting point for that formulation matches exactly the approach of the WCF, particularly as it considers God's covenant as the remedy for man's Fall.

God's Covenant

Chapter 7 discusses the covenant. In contrast (see study below) to some modern interpretive schemes, our faith firmly rests on the unchanging plan of salvation. Moreover, our confessional teaching on the covenant of God begins where Luther left off, noting that the distance between God and his rational creatures is so great that it could never be bridged except by God's own voluntary condescension. God's stooping down, then, is expressed by means of the covenant.

The first covenant was a covenant of ability/works. By that, the WCF means to indicate that Adam, not biased by original sin, had the freedom and ability to keep God's covenant. Had he done so, he—and all his descendants—would have retained eternal life. However, by his freely-chosen Fall, man became disabled. He was incapable of keeping the original covenant. Still, God was merciful, and the Lord initiated a second covenant of disability/grace, whereby a sinner could have eternal life. This covenant of grace required a perfect Mediator and produced faith on our part. This covenant of grace is described by different phrases in Scripture, and it centers on the mediation of Jesus Christ.

This plan of salvation is unified since the time of Adam. Notwithstanding, during the pre-Christ period, all of the sacrifices, promises, types, and ordinances anticipated and pointed ahead to Christ. These were spiritually effectual at their time (since God transcends time) and exhibited the reconciliation between God and man brought by the covenant. Later, after Christ came, the ordinances, sacraments, and means of grace were simpler, more multi-national, and more fully dispensed. However, the WCF makes it plain that there are "not therefore two covenants of grace, differing in substance, but one and the same, under various dispensations." What this means is that any person who could be saved after Adam's Fall was saved by this one plan of grace, was incorporated into the same church by grace, and was converted from his sin nature by grace alone.

Over the past two centuries, a popular theological plan called Dispensationalism has arisen. Early versions of this plan were clearly ruled out by the final sentence of this chapter of the WCF. Dispensationalism, briefly speaking, believes that God works differently in different periods of time. At some times, according to this theory, God saved people who kept the law (although the NT book of Galatians makes it clear that no one can be justified by the law), at others he saved them because they were ethnic Jews, and at others he saved them if they mustered faith in the Messiah. There are many problems with this interpretive system—not to mention the ramifications it brings for end-times views, which can hardly be reconciled with the teaching of Scripture and this confession—but chiefly it disrupts the unity of God's salvation and wrongly erects a wall of separation between the OT and the NT. To see how one mainline Presbyterian denomination critiqued this burgeoning movement over a half-century ago, see the study below.

> *FYI Study (optional) Resource:*
> DISPENSATIONALISM AND THE CONFESSION OF FAITH
>
> The *Ad Interim* Committee [Presbyterian Church in the United States] appointed by the Assembly to consider this question (1941 Min., p. 60; 1943, p. 46) presents the following report.
>
> Before calling attention to certain doctrines, which we believe to be out of accord with the Standards of our Church, we desire to define the terms DISPENSATION and DISPENSATIONALISM. The word "Dispensation" is used by both the Confession of Faith and by Dispensationalism. Both systems use it in the sense of "an administration" of some purpose or plan of God, but they differ on the question of *what is administered.*
>
> That which is "administered" is made very plain in the Confession of Faith (Ch. VII, Pars. V, VI), where, speaking of the Covenant of Grace, we read, "This covenant was differently administered in the time of the law, and in the time of the gospel: under the law it was administered by promises, prophecies, Under the gospel, when Christ the substance was exhibited, the ordinances in which this covenant is dispensed, are the preaching of the word, and the administration of the sacraments of baptism and the Lord's supper; . . . There are not, therefore, two covenants of grace differing in substance, but one and the same under various dispensations."

Here it will be seen that the administration of God's purpose under the law (the OT dispensation) is stated to be different in *form*, as we know it was in organization and ceremony, from the administration under the gospel (our own dispensation), but the point which the Confession of Faith emphasizes is that these two dispensations do not *differ in substance*, but there is *only one and the same Covenant of Grace* to be administered under the various dispensations. Students of the Reformed Faith have differed as to the number of dispensations into which we may properly divide the dealing of God with man since the fall; but they have all agreed, in accordance with our Confession of Faith, that these various dispensations are all administrations of *one and the same Covenant of Grace.*

The opposing viewpoint, on the other hand, as presented by Dr. L. S. Chafer, is as follows: "Since there is so much in the Confession of Faith which is in no way related to this discussion and which is the common belief of all, the issue should yet be narrowed to the difference which obtains between Dispensationalism and Covenantism. The latter is that form of theological speculation, which attempts to unify God's entire program from Genesis to Revelation under one supposed Covenant of Grace. That no such covenant is either named or exhibited in the Bible and that the covenants which are set forth in the Bible are so varied and diverse that they preclude a one-covenant idea, evidently does not deter many sincere men from adherence to the one-covenant theory." (Chafer, *Bibliotheca Sacra*, editorial on "Dispensational Distinctions Challenged," Vol. 100, No. 399, p. 338.)

Thus the "various and diverse" covenants are set over against the "one Covenant of Grace," i.e., one plan of salvation, which is central to our Church's view of the teaching of the Bible. All acquainted with Dispensational thought know what Dispensationalists mean by their rejection of the Covenant of Grace; they do not hold that God has one plan of salvation for all men, but that He had had various and diverse plans for different groups. (Chafer, *Grace*, p. 135). Some of the chief points of divergence will be pointed out below.

DISPENSATIONALISM, therefore, as shown above, rejects the doctrine that God has, since the fall, but one "plan of salvation" for all mankind and affirms that God has been through the ages "administering" various and diverse plans of salvation for various groups.

Such Dispensational teaching is expounded by many in our day, but we shall limit our quotations to the writings of two outstanding exponents of Dispensationalism: Dr. C. I. Scofield (especially as found in certain notes in the *Scofield Reference Bible*) and Dr. L. S. Chafer, who has written extensively on this subject. They both teach a Dispensational view of God's various and divergent plans of salvation for various groups in different ages, although they do not agree on all inferences which may be drawn from this fundamental starting point.

I.   THIS FUNDAMENTAL DIVERGENCE OF DISPENSATIONALISM FROM THE COVENANT THEOLOGY OF THE PRESBYTERIAN CHURCH MANIFESTS ITSELF IN MANY WAYS, SOME OF WHICH ARE THE FOLLOWING:

A. *The Rejection of the Unity of God's People.*
1. The Confession of Faith clearly teaches that God has one people who were brought into saving relation with Him, some under the law, others under the gospel dispensation. The Confession of Faith calls this one people of God "The Church." (*Confession of Faith*, Ch. XXVII, Par. II). Whatever may be the national destiny of the Jewish people, according to the Confession of

Faith their becoming a spiritual blessing to the world and to the Church will be contingent upon their acceptance of Jesus as the Messiah and thereby becoming a part of the Church.

2. Dispensationalism teaches that God has at least two distinct peoples, namely, the Jewish nation and the Christian Church. He has distinctly different purposes for them, and each of these two peoples is united to Him by various and diverse covenants quite different in character. (*Dispensationalism* reprinted from *Bibliotheca Sacra*, No. 372, Vol. 93, p. 396ff., esp. p. 448).

B. *The Rejection of One Way of Salvation.*

1. The Confession of Faith teaches that there is but one plan of salvation—that men are saved only in Christ, by grace through faith. (*Confession of Faith*, Ch. III, Par. V; Ch. VII, Par. III; Ch VIII, Par. VI; Ch. XII, Pars. I, II, IV).

2. Dispensationalism, magnifying the distinction which is made between law and grace (*which Dispensationalists hold to be mutually exclusive*—Chafer, *Grace*, p. 231ff.), agrees that men are NOW saved by grace through faith, but teaches that in other dispensations men have been saved by "legal obedience." The point of testing is no longer legal obedience as the condition of salvation, but acceptance or rejection of Christ. . . " (*Scofield Reference Bible*, p. 1115; also see Chafer, *Dispensationalism*, pp. 415-16; *Grace*, pp. 123, 124-126). It also holds that after the present age of grace, there will be a reversion in the kingdom age to an extreme system of meritorious obligation. (Chafer, *Dispensationalism*, pp. 416, 440, 441, 443; *Grace* p. 223).

C. *The Rejection of One Destiny for All of God's People.*

1. The Confession of Faith teaches that God's people, the righteous, go into "everlasting life" (*Confession of Faith*, Ch. XXXV, Par. II), which is also spoken of as "an everlasting inheritance in the kingdom of heaven." (*Confession of Faith*, Ch. VIII, Par. V). The wicked shall be cast into everlasting torment. Such is the final destiny of the saved and the lost, and the Confession of Faith nowhere suggests that the saved are divided into different and distinct groups which will enjoy different blessings according to the purpose of God.

2. Dispensationalism teaches that the two groups of God's people, the Jewish nation and the Christian Church, are entirely distinct bodies, and in the millennial kingdom will enjoy different blessings, the Jews enjoying earthly and material blessings, and the Church spiritual and heavenly blessings. Some Dispensationalists, like Dr. Chafer, continue this distinction in destiny into eternity, holding that in eternity there are three groups: the lost in hell, the earthly people of God on earth forever, and the Church, the heavenly people of God in heaven forever. (*Dispensationalism*, p. 448).

D. *The Rejection of the Bible as God's One Revelation to His One People.*

1. The writers of the Confession of Faith had not heard of the Dispensational method of "rightly dividing the word of truth" for it was not taught in their day. However, all acquainted with the view of the Reformed Church know that the Church has held that "God, who at sundry times and in divers manners spake. . . unto the fathers by the prophets, hath in these last days spoken unto us by his Son." (Hebrews 1:1, 2). The Confession of Faith states that God has given His people (which the Confession of Faith calls the Church) a unified and progressive revelation, culminating in the revelation in Christ, and most clearly expressed in the New Testament which was written under the guidance of the Holy Spirit who led the Apostles to see the purpose of God in Christ. (*Confession of Faith*, Ch. VII, Par. VI).

2. Dispensationalism rejects both the unity of God's revelation and the fact that God's purpose is "held forth in more fullness" (*Confession of Faith*, Ch. VII, Par. VI) in the New Testament than it is in the Old. Dispensationalism holds that large portions even of the New Testament are for the Jewish nation, not for the Church. In speaking of the Scriptures for the Church, Dr. Chafer says, "The Scriptures addressed specifically to this company are the Gospel by John—especially the upper room discourse,—the Acts and the Epistles." (*Dispensationalism*, p. 443).

The Lord's Prayer and the Great Commission are assigned by some to the Jews of the "tribulation" Period, and not to the Church. (*Grace*, pp. 174, 176, 179, 181).

II   THERE ARE ALSO DISPENSATIONAL DIVERGENCIES FROM THE CONFESSIONAL INTERPRETATION OF THE WORK OF THE EXALTED CHRIST

A. The Confession of Faith speaks of the kingly work of Christ and what is included in the exaltation of Christ. A study, for example, of answers 26 and 28 of the *Shorter Catechism* will show that Christ, "sitting at the right hand of God the Father," is now exercising His kingly function, "in subduing us to himself, in ruling and defending us, and in restraining and conquering all his and our enemies." (It should be noted that the *Larger Catechism*, in answer to question 345, devotes twice as much space to His kingly work as is given to the prophetic and priestly work.)

The second function of the Exalted Christ taught by our Confession of Faith is His coming to judge the world at the last day. This "judgment" naturally is the climax of His victorious activity in "conquering all his and our enemies." All that then remains will be the pronouncement of the final verdict.

B. Dispensationalism rejects or minimizes the present kingly office of Christ, and deviates from the conception of the Resurrection and Judgment set forth in our Standards.
1. Dispensationalism teaches that Christ is not now exercising His kingly power, but is only Head of the Church. It reserves the kingly work of "conquering all his and our enemies" exclusively to the kingdom dispensation, which will follow His second advent. (*Scofield Reference Bible*, note on p. 990).
2. The Confession of Faith speaks of the Resurrection as follows: "At the last day, such as are found alive shall not die, but be changed: and all the dead shall be raised up with the self-same bodies. . ." (*Confession of Faith*, Ch. XXXIV, Par. II). The *Larger Catechism*, in answer to question 88, states that "Immediately after the resurrection shall follow the general and final judgment of angels and men. . ." In dealing with the Judgment, the Confession of Faith says, "God hath appointed a day, wherein he will judge the world in righteousness by Jesus Christ, to whom all power and judgment is given of the Father. In which day, not only the apostate angels shall be judged; but likewise all persons, that have lived upon earth, shall appear before the tribunal of Christ, to give an account of their thoughts, words, and deeds; and to receive according to what they have done in the body, whether good or evil." (*Confession of Faith*, Ch. XXXV, Par. I. See answers to questions 85, 86, 87, 88 of *Larger Catechism*.)
Dispensationalism teaches a series of resurrections and judgments, spaced over more than a thousand years. It is the opinion of your Committee that the above statement of the Confession of Faith does not admit of a multiplicity of resurrections and judgments as taught by many Dispensationalists.

CONCLUSION
It is the unanimous opinion of your Committee that Dispensationalism as defined and set forth above is out of accord with the system of the doctrine set forth in the Confession of Faith, not primarily or simply in the field of eschatology, but because it attacks the very heart of the Theology of our Church, which is unquestionably a Theology of one Covenant of Grace. As Dr. Chafer clearly recognizes, there are two schools of interpretation represented here, which he rightly designates as "Covenantism" as over against "Dispensationalism." (*Bibliotheca Sacra*, Vol. 100, No. 399, p. 338).

> In fact, the divergence of Dispensationalism from the Covenant Theology of our Church is so obvious to Dr. Chafer that he suggests a revision of the Standards of the Church so as to make room for those who no longer hold to the Reformed tradition of a Covenant Theology. (p. 345)

FYI: For other good discussions and critiques of Dispensationalism, see:
- Anthony Hoekema, *The Bible and The Future* (Eerdmans, 1979), pp. 195-218.
- D. A. Carson, *The Sermon on the Mount* (Baker, 1978), pp. 155-157.
- O. Palmer Robertson, *Christ of the Covenants* (Baker, 1984), pp. 201-227.
- John Murray, "Covenant Theology," *Collected Works*, Vol. IV (Banner of Truth Trust), pp. 216-240
- John Gerstner, *A Primer on Dispensationalism* (Presbyterian & Reformed, 1982), pp. 1-37.
- Richard P. Belcher, *A Comparison of Dispensationalism and Covenant Theology* (Richbarry Press, 1986)

Man's Will: Bound or Free (WCF 9)

Many people, who have been raised in our highly democratic and egalitarian society, search through these older confessions in pursuit of some morsel that extols the inherent goodness of man. One will be greatly disappointed in his study of the WCF if that is his goal. Still, some eyes are wider open when they bump across the title of chapter 9 in the WCF. Perhaps it should be re-titled "The Ability of Man" or the "Bondage of the Will" to more accurately reflect its intent—and to prevent the disappointment of libertines.

Chapter 9 of the WCF has two principal parts. First, it gives a generic statement that distinguishes the human will from that of other creatures. Then, it discusses the ability of man in four different states.

The first paragraph of chapter 9 asserts that mankind has a natural liberty, and by that it denies that man is merely a machine or soul-less. Man's will is not forced in the same way that an animal's is. The ability of man involves free choices, but man can never escape his nature. He can choose, but he can never choose contrary to his nature. That nature is then described in paragraphs 2-5 according to different states.

Originally, man was innocent and possessed the freedom and ability to choose what would please God. This was a mutable condition, and theologians speak of it as man "able to sin." Adam, in other words, could have or could not have sinned. After the Fall, however, man lost that ability and could not choose to do good. He was "not able not to sin" and dead in sin. Neither could man contribute to or prepare himself to be reconciled to God. However, conversion introduces the third state—note these are not dispensations or time-periods but states of human ability or lack thereof. In that third state, a sinner is converted and freed from his natural bondage to sin. He is thus "able not to sin," even though he is far from perfect. That perfection comes only upon glorification, the fourth and final state. In that state man has the ability to perfectly and unalterably do good. He is "not able to sin" any longer.

Thus, rather than defending a post-Adam free will, in the sense of having no restraint, the WCF actually exhibits four states of the human will in terms of ability:

- "able to sin." (*posse peccare*)

- "not able not to sin." (*non posse non peccare*)
- "able not to sin." ((*posse non peccare*)
- "not able to sin." (*non posse peccare*)

This prepares us for a consideration of the Five Points of Calvinism. For the reader's convenience, an excellent tract by W. J. Seaton, *The Five Points of Calvinism* is abridged below (Edinburgh: Banner of Truth Trust, 1970; used with permission).

"The Five Points of Calvinism"

We must take our starting point in Holland in the year 1610. James Arminius, a Dutch professor, had just died and his teaching had been formulated into five main points of doctrine by his followers—known as Arminians [note: not Armenians, citizens of Armenia]. Up to this point, the churches of Holland, in common with the other major Protestant churches of Europe, had subscribed to the Belgic and Heidelberg Confessions of Faith, which were both set squarely on Reformation teachings. The Arminians wanted to change this position, however, and they presented their five points in the form of a Remonstrance—or protest—to the Dutch Parliament. The Five Points of Arminianism were, broadly speaking, as follows:

1. *Free will or human ability.* This taught that man, although affected by the Fall, was not totally incapable of choosing spiritual good, and was able to exercise faith in God in order to receive the gospel and thus bring himself into possession of salvation.
2. *Conditional election.* This taught that God laid his hands upon those individuals who, he knew—or foresaw—would respond to the gospel. God elected those that he saw would want to be saved of their own free will and in their natural fallen state—which was, of course, according to the first point of Arminianism, not completely fallen anyway.
3. *Universal redemption, or general atonement.* This taught that Christ died to save all men, but only in a *potential* fashion. Christ's death enabled God to pardon sinners, but only on condition that they believed.
4. *The work of the Holy Spirit in regeneration limited by the human will.* This taught that the Holy Spirit, as he began to work to bring a person to Christ, could be effectually resisted and his purposes frustrated. He could not impart life unless the sinner was willing to have this life imparted.
5. *Falling from grace.* This taught that a saved man could fall finally from salvation. It is, of course, the logical and natural outcome of the system. If man must take the initiative in his salvation, he must retain responsibility for the final outcome.

The Five Points of Arminianism were presented to the Sate and a National Synod of the church was called to meet in Dort in 1618 to examine the teaching of Arminius in the light of the Scriptures. The Synod of Dort sat for 154 sessions over a period of seven months, but at the end could find no ground on which to reconcile the Arminian viewpoint with that expounded in the Word of God. Reaffirming the position so unmistakably put forth at the Reformation, and formulated by the French theologian John Calvin, the Synod of Dort formulated its Five Points of Calvinism to counter the Arminian system. These are sometimes set forth in the form of an acrostic on the word, "TULIP," as follows:

T   Total Depravity (i.e., Total Inability)

U   Unconditional Election
L   Limited Atonement (i.e., Particular Redemption)
I   Irresistible Grace (Calling)
P   Perseverance of the Saints.

As can be readily seen, these set themselves in complete opposition to the Five Points of Arminianism. Man is totally unable to save himself on account of the Fall in the Garden of Eden being a *total* fall. If unable to save himself, then God must save. If God must save, then God must be free to save whom he will. If God has decreed to save whom he will, then it is for those that Christ made atonement on the Cross. If Christ died for them, then the Holy Spirit will effectually call them into that salvation. If salvation then from the beginning has been of God, the end will also be of God and the saints will persevere to eternal joy.

We shall see [abridged below] the truth that Charles Haddon Spurgeon meant when he declared, "It is no novelty, then, that I am preaching; no new doctrine. I love to proclaim those strong old doctrines that are nicknamed *Calvinism*, but which are surely and verily the revealed truth of God as it is in Christ Jesus."

Total Depravity

Surely the thing that should impress us is the fact that this system begins with something that must be fundamental in the matter of salvation, and that is, a correct assessment of the *condition* of the one who is to be saved. If we have deficient and light views about sin, then we are liable to have defective views regarding the means necessary for the salvation of the sinner. If we believe that the fall of man in the Garden of Eden was merely partial, then we shall most likely be satisfied with a salvation that is attributable partly to man and partly to God. The words of J. C. Ryle are helpful: "There are very few errors and false doctrines of which the beginning may not be traced up to unsound views about the corruption of human nature. Wrong views of a disease will always bring with them wrong views of a remedy. Wrong views of the corruption of human nature will always carry with them wrong views of the grand antidote and cure of that corruption."

Fully aware that this was the case, the theologians of the Reformation and those who formulated the Reformed teaching into these Five Points at the Synod of Dort, basing their findings firmly on the Scriptures, pronounced that man's natural state is a state of total depravity and therefore, there was a total inability on the part of man to gain, or contribute to, his own salvation.

The whole personality of man has been affected by the Fall, and sin extends to the whole of the faculties—the will, the understanding, the affections and all else. We believe this to be irrefutably taught by the Word of God, as demonstrated in the Scriptures below. According to the biblical testimony, man, by nature, is:

- Dead (Rom. 5:12)
- Bound (2 Tim. 2:25 ff)
- Blind and deaf (Mark 4:11f)
- Uninstructable (1 Cor. 2:14)
- Naturally sinful: (a) by birth (Ps. 51:5) and (b) by practice (Gen. 6:5).

We must ask, then: Can the dead (Eph. 2:1) raise themselves? Can the bound (see Lazarus) free themselves? Can the blind give themselves sight, or the deaf hearing? Can slaves redeem themselves? Can the uninstructable teach themselves? Can the naturally sinful change themselves? Surely not! "Who can bring a clean thing out of an unclean?" (Job 14:4).

Unconditional Election

Our acceptance or rejection of total depravity as a true biblical statement of man's condition by nature will largely determine our attitude towards the next point that came under review at the Synod of Dort. The same truth was set forth in other creeds, namely in the 1689 Baptist Confession of Faith, which affirms: "Those of mankind who are predestinated unto life, God, before the foundation of the world was laid, according to his eternal and immutable purpose, and the secret counsel and good pleasure of his will, hath chosen in Christ unto everlasting glory, out of his mere free grace and love, without any other thing in the creature as a condition or cause moving him thereunto."

The doctrine of unconditional election follows naturally from the doctrine of total depravity. If man is, indeed, dead, held captive, and blind etc., then the remedy for all these conditions must lie outside man himself [that is, with God]. If some people are raised out of their spiritual death, and since they are unable to perform this work for themselves, then we must conclude that it was God who raised them. If man is unable to save himself on account of the Fall in Adam being a *total* fall, and if God alone can save, and if *all* are not saved, then the conclusion must be that God has not chosen to save all.

The story of the Bible is the story of unconditional election. One can easily consult the narratives about Abraham being called out of heathenism, or Israel selected as a peculiar people (Dt. 7:7), or Jacob chosen in place of the elder Esau (Rom. 9-11). Moreover, our Lord himself spoke about this topic three times in Matthew 24 and also in John 15:6. Of course, this doctrine is also alluded to in passages such as Romans 9:15-21 and Ephesians 1:4-5.

For those who try to transform God's election into a mere foreknowing of man's nice choice to accept the Savior—a good work on man's part by any calculation—the following points should be considered.
1. God's foreknowledge is spoken of in connection with a people and not in connection with any action which people performed. That is to say, irrespective of any action, good or bad, performed by them, God "knew" them in the sense that he loved them and chose them to be his own. It is thus that he foreknew his elect.
2. We are not chosen because we perform such a holy work as "accepting" Christ, but we are chosen so that we might be able to "accept" him (See Eph. 2:10).
3. Neither will it do to say that God foresaw those who would believe (See Acts 13:48). Election is not on account of our believing, but our believing is on account of our being elected.
4. The faith to believe in Christ is given to us by God's regenerating grace. It is the gift of God (Eph. 2:8-9), and it is not of ourselves.

Limited Atonement

This third point not only brings us to the central point of the five, but also to the central fact of the gospel, that is the purpose of Christ's death on the Cross. This is not accidental. The theologians who had set themselves the task of defending the truths of the Protestant Reformation against the attacks of the Arminian party were following a biblical and logical line in their formulations. Since the Bible taught that man, in his natural state, is totally unable to save himself, but that some are undoubtedly saved, the question is "how can any who are saved be saved?" The answer is that the atonement by Christ is stronger than man's sin nature, and it is applied particularly to those God has chosen. This atonement was accomplished through Christ's voluntary submission to the death on the Cross where he suffered under the justice of the Just God and procured the salvation that he as Savior had ordained. On the Cross, then, Christ bore punishment and procured salvation.

The question logically arises: *whose* punishment did Christ bear, and *whose* salvation did he procure? There are three avenues along which we can travel with regard to this:

1. Christ died to *save all men* without distinction. The **Univeralist** view believes that all men will be saved.
2. Christ died to *save no one in particular*. The **Arminian** view believes that Christ merely procured a potential salvation for those who will eventually choose that anyway. Christ died on the Cross but although he paid the debt of our sin, his work on the Cross does not become effectual until one "decides for" Christ and is thereby saved.
3. Christ died to *save a certain number*. The **Calvinistic** view believes that Christ positively died and effectually saved a certain number of hell-deserving sinners on whom the Father had already set his free electing love. The Son paid the debt for these elect ones, satisfies the Father's justice for them, and imputes his own righteousness to them so that they are complete in him.

Christ's death, then could only have been for one of these three reasons: to save *all*; to save *no one in particular*, to save *a particular set*. Particular redemption understands that Christ died to save a particular number of sinners, i.e., those chosen in him before the foundation of the world (Eph. 1:4); those whom the Father had given him out of the world (Jn. 17:9); those for whom he shed his blood to gain remission of their sins (Mt. 26:28 and Mt. 1:21).

This Calvinistic view alone does justice to the purpose of Christ's coming to this earth to die on the Cross. See Eph. 5:25; Rom. 4:25; 1 Cor. 15:22; Is. 53:11.

We do not overlook the fact that there are some Scriptures, which refer to the "world," and many have taken these as their starting point in the question of Redemption. However, when we compare Scripture with Scripture (as suggested by WCF 1:9), we see that the use of the word "world" need not always imply "every man and woman in the whole world." (See, e.g., Jn. 6:37)

Irresistible Grace

This fourth point of the Calvinistic system of belief is the logical outcome of all that has preceded. If men are unable to save themselves on account of their fallen nature, and if God has purposed to save them, and Christ has accomplished their salvation, then it logically follows that God must also provide the means for calling them into the benefits of that salvation which he has procured for them. The Calvinistic system of theology, however, although soundly logical, is more than a system of mere logic. It is a system of pure biblical belief and must rise or fall with a comparison of its tenets and Scripture.

In a recent *Tabletalk* article ("Dead Men Walking," June 2002, pp. 6-7), R. C. Sproul provides a clear discussion of irresistible grace. It depends, he argues, on two main foundations: (1) grace as unmerited favor—if we ever earned it, it would be justice; and (2) God's regeneration as the operation of grace in our lives by the Holy Spirit. Jesus frequently spoke of the necessity of regeneration, but later Semi-Pelagians sought to emphasize a greater human contribution to salvation. These Pelagian cousins presented salvation as synergistic (literally "to work together") in contrast to our Augustinian-Reformed pedigree, which presents grace as the work of God alone. It is only God that can give grace by his divine regeneration, and until that happens, the human being is completely passive, as the WCF affirms elsewhere. Sproul notes that we are as passive as Lazarus was before his resurrection or as Adam was before his creation. Sproul further clarifies:

> Regeneration is not a joint venture. We do not cooperate in it because we will not cooperate in spiritual matters while we are still dead in our sins. Our hearts are totally disinclined and indisposed to the things of God. We love darkness and will not have God in our thinking. . . . We will never choose Christ until or unless we are liberated from that slavery. In short, we are morally unable to exercise faith until and unless we are first regenerated. This is why the axiom of Reformed theology is that regeneration precedes faith. Rebirth is a necessary pre-condition for faith. Faith is not possible for spiritually dead creatures. Therefore, we contend that apart from spiritual rebirth there can be no faith.
>
> At the same time, the doctrine of irresistible grace teaches that all who are regenerated indeed come to faith. The 'irresistible' may be better described as 'effectual.' All of God's grace is resistible in the sense that sinners resist it. But the saving grace of regeneration is called irresistible because our resistance to it cannot and does not overpower it. The grace of regeneration is effectual in that the effect God the Holy Spirit intends to produce actually does come to pass. When the Holy Spirit supernaturally and immediately works to create a person anew, that person is created anew one hundred times out of one hundred. All who receive this grace are changed. All are liberated from the bondage to sin. All are brought to saving faith. The outcome of this work never depends upon the work of the unregenerate flesh. The grace is operative, not co-operative.

Once that divinely-effected rebirth is worked by God alone (monergism), the "rest of the Christian life is synergistic. But the transformation of the person from death to life, darkness to light, bondage to liberty is done by God alone, effectually and irresistibly," which is why we confess *soli Deo Gloria.*

In the same issue of *Tabletalk*, Al Mohler notes the practical value of this biblical teaching: "The denial of irresistible grace leads to a human-centered understanding of the Gospel, produces pride in the hearts of sinners, and encourages manipulation in evangelism. We are heralds assigned to preach a message, not salesmen charged to market a product." (p. 16)

Perseverance of the Saints

The doctrine of the perseverance of the saints is as precious to the believer as it is biblically clear. Some man-made theologies that award more determination to the will of man than to the will of God have difficulty reconciling this biblical teaching with the clear scriptural testimony. However, it is quite clear that when God begins a good work in us, he sees it to completion—all the way until the time of Jesus' return (Phil. 1:6). This and many other passages put this doctrine within the reach of every believer who will avail himself to God's Word on the subject.

Many verses may be consulted, and Officers should be at ease with sharing this aspect of our faith. Among the verses we have found helpful are:

- Romans 8:32-39
- Col. 1:13
- John 10: 27-29
- John 6:54
- 1 Pet. 1:4-5

This comforting biblical teaching is based on several things. It understands regeneration as causing a permanent change in our nature (Jn. 3:1-8). Also, since Christ's death was all-sufficient (Heb. 9:25-28), once he atones for our sin, there is no reversal of that. So certain is our standing with Christ once he adopts us that, as Romans 8 tells us, nothing, no scenario or combination of events—not even stupendous things like "death nor life, neither angels nor demons, neither the present nor future, nor any powers, neither height nor depth, nor anything else in all creation, will be able to separate us from the love of God that is in Christ Jesus our Lord" (Rom. 8:38-39). Those in whom God begins his work of salvation, those who are called, justified, and elected, will also stay with God until the end, to glorification (Rom. 8:30).

John Calvin certainly did not discover or invent this doctrine; God himself reveals it. And its comfort and implications are large for believers and Officers in the church. This gift permits sincere and tender consciences from worrying if God, like many fickle human lovers, will one day fail to be our Saving Spouse. But the more we know the salvation which our God brings, the more clearly we see that he will be faithful to the end, that he will not deny himself (2 Tim. 2:13), and that we can be assured that "If we died with him, we will also live with him; if we endure, we will also reign with him" (2 Tim. 2:11-12).

Session #3a

The Doctrine of Christ and Soteriology

I normally spend little time explaining the particulars of WCF chapter 8. Very few evangelicals find anything disagreeable in these paragraphs. The early paragraphs treat the following subjects. The Lord Jesus, the Second Person of the eternal Trinity, in accord with God's eternal purpose, voluntarily (8:4) kept the law perfectly and fulfilled for us all that Adam did not do (Rom. 5:12-19). He was sinlessly perfect (Heb. 4:15) and fully satisfied the Father's justice, purchasing "not only reconciliation, but an everlasting inheritance in the kingdom of heaven, for all those whom the Father had given him" (Jn. 17:4, 6, 9, 12 and 15; WCF 8:5). His substitutionary death on the cross gained salvation for us. Christ was our prophet, priest, and king. The writers of the WCF desired to make it plain that to all those for whom Christ had purchased redemption, he also certainly and effectually applies that redemption, while also making intercession for them (Heb. 8:2), reveals the mysteries of salvation to them, working in a manner that persuades them to believe, and overcomes all their foes by his power and wisdom. All of this is done by Christ in a manner which is most compatible with his wonderful and unsearchable plan of working (Rom. 11:33-35).

About the only controversial section of chapter 8 is the reference to the design of Christ's atonement as applying only to those whom the Father gave to him. That, too, is rooted in almost an exact quotation of several verses from the High Priestly prayer of Jesus in John 17. The WCF phrases it that Christ actually "purchased not only reconciliation but an everlasting inheritance . . . for all those whom the Father hath given unto him." (WCF 8:5) Among the verses that one might consult to reflect this definite atonement perspective are: Mt. 1:21; Mt. 20:28; John 6:37-39; Rom. 8:29-33; John 10:15 f; and John 17:9-10.

> **John Murray on** *Redemption Accomplished and Applied*
> Professor John Murray communicated the beauties of the work of Christ in his monograph *Redemption Accomplished and Applied* (copyright Eerdmans Publishing Co., Grand Rapids, MI, 1955; used with permission). In that work, he discusses various theories of atonement that are insufficient and draws out the implications of these inadequate views. He also treats the biblical vocabulary on the subject well. Over the years, I have recommended one chapter in particular from that work (chapter IV, pp. 59-75) to our Officer trainees. Below is a summary of it.
>
> Murray states the question as "For whom did Christ die?" He acknowledges that several verses seem, on the surface, to imply that Christ died for every human being. Among those that are sometimes used to reach this conclusion are Isaiah 53:6, Heb. 2:9, and 1 John 2:2. However, mere proof-texting of such a key doctrine is insufficient, for that interpretation demands that every time the Bible uses the words "all" or "every" it *must* mean each and every individual. Murray observes, though, that from "beginning to end the Bible uses expressions that are universal in form but cannot be interpreted as meaning all men distributively and inclusively." He cites Romans 11:12 as one such interpretation that would "make nonsense. . . . When Paul used the word 'world' here he meant the Gentile world as contrasted with Israel. The context makes this abundantly plain." That is a restricted sense that does not men all men distributively. Other examples of similar interpretation are Romans 5:18, 1 Corinthians 6:12 and 10:23. In these verses "all things" are limited by the context. So,

Murray writes, "it will not do to quote a few texts from the Bible in which such words as 'world' and 'all' occur in connection with the death of Christ and forthwith conclude that the question is settled in favor of universal atonement." Murray's explanation of this point in reference to Hebrews 2:9 is particularly helpful. In that passage, "everyone" refers to the sons brought to glory. Those are the ones for whom Christ died, but "there is not the slightest warrant in this text to extend the reference of the vicarious death of Christ beyond those who are most expressly referred to in the context. This text shows how plausible off-hand quotation may be and yet how baseless is such an appeal in support of a doctrine of universal atonement."

Certainly, as Murray notes, Christ's mediatorial dominion brings spin-off blessings to both the elect and the non-elect. The rejection of the doctrine of universal atonement does not mean that unbelievers receive no benefits. The real question is: "on whose behalf did Christ offer himself a sacrifice? On whose behalf did he propitiate the wrath of God? Whom did he redeem from the curse of the law, from the guilt and power of sin, from the enthralling power and bondage of Satan? In whose stead and on whose behalf was he obedient unto death, even the death of the cross?" These Murray sees as the real questions, to wit: "The question is precisely the reference of the death of Christ when this death is viewed as vicarious death, that is to say, as vicarious obedience, as substitutionary sacrifice, and expiation, as effective propitiation, reconciliation, and redemption. In a word, it is the strict and proper connotation of the expression 'died for' that must be kept in mind." (See if 1 Thess. 5:10, 1 Cor. 15:3, and Gal. 2:20 are best interpreted to mean universal salvation)

Murray suggests that a little reflection on the meaning of the term "redemption" shows the impossibility of universal atonement. For this biblical term does not mean "redeemability" or to be set in a redeemable position. Instead, it means that Christ purchased and procured redemption (See Rev. 5:9; Heb. 9:12; Tit. 2:14), and it "is to beggar the concept of redemption as an effective securement of release by price and by power to construe it as anything less than the effectual accomplishment which secures the salvation of those who are its objects. Christ did not come to put men in a redeemable position but to redeem to himself a people."

The same is true for other terms like expiation, propitiation, and reconciliation (Cf. Murray's treatment of these terms in other chapters within this same excellent monograph). Christ did not die to make folks expiable or potentially to propitiate the Father's wrath based upon the exercising of a human option. Murray put it this way:

Christ did not come to make God reconcilable. He reconciled us to God by his own blood. The very nature of Christ's mission and accomplishment is involved in this question. Did Christ come to make the salvation of all men possible, to remove obstacles that stood in the way of salvation, and merely to make provision for salvation? Or did he come to save his people? Did he come to put all men in a salvable state? Or did he come to secure the salvation of all those who are ordained to eternal life? Did he come to make men redeemable? Or did he come effectually and infallibly to redeem? The doctrine of the atonement must be radically revised if, as atonement, it applies to those who finally perish as well as to those who are the heirs of eternal life. In that event we should have to dilute the grand categories in terms of which the Scripture defines the atonement and deprive them of their most precious import and glory. This we cannot do.

Murray notes that Jesus' statement in John 6:38-39 indicates that our very security in Christ depends on the effectiveness of his atonement, and that the persons contemplated in Christ's atoning purpose are the same as those who finally realize salvation. Murray clarifies that the terminology 'limited atonement' may or may not be fair. It is very easy to prejudice an important issue with either a slander or a misrepresentation. However, "unless we believe in the final restoration of all men we cannot have an unlimited atonement. If we universalize the extent we limit the efficacy." He argues:

If some of those for whom atonement was made and redemption wrought perish eternally, then the atonement is not itself efficacious. It is this alternative that the proponents of universal atonement must face. They have a 'limited' atonement and limited in respect of that which impinges upon its essential character. We shall have none of it. The doctrine of 'limited atonement' which we maintain is the doctrine which limits the atonement to those who are heirs of eternal life, to the elect. That limitation insures its efficacy and conserves its essential character as efficient and effective redemption.

It is also incorrect to think that our doctrine is incompatible with evangelism. Says Murray: "The truth really is that it is only on the basis of such a doctrine that we can have a free and full offer of Christ to lost men. What is offered to men in the gospel? It is not the possibility of salvation, not simply the opportunity of salvation. What is offered is *salvation*." In evangelism, Christ himself is offered as the One who made full, perfect, and sufficient atonement for all our sins. What he did on the cross is so powerful that his salvation is not merely possible. "It is that doctrine alone that allows for a presentation of Christ that will be worth the glory of his accomplishment and of his person." He is offered as the Procurer and Securer of redemption, as the all-sufficient Savior. A person is then invited to trust exclusively in him for salvation as he is offered in the gospel—not in any merit, act, or choice of man.

Murray notes that there are many passages that could be drawn upon to illustrate further how widely the Bible teaches this concept. He then draws on an exegesis of Romans 8:31-39 (which is worthy of the readers full review) and many other NT verses, which teach that those for whom Christ died have also died in Christ (cf. Rom. 6:3-11; 2 Cor. 5:14-15; Eph. 2:4-7; Col. 3:3). As to the Romans 8 passage, Murray succinctly observes that the "us" in those verses can only apply to the elect, a group limited by God's decree, for we "may not extend the scope of the sacrifice of the Son beyond the scope of all the other free gifts . . . To put it briefly, those contemplated in the sacrifice of Christ are also the partakers of the other gifts of saving grace."

One should also be sure to grasp the sound argument that all who died in Christ also rose with him (cf. Rom. 6:3-11; 2 Cor. 5:14-15; Eph. 2:4-7). Murray puts it this way:

All for whom Christ died also died in Christ. All who died in Christ rose again with Christ. This rising again with Christ is a rising to newness of life after the likeness of Christ's resurrection. To die with Christ is, therefore, to die to sin and to rise with him to the life of new obedience, to live not to ourselves but to him who died for us and rose again. The inference is inevitable that those for whom Christ died are those and those only who die to sin and live to righteousness. Now it is a plain fact that not all die to sin and live in newness of life. Hence we cannot say that all men distributively died with Christ. And neither can we saw that Christ died for all men, for the simple reason that all for whom Christ died also died in Christ. If we cannot say that Christ died for all men, neither can we say that the atonement is universal . . . The conclusion is apparent—the death of Christ in its specific character as atonement was for those and those only who are in due time the partakers of that new life of which Christ's resurrection is the pledge and pattern. . . . Those for whom Christ died are those for whom he rose again and his heavenly saving activity is of equal extent with his once-for-all redemptive accomplishments.

Murray (and John Owen in *The Death of Death in the Death of Christ*) does an equally good job of addressing other challenging verses such as 2 Corinthians 5:14-15 and 1 John 2:2. Murray's chapter concludes:

We can readily see, therefore, that although universal terms are sometimes used in connection with the atonement these terms cannot be appealed to as establishing the doctrine of universal atonement. In some cases, it can be shown that all-inclusive universalism is excluded by the considerations of the immediate context. In other cases there are adequate reasons why universal terms should be used without the implication of distributively universal extent. Hence no conclusive support for the doctrine of universal atonement can be derived from universalistic expressions. The question must be determined on the basis of other evidence. This evidence we have tried to present. It is easy for the proponents of universal atonement to make offhand appeal to a few texts. But this method is not worthy of the serious student of Scripture. It is necessary for us to discover what redemption or atonement really means. And when we examine the Scripture we find that the glory of the cross of Christ is bound up with the effectiveness of its accomplishment. Christ redeemed us to God by his blood, he gave himself a ransom that he might deliver us from all iniquity. The atonement is efficacious substitution.

This essay, which should be read in full by every ordained Officer, magnifies the greatness of the salvation of Christ. It does not beggar the concept, nor make it dependent on the will of man.

How Great a Salvation!

Having taken stock of the work that Christ did on the cross, the WCF then progresses to discuss how that redemption is applied in chapters 10-18.

One of the most contested areas of Christianity prior to the time of the Westminster Assembly was the manner in which God saved people. It may be hard for us living many centuries later to understand the difficulties, but there were many. The single largest source of confusion was the teaching on the manner of salvation, which evolved over centuries in the Roman church. One key to grasping the divines' statements on salvation is to see that they were careful to draw out these themes in contrast to the prevailing Roman Catholicism of the day.

Interestingly, WCF chapters 9-18, those sections that are most directly concerned with God's manner of saving his people, were some of the least controversial, and consequently least discussed. In contrast to the more controversial sections on God's decrees, and the lengthier treatise on Scripture, these portions attracted few heated debates when the committee reported these to the floor of the Assembly. Considerably less time was spent on these chapters of eternal significance than on the topics of government, sacraments, Christian liberty, and the sovereignty of God.

The reason there was so little controversy over these chapters is found in the wide agreement that these divines had with one another and with Scripture. It calls for little debate when the members agree, and more importantly, agree with Scripture, the common authority. So the fact that there was so little controversy surrounding these chapters is a lasting testimony to the unanimity among these leaders.

Of course, they understood that God's entire work of salvation was attributable to the "voluntary condescension on God's part" (7:1), which was expressed by way of the covenant. These divines were keenly aware that the distance between God and his creatures was so vast that the creatures could never somehow evolve upward or eventually climb up to his expectations. Hence, God had to take the initiative in salvation. Had he not, we never would have been saved. That is fundamental to the Westminster view of salvation. If God had not acted first, we would not have acted at all.

The manner of God's saving is also inseparable from the person and work of Jesus Christ. The divines' consistency can already be felt, as they tie together the precious work of salvation with the earlier teachings on God's sovereignty and election. In keeping with those earlier biblical truths, they seek to portray the manner of salvation as based in the work and power of God, not based in the work and power of humans, the church, or experience. In contrast to the Romanist teaching that salvation came through the Church, and in contrast to Protestant extremists' teaching that salvation came from elevated mystical experience, and in contrast to the new-found faith of their day, which stressed that humans worked salvation out as a by-product of their own free and rational choices, these scriptural leaders donated to the church a superb declaration that stressed that salvation was of the Lord (Jon. 2:9).

In our own times, we could benefit by a renewal of this emphasis. How many times have we seen around us (or perhaps been guilty ourselves of promoting) a version of works-salvationism, which implies that it is really up to individuals to determine their own destinies? In that process, somehow amazing grace gets lost. If we do not clearly communicate and practice the kind of faith that depends on God from first to last (Rom. 1:17), we diminish the gracious manner of God's salvation. It is not due to our works (Rom. 9:16) nor our efforts that we have God's salvation; it is the gift of God (Eph. 2:8 and Rom. 4:1-8). I think an early twentieth century preacher would have agreed with these chapters by the divines, when he (Donald Barnhouse) said that all who allow for any contribution from man in salvation may as well pervert the gospel chorus into:

Jesus paid 90%.
10% to him I owe.
Sin lost most of its stain,
He washed in pink again.

The Assembly divines knew this salvation "so rich and free" from their own experiences as well as from the study of Scripture. These Puritans knew salvation about as well as any. And they sought to set forth those truths in the WCF. Not only did they engrave these in the Western mind, but they also were faithful to preach these to the leaders of their government, especially when they were given opportunity to preach before Parliament.

In each of the individual chapters in WCF 10-18, one biblical step in salvation is discussed at a time. As will be seen below, the authors who drew up these wordings were familiar with other Reformed statements on these subjects, with some even being experts on individual topics (e.g., Anthony Burgess on justification). Some had even written prolifically on certain topics, so there was certainly ample expertise in the room.

Moreover, these Christians had a better and more comprehensive grasp than many modern Christians. These forefathers, writing 350 years ago, evidenced a great appreciation for the wholeness and connectedness of God's salvation. Since it is his salvation given to his people, it should be communicated as he lays it out in scripture. One of the frequently ignored aspects of biblical teaching is that the various parts of God's salvation are related to one another. That is to say that when God saves a person, he not only gives forgiveness and redemption, but also freely gives justification, sanctification, adoption, and will keep us until the end.

The Pattern of Salvation

Theologians have spoken of this as the "order of salvation" (Latin: *ordo salutis*), and it is indeed a biblical concept that is represented here. Before looking at the individual parts (as the WCF does), first make sure you are aware of a few passages in Scripture that indicate this normal connected pattern of salvation. Although a person may not be fully conscious of each individual step, it is important to see how the Scripture does teach such a pattern or order. If we can sense this big picture, then the parts fit together a little better.

Several passages allude to this pattern. John 1:12 is a common memory verse for many new Christians. Like several others, it is a shame that we don't go on to memorize the next part. We are pleased to assure our listeners that if they will receive Christ and believe on his name, they will have the right to become children of God. The public process is to "Receive-Believe-and-Become." However, the very next verse goes on to explain that before we can do any of those things, something invisible must happen to us first. There is an order of salvation, and verse 13 speaks of those who become God's children. Yet they do not become that way because of natural birth or of some decision or will of a human father. God's children are "born of God." Rebirth is more fundamental and must come first before we "Receive-and-Believe." In fact, we will neither receive nor believe until we are first born again. That's what Scripture and Confession teach.

John 3, the well-known episode with Nicodemus, contains a definite order. Jesus himself says that things must follow a certain order if a person hopes to see the Kingdom of God. That will not come unless there is first a rebirth process. The Lord of our salvation announced the steps and pre-requisites: "No one can see the Kingdom of God unless he is born again . . . No one can enter the Kingdom of God unless he is born of water and the Spirit" (Jn. 3:3, 5). Thus being born again precedes any spiritual insight or inheritance of eternal life. Rebirth (or regeneration) must come first, and not vice-versa.

Romans 10 also teaches a pattern. Verse 13 of that chapter promises that anyone "who calls on the name of the Lord will be saved." However, as that section of Scripture continues, it makes it clear that this act of confession only occurs following other basic aspects related to our salvation. As that passage works its way backwards in chronology, it tells us that no one makes that confession without internal belief (10:14), and that such belief will not be there unless the person "hears" the call. And people will not hear the call, without the preaching of God's Word, and the preachers of God's Word must be commissioned (10:15) to go and bear the good news. The chain in this passage is that the Church sends preachers, who preach the Word so that people can hear the message. After hearing the message, those who are God's people will believe and then will confess the Lord. And assuredly, all who call on the Lord will be saved. This is the order of salvation in Romans 10.

Perhaps one of the clearest places where this is explained is Romans 8:28-32. The first verse in that passage is a treasured memory verse, especially for times of trouble. Yet often, memorizers leave off some of the best parts. As we go on to continue to read Romans 8:28, it speaks of those who are "called according to God's purpose." This verse is not applicable to all people, but specifically to the domain of God's people who are called according to his purpose. The first step in this revealed order is God's purpose (or "decree" as WCF speaks of it). Then and only then does it move to those who are called. In addition, this passage goes on to show that those who have been called according to God's purpose are also then the objects of his predestination, his calling, his justifying, and his glorifying (all in 8:30). Hence God, beginning with his purpose (decree), predestines, calls, justifies and keeps; so that all who are somewhere in the midst of that process can certainly know that all things will work together for good. This order of salvation gives meaning to the assurance to which so many of us cling in that wonderful memory verse.

Also to see the interconnectedness of Christian experience, one could study Romans 5:3-5 and 2 Peter 1:5-9. In both of those, growth in grace, or the maturation of Christian virtues, are heaped upon one another as God does his work in our lives. Apparent in Scripture is a basic pattern in which God takes us from death to life, from unbelief to trust, and this "so great salvation" (Heb. 2:3) is a package deal that flowers into many different aspects and into eternity.

Assuming the great teachings already laid out in God's decrees (WCF 3), the covenant (WCF 7), and the person and work of Christ (WCF 8), the WCF teaching on the order of God's salvation begins with "effectual calling." Effectual (or in other places "efficacy") means that something truly takes effect in reality. It works. It is the opposite of theoretical. Effectual calling is that calling by God to forsake our sins and come to him, which really takes effect. As Jesus taught us, "Many are called [outwardly, and not really taking effect], but few are chosen [only those effectually called]" (Mt. 22:14). While many outwardly hear the gospel message, only some respond. Those who respond are the ones whom God calls in real effect.

Frequently the Scriptures speak of the "called" of God (e.g., Rom. 1:1), or being called by God (2 Pet. 1:10). A number of leading bible commentators have noticed that in the NT Epistles, the phrase "called" is only used of true Christians, who have been effectively drawn to God. The WCF is quick to remind us that this calling, just like our whole salvation, is not creditable to us, to our efforts, or even to our response to God. It is not we who save, but God. Chapter 10 tells us that this effective call is from "God's free and special grace alone, not from anything at all foreseen in man, who is altogether passive therein, until being quickened (See Eph. 2:4-5) and renewed by the Holy Spirit, he is thereby enabled to answer this call, and to embrace the gospel . . ." (10:2).

Ephesians 2:1-10 is a fine passage to consult, since it incorporates nearly all of the individual steps of salvation. The first 3 verses of this passage indicate that before any person comes to Christ, that person is "dead in transgressions and sins" (2:1), a follower of the "ruler of the kingdom of the air, the spirit who is now at work in those who are disobedient" (2:2), intent on "gratifying the cravings of our sinful nature" (2:3), and "by nature, object of wrath" (2:3). This was our pre-Christian state, and we could not have the faith of Ephesians 2:8-9 without a dramatic interruption by God.

Into this sin-dominated life comes God's rich mercy (Eph. 2:4). While we were still dead (cf. also Rom. 5:6-10), prior to our seeing the kingdom of God (Jn. 3:3, 5), God who is rich in mercy "made us alive with Christ even when we were dead in transgressions—it is by grace you have been saved" (2:5). As to order, God's work comes before our conscious faith. We are reborn, or "made alive with Christ"; then we can respond in faith, following rebirth. In addition, after this rebirth, the outworking of this salvation continues into the "coming ages" so that Christians can live lives that "show the incomparable riches of his grace" (Eph. 2:7).

Then verses 8-10 inform us that grace is foundational, i.e., that this grace which comes from God generates even our faith "—and this [is] not from yourselves, it is the gift of God" (2:8). These verses are clear that the work of salvation is in no way from ourselves, nor from our own works (2:9). The entire work is begun and affected by the mighty grace of God. This work does not end only in our salvation; it extends to our living out a Christian life as the "workmanship of God," who have been created in Christ Jesus to do good works "which God prepared in advance for us to do" (Eph. 2:10). Hence we can see the order of salvation and the scope of God's work in these verses.

Effectual Call
Chapter 10 of the Confession also notes that it is only those whom God has predestined to life that he effectually calls. Is this not the biblical teaching found in Romans 8:28-32? Those, and only those whom he effectively calls out of their state of sin and death, have their minds enlightened so as to "savingly understand the things of God, taking away their heart of stone, and giving unto them a heart of flesh; renewing their will, and, by his almighty power, determining them to that which is good" (10:1). This is God's effective calling, a beginning step in our conversion. In this strong and sovereign act of God, Christians still come to him "most freely, being made by his grace" (10:1). God determines and calls; and he also makes us willing to come freely. There is no contradiction, and the authors of the WCF knew this. Possibly they were ahead of many of us. God's grace is even so powerful and broad that he is capable of saving elect infants and others not capable of being ordinarily called by the Word. Far from being a narrow faith, ours is more comprehensive than those which make the determination of salvation dependent on maturity, intellect, or a human decision.9

---

9 While some are put off by the assertions in WCF 10:3, it should also be recalled that, whether infants or adults, all persons are not elected by God. The second part of WCF 10:3 is actually the categorical principle, and one might wish that second part had occurred first for clarity's sake. If it did, it might more properly reflect a comprehensive statement of this point, which might well read: "All other elect persons, who are incapable of being outwardly called by the ministry of the word, even including to elect infants, dying in infancy, are regenerated and saved by Christ through the Spirit, who worketh when, and where, and how he pleaseth." Then section four would flow well, too. If,

Justification

The next ordinary step in God's salvation is justification. Many have been taught from a young age that this means roughly the same as the slurred sentence "Just as if I'd." In this way we see that to be justified is to be seen by God "just as if I'd" never sinned. Such a simple definition is still helpful as it stresses that justification is essentially an act that God alone does. We have no part in our justification. It is a legal pronouncement, with God acting as Judge. To be justified is to be pronounced free from the penalty of sin, which we truly deserve.

Another way to understand the meaning of justification is to be familiar with modern printing techniques or most word processors. When some text is being typed, most word processors have a function called justification. (What a thrill to see such biblical words in so many computer manuals!) The justification function is a fancy process by which the computer lines up all the characters you have typed to make them all align perfectly on the right margin. To do this, the "justifier" takes each individual character and moves it so that it lines up to meet the predetermined standard. In a small way that may be a picture for us about God's justification. He takes our sin, the entire account, and makes it all line up perfectly in the end. We are justified, made to line up so as to meet God's standards of righteousness, which we did not meet in our own. It takes a powerful Justifier; thus the Bible confesses that Jesus is both the just and the Justifier (Rom. 3:23-25). If we can remember that God alone justifies us, many other theological factors will be sorted out right.

The WCF has a superbly crafted explanation of this process of justification, which was the same in most respects for the saved of God in the Old Testament as well as in the New (11:6). This justification is not rooted in persons but in keeping with earlier teachings, "God did, from all eternity, decree to justify all the elect . . ." (11:4). When Jesus died on the cross, he fully discharged "the debt of all those that are thus justified, and did make a proper, real, and full satisfaction to his Father's justice in their behalf . . . not for anything in them; [but] . . . only of free grace" (11:3). If it is asked, "Is all this biblical, or the invention or tradition of imaginative theological minds?" one could consult the following NT verses, which teach:

- that Christians are justified based on the forgiveness which comes only from Jesus (Acts 13:38);
- that we are justified by grace, based on "the redemption that came by Christ Jesus" (Rom. 3:24);
- that God demonstrates his justice through justification, in that he is the one who justifies (Rom. 3:26) in light of his punishing Christ in our place;
- that we are justified through a non-works instrument, faith (Rom. 5:1);
- that the opposite of condemnation, i.e., justification is ours in Christ (Rom. 8:1);
- that since it is God who justifies, no one can separate the believer from his Lord (Rom. 8:33-39).

These standards are also careful to point out that faith rests on Christ alone as the instrument of justification (Gal. 3:10-12), and true belief unites faith and work in biblical balance. If one revisits Ephesians 2:10, it will be clear how God works all of grace, which if rightly understood, leads to lives of obedience.

---

therefore, the controversial paragraph is set in its context, it becomes clear that the aim of the divines is to comment on how wide and effective God's calling is—far beyond any human limitations—and that it can even reach to cases of infant mortality, although it would not presume that every single case of infant mortality is co-extensive with divine election.

This profound section on justification makes it clear that this process does not somehow infuse righteousness in the believer (the Roman Catholic view; cf WCF 11:1) as if righteousness were a substance pumped at a gas station, but instead that justification is God's pardoning of our sins, as he accounts us as righteous. We're back to "just as if I'd" never sinned. He does this for the sake of Christ alone, in that Jesus and the Father covenanted for a group of people before the foundation of the world, and on the last night of Jesus' earthly life, he presented God with the claim to redeem "all that you have given me" (Jn. 17:4, 6, 9). None of us are justified because of the act of believing, or some later obedience, or for anything within us. We are only justified at the will of God, by the good pleasure of the Father, who is satisfied with Christ's obedience on our behalf. All of this is the gift of God, including believing (11:1). However, once a person is truly justified, WCF 11:2 sounds reminiscent of a harmonization of Paul and James, as it asserts that true faith "is not alone . . . but is ever accompanied with all other saving graces, and is no dead faith, but worketh by love."

Christ fully paid our sin debt and satisfied the Father's righteous standards (WCF 11:3), whereas we never could. Accordingly, "the exact justice and rich grace of God might be glorified in the justification of sinners."

Adoption
And the work of God in our lives does not end with justification. God still has more to give his children. Chapter 12 of the Confession (which is both the smallest and often most overlooked) goes on to speak of the biblical teaching of adoption. After a Christian is effectively called and justified, he is also adopted. God does not just legally save us; he also incorporates us into his very own family. As Psalm 68:6 tells us of one of God's blessings, "He sets the lonely in families." In this case, God puts us into his own family.

The divines at Westminster knew that all who are justified are also adopted and given the liberties and privileges of the children of God, have his name put upon them, receive the spirit of adoption (Rom. 8:15-17), have access to the throne of grace (Heb. 4:14-16 and Rom. 5:1-2) with boldness, are enabled to cry Abba, Father (Gal. 4:6; Rom. 8:15), are "pitied, protected, provided for, and chastened by him (Heb. 12:5-8), as a father; yet never cast off . . . and inherit the promises, as heirs of everlasting salvation." These authors were not writing arid theological propositions. They knew the comfort of the teaching of adoption and wanted their flocks to know this edifying doctrine, as a staple of the Christian life. More practical teaching can scarcely be found.

In our own times, as abortion has become so rampant, many Christians have become more acquainted with adoption—even though it is not a brand new innovation. An Elder in our congregation adopted his son in the 1950s. There is no way that he could possibly love any son more. All adoptive parents feel the same way. Adoptive children are not second-class children at all. The Scripture teaches that each Christian is adopted into the family of God and given stupendous privileges. The Westminster divines elevated this teaching and realized that it was vitally important. We are thankful they had such insight to do so. However, even greater than this single chapter on one benefit of our great salvation is the more comprehensive teaching on how God continues to infiltrate us with holiness thereafter. One of the beauties of this system of doctrine is that, while many modern approaches emphasize only one aspect of the *ordo salutis* (often to the minimization of other glorious aspects of sanctification), these Westminster Puritans were very well-rounded and emphasized as comprehensive an approach as possible. Presbyterian piety, if rightly understood, is actually very full and beautiful, in contrast to being narrow or burdensome. The doctrine of adoption, although perhaps not a theological *summa*, is one part of that whole.

Sanctification

Following upon the heels of adoption is the work of being made holy (or sanctification). This sanctification affects all parts of the whole redeemed person, yet is not perfect in this life (13:2). The Confession represents Paul's teaching in Romans 7 very well, namely, that even the best of Christians are at times besieged by impulses that are less than holy. And at times we cannot fathom why we do the very things we do not want to do—and fail to do those things which we know we ought to do. These great leaders three and a half centuries ago were also realistic enough to guard against some type of perfectionism. They had learned from Scripture and their own experience that in this spiritual battle, flesh against Spirit, even in the best of believers corruption remains for a time and may occasionally prevail. We will sin, and to deny that is to argue with scripture (Cf. 1 Jn. 1:8). Rather these Westminster pastors warned of a "continual and irreconcilable war, the flesh lusting against the Spirit, and the Spirit against the flesh" (13:2).

Sanctification applies only to those who have been effectively called, regenerated, and who have been given a new (2 Cor. 5:17) heart within them. All such Christians are further sanctified "by his [Christ's] Word and Spirit dwelling in them" (13:1), and there is gradual Christian growth. This captures the clear scriptural teaching that each person who is born again is also filled with the Holy Spirit. There certainly are, and should be, lifelong seasons of renewal and deepening. Nevertheless, Christians receive the Holy Spirit in connection with salvation—and not as a later blessing. Sanctification is part of the package deal, which we call the order of salvation.

As the Bible teaches, so these authors wrote. All who have been baptized into Christ have been baptized into his death and resurrection (Rom. 6:3-4). This spiritual baptism refers to each Christian. Furthermore, no one can confess Jesus as Lord without the Holy Spirit (1 Cor. 12:3) first renewing his mind to make that statement. First comes renewal, then confession, as the order of salvation. Likewise, first comes calling, justification, and adoption. To all those who have those graces, sanctification comes as well. God justifies exactly none that he does not also sanctify. And even though no person becomes perfectly sanctified in this life (13:2), God progressively works in us (13:3), and "the saints grow in grace, perfecting holiness in the fear of God."

Saving Faith

The next topic that the Confession takes up in sequence is Saving Faith, followed by repentance. We do not cooperate with God at all in the effective call, justification, or adoption. Like submerged parts of an iceberg, these are below the surface but very real. These parts of the salvation process are totally and exclusively his works. And in one sense, sanctification is definitive, and performed by God (e.g., 1 Cor. 6:10). The WCF places the individual aspects of salvation in order, beginning with those steps, which God alone does, and then moves into the realm in which we are conscious and cooperative. That is likely the reason for the order of these chapters, once again underscoring the sovereign determination of God in salvation.

After a person has been called, justified, adopted, and sanctified by God, then it may dawn on us what has happened. At that time we are called (and now able) to exercise saving faith, because we have been made new creatures. The proverbial tip of the iceberg then appears. Accordingly, the

14th chapter of the WCF gives us an excellent and most practical definition of saving faith. Saving faith is the kind of faith that is not mere acknowledgement of spiritual generalities. It is one which "believes to be true whatever is revealed in the Word, for [as] the authority of God himself speaking therein; and acts differently on that which each particular passage contains; yielding obedience to the commands, trembling at the threatenings, and embracing the promises of God for this life, and that which is to come" (14:2). Such saving faith is not merely giving assent to truths about God, but superior to the assent of demons (Jas. 2:19), it touches the realm of behavior, and we "act differently," "trembling at threatenings," and honoring the Word of God. That is saving faith, the kind of faith that is given to all the elect, in which they are "enabled to believe . . . the work of the Spirit of Christ in their hearts" (14:1). To all whom the Father calls, justifies, adopts, and sanctifies, he also gives saving faith which "is increased and strengthened" (14:1) and "gets the victory" (14:3). Also, to all those to whom God gives these, he grants repentance.

Repentance
Repentance is "an evangelical grace" (Note: not work) which should be known by every saint. It is a true hatred of the "filthiness and odiousness of sin, as contrary to the holy nature, and righteous law of God" in which a redeemed person is so grieved that they turn away (The biblical word for repentance refers to a 180 degree reversal or turning away) from sin (15:2). Every Christian is to make repentance not only at conversion, but also afterward, and is to "repent of our sins particularly" (15:5). The divines also wanted it clearly understood that such repentance itself was not some satisfaction for sin, nor an assistance to grant us pardon (15:3).

Repentance unto life is a grace, by which a sinner is able to see his sins as God sees them—as filthy and hateful—and as involving great danger to the sinner because they are completely contrary to the holy nature and righteous law of God. Understanding that God in Christ is merciful to those who repent, the sinner suffers deep sorrow for and hates his sin and also determines to turn away from all his sins. This chapter also teaches that repentance is required, that particular repentance is needed, and that nothing is too large or small for repentance. Private confession, although not to a priest, also has its place.

The Roman Catholic view was at the forefront of discussions about both repentance and good works. Chapters 15 and 16 of the WCF are best understood as in opposition to the Romanist tradition. These godly men wanted to make sure that their sheep were not in bondage to the system, which taught that penitence was a sacrament, or that a person could accumulate enough good works10 to be in good stead with God.
It is certainly true, as we have already seen in Ephesians 2:10, that any truly born again person is expected to grow in doing good. Jesus taught that those who were truly his sheep would not be so in word only, but those who did the works of the Father (Mt. 7:21-23). God expects us, once born again and filled with the Spirit, to serve him in this world and to do those things that he commands (16:1). But never are works the basis for our salvation, nor our sanctification.

Perseverance and Assurance

---

10 I normally spend very little time discussing WCF 16, because it has not been a pressing problem among evangelicals for centuries. It is usually enough to acquaint Officers (if not already) with erroneous Romanist views prior to the Reformation. Most of WCF 16 is aimed at those errors and continues to have application in situations where works are over-emphasized, which I have to say, when compared to historic excesses doesn't seem to be a predominant trend in most Presbyterian churches today.

The final two chapters in this section involve the perseverance of the saints and assurance of salvation. We have already seen in Romans 8:32 that not only does God call, decree, predestine, and justify, but moreover, that those who are the objects of this grace are also "glorified." This refers to the final state, when even our bodies will no longer show any defects of sin. This act of God, which is given to all "whom God has accepted in his Beloved (Col. 1:13), effectively called, and sanctified by his Spirit" (17:1), assures that such people, "can neither totally nor finally fall away from the state of grace, but shall certainly persevere to the end, and be eternally saved" (17:1). Whether we call this "eternal security," or "once saved, always saved," or the "preservation of the saints," it is still a thoroughly biblical teaching, as the divines so well understood.

It is taught in John 10, when Jesus says, "My sheep listen to my voice; I know them, and they follow me. I give them eternal life, and they shall never perish; no one can snatch them out of my hand . . . no one can snatch then out of my Father's hand" (vss. 27-29). Earlier, our Lord had taught that if we feed on Christ, he will keep us until the last day and raise us up (Jn. 6:54). Paul assures the Christians at Phillipi that when God begins a good work (of salvation) in people, he will also continue it until its completion (Phil. 1:6). Peter speaks of an "inheritance that can never perish, spoil or fade—kept in heaven for you who through faith are shielded by God's power" (1 Pet. 1:4-5).

Once we are born again, there is no later change in our nature (Jn. 3:1-8). And since Christ's death was once and for all (Heb. 9:25-28), in that all who are Christians have died with him (Rom. 6:4-8), we die to sin once and from then on are irrevocably members of God's family. We are given the utmost assurance; in fact, Romans 8 tells us that nothing thereafter can possibly "separate us from the love of God that is in Christ Jesus our Lord" (Rom. 8:38-39). Those in whom God begins his work of salvation, those who are called, justified, and elected, will also stay with God until the end, to glorification (Rom. 8:30).

Although God gives perseverance, the WCF is astute enough to warn us that there will be difficult times (17:3); not all will be a bed of roses. Still, we receive great comfort from the basis of this perseverance. I have used WCF 17:2 repeatedly in counseling sessions with tender-hearted Christians to encourage them to recognize the true basis of their faith: not in themselves, but in God. I believe the Assembly divines knew the value of this as well; for they taught that our perseverance, far from depending on us, depended on the following anchors, which were far more faithful than ourselves. This perseverance as the WCF teaches (17:2) depends "not on our own free will, but upon:
- the immutability (unchangeableness) of the decree of election (Rev. 13:8);
- the free and unchangeable love of God the Father (Eph. 1:4-5; Rom. 8:39);
- the effectiveness of the merit and intercession of Jesus Christ (Heb. 7:25 and Rom. 5:8);
- the indwelling spirit (John 15),
- the [implanted] seed of God within them (1 Jn. 3:9);
- the nature of the covenant of grace (Heb. 6:17-18).

Such perseverance is a gift of God and allows us to be delivered from the fear that God will cast us off later. The more we know the depth of the salvation that God gives, the more clearly we see that he will be faithful to the end, that he will not desert his saved ones. We may rest assured that "if we died with him, we will also live with him; if we endure, we will also reign with him" (2 Tim. 2:11-12).

The Assembly was in line with the similar sentiment of the earlier Synod of Dort, on the practical value of perseverance: "Satan hates it, the world laughs at it, ignorant men and hypocrites abuse it, and erroneous spirits impugn it; yet the spouse of Christ hath always most tenderly loved, and constantly defended it, as a treasure of invaluable price. Which that she may do, God will provide and bring to pass: against whom neither can any counsel avail, nor strength avail."

The final chapter in this section on God's salvation is on assurance. Although there may be times or seasons in our life when this assurance is shaken at low levels, or besieged (WCF 18:4), still it will not be totally absent. So strong is this assurance that, according to the Confession, it is not a bare conjecture nor based on probability (18:2). It is an infallible assurance based on the following (Again, our benefits are not dependent on things we do, but on what God does.):

- the divine promises of salvation (Gal. 3:18);
- the inward evidence of those graces (Gal. 5:22-26);
- the testimony of the Spirit of adoption confirming that we are God's children (Rom. 8:15-17);
- the indwelling Holy Spirit, who is the deposit of our inheritance (Eph. 1:13-14).

The Confession recognizes that this assurance is sometimes counterfeited (Heb. 6:4-6) by hypocrites and presumptuous people, but that all who truly believe in the Lord will have some measure of this assurance. God does not want his children to perpetually wonder whether or not they are accepted in the beloved. Once we are saved, God's Spirit also assures us of God's faithfulness to keep us. Toward the end of his life, the apostle John believed that we could know that our salvation was certain. In 1 John 5:13 he informs us that he was writing these truths so that we may *know* (not guess) that we have eternal life.

This, God's salvation, is generous, one which extols his sovereign power, and one which is by grace from first to last. If we understand this, perhaps we can also understand why the composer J. S. Bach, who shared these views, signed his compositions with the words *soli deo gloria*, the Latin for "to God alone be the Glory." The members of the Westminster Assembly certainly knew this well. If we can agree with their thoroughly scriptural views, we can breathe a great sigh of relief, and walk with confidence, assurance, and a smile of joy on our faces.

Homework reading:
    Read the article by John Murray from his *Redemption Accomplished and Applied*.
    For next week, read the article by Robert Rayburn on the Sabbath.

Session #4: Practical Theology

Much of the latter half of the WCF deals with a range of practical matters related to Christian living and the role of the church. Chapters 19 and 20 deal with the law and liberty. Other chapters in the final third of this Confession deal with worship, the Sabbath, oaths, politics, marriage, and the church and her sacraments.

The Law

Chapter 19 is a superb statement on the applicability and usefulness of the law for all believers and all times. Far from being unimportant for ethics and Christian spirituality, the law of the Lord is perfect, reviving the soul (see Psalm 19). The first paragraph of WCF 19 reminds us that this law, even though not overtly identified as such, was present even in Eden before Adam's Fall. This was part of the covenant of ability, i.e., Adam had the ability to keep it prior to the Fall. Written on man's heart from the beginning as "a perfect rule of righteousness" (WCF 19:2), the law was further codified in writing at Mt. Sinai in the Ten Commandments. These commandments, as is often noted, may be divided into *tables* and *types* of law.

The *tables* of the law (WCF 19:2) are the first table, which includes the first four commandments that regulate our duty toward God, and the second table, which contains moral commandments directed at our behavior to other men. The NT never treats the moral commandments as passé.

The *types* of the law are (1) moral, (2) ceremonial, and (3) judicial (or political). The *moral* law, summarized in the Ten Commandments, addresses how we should treat one another as fellow creatures. These moral commandments (WCF 19:5) are always binding—the moral fabric of human relationships is so designed and unchanging—and they apply both to believers and unbelievers. Those moral aspects of the law are for all time because they reflect the authority of the Creator and the approval of our Redeemer (19:5).

The *ceremonial* laws (19:3) are all those worship and ritual codes, including aspects of feasts, Kosher laws, cleansing laws, etc., which were designed to point to the sacrifice of Christ. Once Jesus fulfilled those on the cross, there is no additional need to continue those aspects, which were designed for Israel as an infant church ("the church under age"). Thus, the ceremonial law is no longer binding, and the early church resisted its reimposition. These are "now abrograted under the New Testament."

The *judicial* or *political* laws were those civil statutes revealed by God for the post-Mosaic nation of Israel (see, for example, Exodus 21-23 for case laws based on the Ten Commandments in Exodus 20). These were designed only for strict application in the nation-state of Israel as God prepared them for the coming of the Messiah, much like the ceremonial laws were. The authors of the WCF also believed that those aspects of the political law "expired together with the state of that [OT Israel] people" (WCF 19:4). However, there are certain portions of good government that were contained in these earlier codes, and the "general equity" or material equivalence in substance should be honored wherever applicable. Those who believe that the entire codification of the OT case law is binding for every civil government today find themselves slightly afield of this teaching that only the "general equity" is perpetually binding. The divines, for example, did not attempt to have the sitting legislature—right across the street from them—enact the Mosaic code as their statute law. Some Puritans in colonial New England, however, may have been closer to that view, but the WCF itself only specifies the moral law as the continuing part of the OT law.

The balance of this chapter states that these proper uses of law are not at all contrary to the grace of the gospel (19:7). Anyone who seeks to pit grace and law as enemies or functional opponents in sanctification has to take exception to this final paragraph, which wisely asserts that these two "sweetly comply" as "the Spirit of Christ" subdues and enables our wills to freely and cheerfully pursue the will of God revealed in the law. Of course, this is not to be pursued as a covenant of human ability, for we need the inner work of the spirit to love the law. Still, the law is useful to:

- Inform us of our duty and the will of God;
- Reveal the sinful pollutions of our heart and nature;
- Convict us of our sin;
- Humble us and teach us to hate our sin;
- Prove our need for Christ and his salvation, which is based on his perfect obedience;
- Restrain corruption even among the regenerate;
- Illustrate what our sins deserve.

Thus understood, the law of God is not a bad tool of sanctification. Why would any believer not want to be refined by this divinely-designed tool of sanctification, unless he was seeking to avoid God's high standards for spirituality? In fact, the WCF is a sound and needed antidote to the various antinomian approaches today, and it anticipated their wrong-headed approaches with its conclusion in WCF 19:6: "So a man's doing good and refraining from evil, because the law encourages the one and deters the other, is no evidence of his being under the law and not under grace." The two "sweetly comply," and Officers ought to guard the flock from imbalanced or experimental approaches that do not keep these two strong forces married.

Christian Liberty

This chapter is a hallmark of our standards. Like Martin Luther a century earlier, these divines wanted to make sure that their audiences realized that they were not trying to create new law and set up new moral strictures. The chapter on Christian Liberty differentiates several key concepts. To begin with, it defines the liberty that Christ has for believers as deliverance from sin's guilt, the wrath of God, and the curse of the law. These are, as most quickly recognize, spiritual liberties as contrasted with civil or physical liberties. The various aspects of spiritual bondage are overcome. Christians have a larger amount of liberty because, as the previous chapter asserts, the judicial and ceremonial laws have expired. We are thus freed from "the yoke of the ceremonial law" and have greater access to the throne of grace.

The second paragraph of this chapter affirms that only God rules over one's conscience. Accordingly, he has liberated it from man-made traditions, doctrines, imperatives, and regulations, which are in any way additional or contrary to his Word. The believer is under no obligation, therefore, to yoke his conscience to non-divinely-ordained truths. To do such, even if well-intentioned, may have the affect of betraying Christian liberty or destroying a reasonably conscientious approach to life.

That being said, however, this view does not encourage license. To use the doctrine of Christian liberty—either in deed or by word—to justify something not permitted by God or to cause others to stumble is a serious misuse of it. The Officer candidate is to remember the apostolic teaching in Romans (and elsewhere) to avoid causing a weaker Christian to stumble.

Christian liberty, if kept in its proper perspective is a large gift to the church. To push it to extremes, however, whether in morals, doctrine, or worship is a misappropriation of something that God intended to be beneficial. The following chapter of the WCF shows, for example, that worship is not to be performed in a libertine fashion; instead, it is to be ordered—ordered to the glory of God, not the whim of man, just as morality is.

Worship and the Sabbath

Chapter 21 treats two critical subjects: worship and the keeping of the Sabbath day. Reminiscent of the maiden paragraph of our confession, this first paragraph assumes that the light of nature has made certain aspects of God's existence plain. Although his supremacy should be clear—even from nature—the permissible way of worshiping God has not come from the revelation of creation. Instead—and particularly in light of man's fallen nature (cf. WCF 6)—the proper worship of God is not left merely to the imaginations or devices of man. The "acceptable way" (note, this is not terribly pluralistic) of worshiping God is revealed by himself and limited to what Scripture reveals (21:1). Worship is far too important to be done without divine instructions; and man is far too fallen to fabricate for himself—no matter how enthusiastic, artistic, or well-meaning—ways to worship God. Thankfully, God has left behind ample revelation within the pages of Scripture for sincere worshipers to know what to do.

To begin with, of course, worship is only appropriate for the Triune God—never to saints or other creatures (21:2). Moreover, worship must always be involved with the mediation of Christ alone. That standard means that we must constantly study, reform, and compare our worship to the priestly work of Christ—not to the trends of the day or perceived needs of the people. *The Mediator is always more important than the media.*

Several component parts of worship are then identified in WCF 21:3. Among the ongoing parts of biblical worship are: prayer (21:3-4), Scripture reading, sound preaching (and, note, the role of the audience is to give a "conscionable hearing"), and biblically-sentimented singing (21:5). The Psalms are mentioned and were the norm for much of the Christian world of the day, but it is not necessary to exclude all other kinds of biblically-sentimented singing. God-honoring hymns and music may also be employed (see Psalm 150). Again, the key for acceptable music is that it meets the standard of honoring God's revelation.

The sacraments are also a part of worship. Although mentioned in this paragraph (also with oaths, vows, fastings, and other special aspects of worship), merely in the words "the due administration and worthy receiving," no particular frequency of administration is given for the sacraments. Obviously, the sacrament of baptism depends on candidates and is not performed at any fixed frequency; moreover, the frequency of the Lord's Supper is left to the discretion of the Session. Throughout various Reformed communions, the Lord's Supper is celebrated annually, quarterly, monthly, weekly, or whenever the Elders see most practical. There is no—and the larger Reformed tradition has not dogmatized on this—absolute on this matter of worship, and the WCF wisely avoided dogmatizing on this.

A second time this chapter uses the terms "acceptable" in paragraph 6. In this case, neither prayer nor worship is made more acceptable because of the place where it occurs. Rather, God's spiritual nature is highlighted, and he is to be worshiped in spirit and in truth (Jn. 4:24), whether privately, by families, or corporately. It is assumed that private devotions and family worship will both be regular and that they will contribute to a more solemn "public assembly," which is not to be characterized by carelessness or neglect.

The Regulative Principle is still very important for growing and stable churches today. If it is not employed, worship services will frequently drift like vessels without anchors. Although it does not prescribe all particulars for the service—*circumstances*, such as time of worship, selection of hymns, the use of a robe (or not), and many other features that are properly left to the discretion of the Elders—the Regulative Principle can protect a church from faddishness, ideas that are not maturely considered, man-centered focal points, and undue emotionalism or subjectivism.

The final two paragraphs of this chapter on worship address the Sabbath. *First*, a biblical review is given for this institution (21:7). It began at creation and followed God's own pattern of working six days and resting one. At the time of Christ (who kept the Sabbath himself, not dreaming that it was passé in any sense) and to honor his resurrection on the first day of the week (then Sunday), the Christian Church began to observe the Sabbath, which is useful for all ages, on the first day of the week. The keeping of the Sabbath is expected until the end of the world.

Second, practical considerations for a proper keeping of the Sabbath are provided in WCF 21:8. Among these are that people should prepare ahead of time so that the Sabbath will not be hindered by mundane duties, which could be done at other times. The purpose is for believers to have "a holy rest all the day" from their normal vocations. The activities which are appropriate for the other six days, including thoughts, recreations, and worldly jobs are to be abstained from as much as possible so that God's family can rest, worship, and serve him in works of necessity (works of necessity may include those who protect the citizenry and medical personnel, for example) and mercy. Some people think the WCF is too explicit on abstaining from recreations on the Sabbath, and this paragraph is best understood within its context as calling God's people away from worldliness in many forms. When written in the 17th century, certain recreations were beginning to affect church attendance. Of course, when compared to today's normal Sunday recreational opportunities, those were much smaller in scale. The fourth commandment is God's gift to man (see Mk. 2), and we should receive it as such, call it our delight, and keep it holy. It is a chief tool to further the godly aims of human worship.

We rarely devote much time to the subject of **oaths and vows**, since most of the comments were directed at Reformation-era controversies. On the one hand, the Anabaptists were overly-literal, thinking that the Bible proscribed all vows and oaths. This "left-wing" of the Reformation also believed that Christians could not serve as elected officials or in armies (the descendants of Anabaptists are still officially pacifist). The WCF denies both of these in 22 and 23:2. On the other hand, the Roman Catholics would take vows, specifically for poverty, celibacy, and submission to their clergy (22:7), which were neither scriptural nor wise. The Confession warns against these as "superstitious" and "sinful snares."

However, vows may be taken, says the Confession, under the following conditions:
  (a) either in worship (e.g., marriage, the sacrament of baptism, or ordination; cf. 22:1) or in proper civil contexts (22:2);

(b) in the name of God (22:2);

(c) only after thought or "never vainly or rashly" (22:2);

(d) deliberately and if able to perform what is sworn (22:3);

(e) performed with faithfulness (22:5); and

(f) "in the plain and common sense of the words, without equivocation or mental reservation."

This final phrase is especially relevant to vows for church Officers and members. Each should know what he is engaging himself to do and should count the costs before entering into a covenantal oath. Particularly important for our consideration are the Officers' vows, which will be discussed later under our church's constitution. However, for now, it should be noted that each man who serves must be able to apply the conditions above to his particular set of vows "without equivocation or mental reservation."

Civil Government

Chapter 23 contains one of the finest theological statements on politics from early modernity. The opening paragraphs—instead of affirming government "of the people, for the people, and by the people"—affirm a more God-centered approach, noting that God has ordained civil government as its own dignified sphere to be "under him, over the people, for his own glory, and the public good." (23:1) As already observed, the WCF approves participation in civil government as lawful (23:2). Whenever Christians serve in government, they should "especially maintain piety, justice, and peace" according to the civil laws. They do not, in other words, put their light under a bushel if serving in the public sector. In keeping with Romans 13, they may engage in just wars. Civil Government was also ordained to punish criminals and to defend and encourage right civic action.

Citizens, in turn, were to pray for their governors, honor them, pay taxes, and submit to them—all as taught in Romans 13:1-7. Even if a civil ruler does not share our religious faith, citizens are not automatically justified in resisting him; that must only come about in rare and extreme situations.[11]

While one of the beauties of the WCF is its appreciation of the proper role of civil government, it also denied certain roles to politicians. They were not to perform the unique "marks" given to the church, including preaching, discipline, or the administration of the sacraments. In sum, they were not to interfere in matters of the faith. However, they should serve (as Is. 49 taught) as "nursing fathers," who were to protect the Church without establishing (this is a prime example of what the First Amendment means by an 'establishment of religion') a particular sect. In fact, our Confession calls on the civil government to protect equally all ecclesiastical clergy. Civil rights, such as personal protection and libel restrictions, were to be upheld by the civil governors, as were the freedom of church assemblies "without molestation or disturbance." (23:3) The civil government is to ensure, not hinder, the free internal operations of lawful religious societies.

Of course, if this sounds fairly Americanized, it is. The original wording granted considerably more power to governors to convene a synod, just as Parliament did at Westminster in 1643.

---

11 Since this is such an involved topic, I will refer the student to my book *The Genevan Reformation and the American Founding* (forthcoming 2003) for fuller discussions of the view of Calvin and other Puritans on the role of civil government. This book may be ordered from Amazon.com.

Even though that led to spectacular products, Americans a century later thought it wiser not to permit the civil government to convene a church meeting. History has proven them wise in that regard.

The original wording below shows the difference of sentiment, particularly the larger role in religious affairs afforded to the Parliament.12

AMERICAN WCF 23:3

III. Civil magistrates may not assume to themselves the administration of the Word and sacraments; or the power of the keys of the kingdom of heaven; or, in the least, interfere in matters of faith. Yet, as nursing fathers, it is the duty of civil magistrates to protect the church of our common Lord, without giving the preference to any denomination of Christians above the rest, in such a manner that all ecclesiastical persons whatever shall enjoy the full, free, and unquestioned liberty of discharging every part of their sacred functions, without violence or danger. And, as Jesus Christ hath appointed a regular government and discipline in his church, no law of any commonwealth should interfere with, let, or hinder, the due exercise thereof, among the voluntary members of any denomination of Christians, according to their own profession and belief. It is the duty of civil magistrates to protect the person and good name of all their people, in such an effectual manner as that no person be suffered, either upon pretense of religion or of infidelity, to offer any indignity, violence, religious and ecclesiastical assemblies be held without molestation or disturbance.

ORIGINAL WCF 23:3

III. The civil magistrate may not assume to himself the administration of the Word and sacraments, or the power of the keys of the kingdom of heaven: yet he hath authority, and it is his duty, to take order, that unity and peace be preserved in the Church, that the truth of God be kept pure and entire; that all blasphemies and heresies be suppressed; all corruptions and abuses in worship and discipline prevented or reformed; and all the ordinances of God duly settled, administered, and observed. For the better effecting whereof, he hath power to call synods, to be present at them, and to provide that whatsoever is transacted in them be according to the mind of God.

Marriage and Divorce

The section on social and ethical concerns is rounded out with a discussion of marriage and divorce in chapter 24. The opening paragraph defines marriage as a lawful union between one man and one woman. Obviously, same-sex marriages—clearly forbidden in Scripture—were not acceptable to these Puritans. The purposes of marriage were to provide mutual help, avoid immorality, and provide for reproduction, biologically and spiritually (24:2). Believers should only marry those who maintained the true faith and were to avoid marriages with unbelievers, idolaters, or those who clung to Roman Catholicism. Incest, or marriage to a near-relative was forbidden in 24:4. Originally WCF 24:4 added (which our version has deleted): "The man may

12 A comparison of changes within the WCF from its original may be found at: http://opc.org/documents/WCF_orig.html.

not marry any of his wife's kindred nearer in blood than he may of his own; nor the woman of her husband's kindred nearer in blood than of her own."

The grounds for dissolving a marriage were few and far between. Discovery of sexual sin before or after the engagement is a ground for dissolution of marriage in keeping with the OT. Or if adultery occurred after the marriage, the innocent party is free to divorce and remarry in the Lord. These earlier pastors also realized that there is little new under the sun: people would connive to find ways to rationalize easy divorce. But, God takes these marriage covenants so seriously, that there are only two biblical grounds for divorce recognized by the WCF: (a) actual adultery of some kind (not merely 'looking at a woman with lust in your heart'); and (b) willful, irremedial desertion by the unbelieving party in a marriage, as in 1 Corinthians 7. Only those cases have been recognized by our Confession as biblical grounds for divorce.[13]

From this short lesson, it may be seen that the WCF and its authors were not concerned merely with heady, theological matters. It also speaks to matters of ethics, leisure, worship, truthful speech, Christian liberty, and the continuing value of the law. Few creedal statements address the breadth of areas this one does with as much scriptural faithfulness and comprehensiveness in succinct wording.

---

[13] One PCA General Assembly (1992) sought to amend the WCF at this point to recognize divorce as lawful on the grounds of physical abuse. However, the requisite constitutional requirements (2/3 of the presbyteries) were never reached to amend the WCF to add that ground.

Session #4a
The Church and Its Sacraments

To begin our discussion of this topic, we might want to file this nugget away: Even though our period of history seems to give much confidence to the numerous "new organizations, clubs, and societies almost beyond number, with all sorts of objects and of every name, for men, women, and children," still "man has never devised any organization equal to the Church in its educating and uplifting power."

Jesus said, "By their fruits you shall know them." That is true not only in terms of an individual but also in terms of the societal effect of an organization. In this session we hope to examine the chief vehicle that expressed the teaching coming from the Westminster Assembly—the Church. We will concentrate on the teaching and impact of the Westminster Confession of Faith in three key areas: (1) The Church, (2) The Sacraments, and (3) Church order. In each of these areas the Westminster faith had a definite and large impact. In these three areas we see the principles of the Westminster faith put into practice, the doctrinal skeleton takes on flesh, and the rubber meets the road. These are the consistent outworkings of the earlier theological truths and may serve as the chief tests of the truth of a faith. Let us explore each of these in light of the statements by the Assembly on these areas.

The Church

The Westminster divines wrote in a time when the church was the primary organization for expressing and living out the faith.[14] Long before other voluntary societies and para-church groups had been established, it was unthinkable for any organism except the church to be the chief expression of the Christian faith. The Westminster Assembly defined the church in broad terms, but it is helpful for us to understand that the church is not merely a formal or external organization. It flows from an inner life as a unique institution in society and in the history of the world.

The teaching of the Westminster Assembly on the church and the church's understanding of it flowed from the rich apostolic doctrine of the communion of saints. This communion of saints is the strongest degree of fellowship, causing those who are saved by God to see their lives more in terms of the corporate Body of Christ than in terms of an individual's interests. Many churches routinely confess in the Apostles' Creed that they believe in the communion of saints, yet few of us have as sophisticated a view or practice of the communion of saints as these divines did. Chapter 26 of the WCF says that, "All saints are united to Jesus Christ their head by his spirit and by faith . . . [and] have fellowship with him in his grace, sufferings, death, resurrection, and glory: And, being united to one another in love, they have communion with each other's gifts and graces, and are obliged to the performance of such duties, public and private, as do conduce to their mutual good, both in the inward and outward man" (WCF 26:1). As we compare this teaching with Scripture, we find that it is indeed compatible with what the Book of Acts represents as the earliest Christian fellowship (Acts 2:45; 4:32 ff.) The Confession understood that for the church to be the church as God intended it to be, it would have to exhibit the strong communion of saints. It would be God's society.

---

14 Portions of this discussion are taken from my *Windows on Westminster*, Copyright © 1993, Great Commission Publications, Suwanee, Georgia; used with permission.

Furthermore saints are, according to the Confession, encouraged to assist one another in spiritual services so as to build up the body of Christ, even to "relieving each other in outward things, according to their several abilities and necessities" (26:2). This communion of saints is an opportunity for evangelism, for extension of the gospel, for diaconal ministry, as well as for building up believers. It was the Apostle Paul who encouraged the church to "do good unto all people, particularly to those in the household of God" (Galatians 6:10). Of course, this communion of saints does not take away or infringe against the possession of personal property, as if a socialistic approach to property was taught in Scripture (26:3). The Westminster divines conceived of the church as an active society-within-a-society, ministering to the needs of the saints.

It is important to understand just what the forefathers at Westminster understood by the church. In their excellent chapter on the church they make a distinction in the beginning between the invisible and the visible church, with the invisible church as the sum total of the elect who have been "gathered into one head who is Christ, who is also the spouse, the body, the fullness of him who fills all in all." And somehow, the whole of this Spirit-indwelt society is greater than the sum of its individual parts. In this first definition of the church we see the Westminster authors taking a consistent step to define the very nature of the church, as rooted in the counsel and decree of God. The most basic definition of the church is that society which is created by God through his strong and sovereign election. The church therefore is not defined "from below," as if it is identified chiefly in terms of its outward manifestation, appearance, structure, sacraments, or doctrine, but rather it is primarily identified with the work of salvation that God performs for his elect. The whole number of the elect, therefore, equals the invisible church.

In contrast, the visible church is the external church (both in the Old Testament and in the New Testament—WCF 25:2), consisting of all those in the world (That is the meaning of "Catholic") who profess the true religion, as well as their children. The Confession is thoroughly covenantal to define the church as including not only believers but also their infant seed. Moreover, this church is the "Kingdom of the Lord Jesus Christ, the house and family of God, out of which there is no ordinary possibility of salvation" (25:2). Thus the high position of the church is to be that ordinary mechanism which nourishes and accompanies salvation. It was unthinkable to the biblical students at the Westminster Assembly that a person might be saved and then not be a part of the household of faith. In addition, to this outward society are given the sacraments, the ministry of preaching, and the duty of building up the saints until Christ returns again (25:3).

Individual congregations are more or less pure according to a definite standard. The WCF sets forth three of those standards, which are sometimes called the "Marks of the Church." In WCF 25:4 the determination of the purity of the church is made in light of how (1) The Gospel is taught and embraced, (2) The Sacraments are administered, and (3) Public Worship is performed.

It is also admitted that, even among those churches which are most in pursuit of the purity of the gospel, still there are no perfect churches, and even the best of churches are "subject to both to mixture and error" (WCF 25:5). As a result, some churches have degenerated so as to forfeit their claim to being genuine churches of Christ, resulting in actually being "Synagogues of Satan" (WCF 23:5, cf. also Revelation 3:9). Yet in the midst of this mixture of truth and error, God is faithful to his church, and as the Confession assures, his church will never be left on earth without a witness and without worship to give him glory. Finally the Confession, in stark contrast to the

Roman Catholic tradition, explicitly confesses that, "there is no visible head of the church except the Lord Jesus Christ, and that the Pope of Rome could not in any sense be head of that."

The church is God's society. In an age characterized by heightened individualism, the Confession's teaching—that God's sovereignty and salvation results in saints' inclusion in his society—is a healthy corrective for many of us. According to the WCF, God puts us in a social entity, a society to grow and serve him. His structured and vital society is the chief vehicle for living out the faith expressed earlier in the WCF. This society then becomes salt and light to various societies.

The Sacraments

One of the primary callings and exclusive responsibilities of the church is to administer the sacraments. In fact, Christ never assigned the administration of sacraments to any other agency except the church. As the Confession teaches, the sacraments are those directly instituted holy signs and seals of the covenant of grace which Christ has explicitly ordered for the church to carry out until his return (WCF 27:1). The uses of the sacraments, according to the authors of the Assembly, were as follows: "To represent Christ and his benefits; and to confirm our interest in him: and also, to put a visible difference between those that belong unto the church and the rest of the world; and solemnly to engage them to the service of God and Christ, according to his word" (WCF 27:1).

The divines at Westminster were most interested in making sure that the confusions evident in the Roman Catholic and some Anglican churches were not perpetuated. They taught that there was a difference between the sign of the sacrament and that for which it stood (27:2). Moreover, they said that any grace which comes through the proper use of the sacraments is not delivered merely because of a magical power within them, nor because of the spiritual piety or ordination of the person who ministers it, but always dependent upon the work of the Holy Spirit and the divine institution of God.

The authors of the Confession of Faith, in contrast to many modern Christians who perhaps have not studied the Scriptures as thoroughly as these divines, understood that there was a strong continuity between the Old and New Testaments. So they confessed that the sacraments of the Old and New Testaments, as far as the spiritual meaning was concerned, were basically the same in substance (WCF 27:5). In keeping with that, there were only two sacraments (in contrast to the Roman Catholic belief in seven sacraments) which were viewed by the Assembly-men as "ordained by Christ our Lord in the Gospel" (WCF 27:4). These two were Baptism and the Lord's Supper.

It is worth noting at this time that the very definition of the sacrament, as with the earlier definition of worship (cf. WCF 21:7), is given in terms of what God reveals. Both worship and the sacraments (and church government in the chapters to come) are all defined with the common thread of teaching—that is to say, they were based on the divine definition. The authors of the Westminster Confession did not consider themselves wise enough, insightful enough, nor holy enough to inventively set out which practices would be acceptable to God in worship, the sacraments, or government. They understood the effect of the Fall and depravity far too well to attempt that. Moreover, they understood that God himself was the divine determiner of what was appropriate in worship and the sacraments. Thus they limited the sacraments to what God through Christ had clearly ordained.

The two sacraments, then, were Baptism and the Lord's Supper. The chapter on Baptism (WCF 28) begins by defining this baptism in keeping with the earlier definition of a sacrament as that which was ordained by Christ. This sign and seal of the covenant of grace signified many other things, among which were, "A person's ingrafting into Christ, of regeneration, of remission of sins, and of his giving up unto God through Jesus Christ to walk into newness of life" (28:1). In keeping with the biblical and apostolic tradition, water was the only element to be used, and baptism was simply to be ministered in the name of the Triune God. The Confession also stated that the total immersion of a person into water was not necessary (28:3) but could be rightly administered by "pouring, or sprinkling water upon the person" (28:3). This was all in keeping with the dominant Old Testament mode of sprinkling with a hyssop branch (cf. Psalm 51:9). Of course not only were adult believers allowed to be baptized, but the infants of one or more believing parents were also to be baptized in keeping with the Old Testament practice of circumcision (WCF 28:4).

So important was the sacrament of Baptism to the authors of Westminster Assembly that they believed that it to be a "Great sin to hold in contempt or neglect this ordinance" (28:5); yet they realized that a person's very salvation was not based on this sacrament being applied to them. They also confessed that the real meaning of baptism was its reference to the Holy Spirit's spiritual work in a person's life. Along with that it was confessed that the working power of baptism was not tied strictly to that exact moment of time in which it was applied (as in an infant's life), but that the grace and promise was truly delivered in due time by the Holy Spirit to the elect, or as the Confession says, "To such (whether of age or infants) as that grace belongs to, according to the counsel of God's own will, in his appointed time (WCF 28:6). Finally the authors of the Confession, in keeping with Ephesians 4, stated that this sacramental application of baptism should be applied to a person only once—as circumcision was and not with repetition.

In our times this teaching on baptism has been debated among many evangelicals who believe the Bible. Although often challenged, it is difficult to find a thorough study of Scripture that shows where the Westminster Assembly authors went wrong. Hence, it would be a good challenge and a worthwhile study for every Christian, who views the Westminster Assembly positively, to go back and re-study these issues and seek to understand the mind of the Assembly.

For Additional Study: *What did the Early Church Think about Infant Baptism?*
An article by P. Robert Palmer ("Another Look at Baptism") from the 1979 *Covenant Seminary Review* notes the following about the early church's understanding about infant baptism. That article, which also excellently argues for infant baptism, supported the ancient practice on the following biblical pillars:

- The unity between OT and NT believers (cf. Ex. 12:6, Jer. 26:17 with Acts 7:38);
- The centrality given to godly households in biblical history to transmit God's redemptive purposes (Ps. 78:4-7; Gen. 9:9; Dt. 28:4, Acts 16:31; Mal. 2:15);
- The very high value placed on children by Christ (Mt. 18:10; Mk. 10:13-16);
- The apostolic treatment of believers' children (e.g., Col. 1:2 with 3:20; 1 Cor. 7:14) as part of the worshiping community;

- The consistent emphasis in the Bible on the family unit worshiping together (Gen. 17:7; Acts 16:15, 31: Acts 10:2; 1 Cor. 1:16);
- The similarity between circumcision and baptism (Col. 2:11-12);

Palmer also sets forth abundant corroboration for the practice of infant baptism from some of the earliest Christian theologians below.

- **Justin Martyr** noted: "We Gentile Christians also, who by him have access to God, have not received the circumcision according to the flesh; but that circumcision which is spiritual . . . We have received this circumcision in baptism."
- **Tertullian** (ca. 200 AD) "leaves no doubt that infant baptism was the established practice among the earliest NT Christians."
- **Origin** (ca. 230 AD) further rooted infant baptism in apostolic practice, confirming that "the church received from the apostles the injunction, or tradition, to give baptism even to infants."
- **Chrysostom** (ca. 400 AD) wrote about the "pain and trouble in the practice of that Jewish circumcision; but our circumcision, I mean the grace of baptism, gives cure without pain; and this for infants as well as men."
- **Pelagius**, although defective in his view of the human will, was an early witness to this. Denying that even the worst imaginable characters might prevent infants from being baptized, he asked, "What can be so impious as to hinder the baptism of infants?"
- **St. Augustine** wrote: "The whole church of Christ has constantly held that infants were baptized. . . . Infant baptism the whole church practices. It was not instituted by councils, but was ever in use."

****

The second sacrament is the Lord's Supper. In the 29th chapter of the Westminster Confession of Faith, great detail is given on the Lord's Supper, primarily in contrast to the Roman Catholic and hierarchical practices of that time. For example, private masses are ruled out (29:4), as is the denial of the cup to the people, the worshipping of the elements, the adoration of the elements, or the re-sacrifice of Christ in the Mass (WCF 29:2). In addition the primary denial of the Roman Catholic view is expressed (WCF 29:6) as the authors of the Confession state that trans-substantiation (that belief that the very elements change their substance from bread and wine into the actual body and blood of Christ) is "repugnant, not to Scripture alone, but even to common sense, and reason" (WCF 29:6).

From these sections, we see how Reformation and Presbyterian Christians seriously took this sacrament to heart, and how they sought to keep the biblical and confessional injunctions. It might be interesting to see how the Westminster Assembly authors set out what would exclude a person for worthy reception of the sacrament. The following infractions of ignorance, which were considered sufficient to disqualify from the Lord's Supper in the 1640s, give us an idea of the seriousness of the sacrament.

1. All that do not know and believe the being of a God and the Holy Trinity. 2. They that are not acquainted with original sin and the fall of man. 3. They that don't believe Christ to be God and man, and our only Mediator and Redeemer. 4. And that Christ and his benefits are

applied only by faith, which faith is the gift of God, and implies a trusting in him for the remission of sins and life everlasting. 5. The necessity of sincere repentance and a holy life in order to salvation. 6. The nature and importance of the two sacraments, especially the Lord's Supper. 7. That the souls of believers do immediately live with Christ after death; and the souls of the wicked immediately go to hell. 8. The resurrection of the body and final judgment.

We have seen in these portions an elaborate description of the church, its sacraments, its preaching ministry, and the great emphasis on reverence, holiness, and awe. That speaks volumes about the Westminster understanding of worship. The sacraments and the church were the chief expressions of their faith. The society of God was given unique signs and seals of his covenant.

The End-Times According to the Westminster Confession: A Sketch

In general, the WCF does not attempt to provide too many specifics or go beyond the Scriptural testimony. In particular and in contrast to some modern schemes, its view of the end-times (eschatology) is rather straightforward and unencumbered. It confesses that Christ will return, and when he does, he will rather rapidly—instead over a long period of time—perform all the events predicted in Scripture.

In the final two chapters, the WCF addresses personal eschatology (WCF 32) and cosmic eschatology (WCF 33). As far as personal eschatology, or what happens at the end-times of an individual's life prior to the Second Coming of Christ, the WCF affirms that our bodies experience normal, physical decomposition (they "return to dust"). Immediately after physical death, however, our souls go directly to one final destiny or the other—there is no third option (32:1)—(1) believers go directly to heaven and are made perfect in holiness, where they await the full redemption of their bodies, and (2) unbelievers are cast into hell, where they experience "torment and utter darkness" until they receive their disglorified bodies as a further and continuing punishment. All who are left on earth until Christ returns (see 1 Thess. 4:16-17) will be raised at that time (32:2); conversely, the bodies of the unjust will be raised to dishonor. These mirror-image destinies are the only two available, and they are irreversible.

The last chapter of the WCF teaches that a final judgment will occur, at which time Christ judges all who have ever lived on earth and the fallen angels. This judgment will, in no way, reverse any of the destinies specified in WCF 32. The purpose of this final judgment is to vindicate Christ, show God's mercy, and after that there will be no more interruptions of godly fellowship. Those who receive everlasting life will always enjoy that union with Christ and his people, while the wicked will suffer "eternal torments."

Along with WCF 32:2, which discusses how people will meet Christ if they are alive when he returns, the only substantive paragraph in the WCF on the end times of human history (33:3) is quite reserved and does not attempt to set dates or identify the anti-Christ (most of the Westminster Assembly, however, thought that was the Pope!). It simply affirms that Christ will come again, that men should be watchful (see Mt. 24:36-39), that God's plan is to keep that day unknown, and that we are to be prepared for an imminent Coming of Christ.

This sketch does, however, rule out certain views. Conversely, the WCF does not seem to envision the following concepts that are widely popular from time to time:

- A rapture of any kind, except as spoken of in WCF 32:2;
- A tribulation period other than normal history;
- A literal millennium, which is not even mentioned in these paragraphs;
- A separate return of Christ after a rapture/tribulation/millennium period.
- Any special treatment of Israelis as contrasted with Christians.

Certain kinds of millennial views, thus, may be inconsistent even with the skeletal teaching of the WCF on this. Hence, it is incorrect to describe the WCF as largely agnostic on this matter; certain notions are definitely embraced and others are not endorsed. Most Reformed Officers since the Reformation have been now-millennialists of one type or another, although some at the Assembly were also Puritan postmillennialists. Earlier in the twentieth century, one denomination (the Bible Presbyterian Church) acknowledged that their view (premillennialism) was inconsistent with the wording and intent of the WCF: thus, they honorably amended their version of the WCF in 1938 to allow for their view, while the OPC and the PCA did not so modify.15 That is one approach to honor the original WCF while also reflecting a denomination's distinctives; of course, it requires the objective meaning of the Confession to be acknowledged and differences to be well defended from Scripture.

****

Note on additional chapters. Two other chapters were added to the versions of the WCF utilized in some denominations in the early 20th century. In 1903, the Northern Presbyterian Church (UPCUSA) sought to soften the clearly predestinarian tone so pervasive in the WCF by supplementing the historic 1648 version with two modern chapters: "Of the Holy Spirit" (chapter 34) and "Of the Gospel and the Love of God in Missions" (chapter 35). While both contain some helpful and faithful ideas, the 35th chapter contains several expressions that are contrary to earlier provisions in the original WCF. Among them is the phrase that "God declares his love for the world" (35:2) without any clear qualification, which is exceedingly difficult to harmonize with WCF 8-18. Moreover, the "Declaratory Statement" adopted that same year makes it clear that the church was seeking to tailor the Confession to concerns of free-willists. Although it may be admirable to seek to answer our objectors, neither are we convinced that the earlier versions led to contradictions that necessitated answering, nor are we certain that such concessions as those contained in these 1903 revisions served to strengthen the church.

The ARP (arpsynod.org) and EPC (epc.org) also adopted these chapters, whereas the OPC, the PCA, and the RPCNA did not.

---

15 For more on this, see http://bpc.org/what/index.html#Confessions.

Session #5   Church Government (WCF 30-31)

God's society was given order or a governmental structure for the church that is unique and separate from civil forms of governing. Milton was indeed correct when he spoke of church discipline as "the execution and applying of Doctrine home." One of the other chief contributions to culture and church life has been the thorough discussion by the Westminster Assembly on the nature and practice of church government. More discussion, debate, and study was devoted to this topic than any other topic. In fact, many commentators and scholars on the Westminster Assembly have spoken of the "Grand Debate" as that lengthy and thorough discussion of the principles of church government. Exactly two centuries after the convening of the Assembly, Thomas Smyth of Charleston, SC, summed up the importance of the subject of government: "The subject of church government became the all-engrossing topic of the day, and, from its close connection with public affairs, a national question. Within a period of twenty years no fewer than 30,000 pamphlets were issued on this subject." As noted earlier there was a range of views on this subject as the Assembly convened, and this variety of opinion continued until the end of the Assembly. However, those who sympathized with this Confession and the majority of its adherents have, for centuries, observed the clear lines of presbyterian polity in this area. Moreover, the original *Directory for Church Government*, also composed by this Assembly (and contained in my *Paradigms in Polity*, pp. 260-277), make it clear that presbyterianism was definitely the majority opinion of that Assembly, even if other small, dissenting parties lobbied furiously for different polities.

It is also important to note then, in light of the extensive debate given to the discussion, that the confessional teaching on church government (found primarily in chapters 30 & 31) is fairly slim. There are two likely explanations for this. The *first* is that the committees formulating the Confession (and the Assembly itself) could not agree on all aspects on church government, although the primary skeletal structure of biblical Presbyterianism is clearly the view of the vast majority. *Secondly*, the Confession here as elsewhere also exhibits the commitment of the divines not to exceed the bounds of scriptural revelation on a particular topic. That is to say, the Assembly men were careful not to go beyond Scripture, desiring only to confess that which was clearly scriptural.

Chapter 30, which begins the discussion of church discipline, affirms first that Christ as King and Head of the Church has erected a government for his society, a specific church government that is distinct from the civil government (WCF 30:1). Within this church government, Christ has ordained certain leaders and has given to them the keys of the kingdom (cf. Matthew 16:19, 18:18). To these church Elders are given the power, which Christ had spoken of as to declare that sins are forgiven or that sins are retained (Jn. 20:23). Moreover, to these leaders of the society (not just to private individual members), the ministry of the gospel and church discipline are given.

About a half a century before the Westminster Assembly, Thomas Cartwright, an early British Presbyterian expressed the basis for this orderly discipline this way: "The discipline of Christ's church that is necessary for all times is delivered by Christ, and set down in the holy Scriptures. Therefore the true and lawful discipline is to be fetched from thence, and from thence alone. And that which resteth upon any other foundation ought to be esteemed unlawful and counterfeit. Of all particular churches there is one and the same right order and form: therefore also no one may challenge to itself any power over others; nor any right which doth not alike agree to others."

Church discipline is an often ignored subject in modern churches, but it was not so in the seventeenth century. The Westminster Assembly authors realized the necessity of church discipline and taught that such church discipline was necessary "for the reclaiming and regaining of offending brothers, for deterring others from like offenses, for purging out the leaven which might infect the whole lump, for vindicating the honor of Christ, and the holy profession of the gospel, and for preventing the wrath of God which might fall on the church should it continue in disobedience" (WCF 30:3). A healthy view of church discipline is a needed corrective in our own time, and no society can function without it. The Christian should sincerely study the following Scripture texts to see how clear and undeniable church discipline is as a duty both to individuals and to the church: Matthew 18:15-18, Titus 3:10, 1 Corinthians 5, and I Timothy 5:20 & 1:20. Even more so, ordained Officers must understand the biblical practice and rationale for this ongoing ministry (For more on this, see below under Session #6).

The purposes of church discipline are never to glorify the Elders or to seek vengeance; instead the goal is for these leaders to reclaim a Christian brother (Gal. 6:1). Thus the Confession sets out the possible modes of church discipline as admonition, suspension from the Lord's Supper, and excommunication, according to the nature of the crime and the behavior of the person (WCF 30:4). Church discipline was hotly debated at the Westminster Assembly, because it was realized that if authority was truly given by Christ to these Officers, as basic Presbyterianism has long asserted, then there was a type of authority given to the church which was not given to individuals. The few Independents at the Assembly sought to disconnect that authority from having any more than advisory power, but the vast majority of the Assembly refuted that, holding fast to their view that believers should be submissive to their Officers (1 Peter 5:1-5), and moreover that Christ had indeed established more than a mere counseling or advisory power to be given to the church.

If the church was to be an aggressive and growing society it was understood that, in a world in which depravity existed, the church would of necessity, in obedience to her Master, carry out church discipline. The primary reasons that we do not exercise church discipline today are because we are afraid that others might reject us for a strong and uncompromising stand, the fear that some-how church growth might be inhibited (however cf. Acts 4 & 5), and/or perhaps a laziness, or even an unwillingness to take our stand with Christ. Church discipline was non-negotiable to the church in the NT, and we should also have a renewed appreciation of that needed mark of the church today. Discipline and structure are essential if any society wishes to continue or maintain any virtues. God's society has been given its own order.

Another part of church government was the relationship of different levels of governing bodies. According to the Confession, to expedite government and more appropriately build up the church, God had ordained assemblies, which were also called synods or councils (WCF 31:1). These were exclusively ecclesiastical meetings and were not to be confused with the civil government. Ecclesiastical Elders were to call together these assemblies.

According to the Confession, these ecclesiastical councils were not to inter-meddle with the affairs of the state, except to give their humble and biblical advice (31:5). Instead they were to determine controversial matters of faith or conscience. They were also to develop directions for the better ordering of the worship of God and to "authoritatively determine" complaints "in cases of maladministration" (31:3). When an assembly determined those decrees or cases, as long as they were in keeping with the Word of God, they were to be received with reverence and submission, not merely because they agreed with the Word of God, but because of the cumulative effect of the many advisors giving council (WCF 31:3). This is God's society at work.

The practice of the church is perhaps best understood when we look at the outward manifestation, the government of the church. On government, A. W. Mitchell observed that God had "not left this important concern to be regulated by the wisdom or caprice of fallible men." He noted the two radical principles of biblical church government as: (1) the parity of ministers, and (2) the regulation of all matters by the whole body, comprehending the subordination of inferior to superior judicatories. The essential principles of Presbyterianism were laid out in propositional form and debated with thoroughness by the Westminster Assembly for a long time. Following the normal committee format for reporting, below is a summary of the major propositions recommended by the second and third committees:

> In inquiring after the Officers belonging to the Church of the New Testament, we first find that 'Christ, who is Priest, Prophet, King, and Head of the Church, hath fullness of power, and containeth all other offices, by way of eminency, in himself; and therefore hath many of their names attributed to him.' To this sacred and comprehensive proposition they appended a number of Scripture proofs, in six divisions. The following names of Church-Officers were mentioned as given in Scripture to Christ:—1. Apostle; 2. Pastor; 3. Bishop; 4. Teacher; 5. Minister, or *diakonos*; but this last name was rejected by the Assembly, as not meaning a Church-Officer in the passage where it is used. The report of the third committee was similar in character, ascribing, in Scripture terms, the government to Jesus Christ, who, being ascended far above all heavens, 'hath given all Officers necessary for the edification of his Church; some whereof are extraordinary, some ordinary.' Out of the scriptures referred to they found the following Officers:—Apostles, Evangelists, Prophets, Pastors, Teachers, Bishops or Overseers, Presbyters or Elders, Deacons, and Widows.

These principles became the primary carriers of the underlying beliefs of the church. They were the outward manifestation, the organized vehicle of communicating the faith. The Westminster Directory of Government summarizes its scriptural basis, in terms of Christ, and our constitution (see Preface I in the BCO) wisely incorporates this same approach:

> JESUS CHRIST, upon whose shoulder the government is, whose name is called Wonderful, Counsellor, the Mighty God, the Everlasting Father, the Prince of Peace; of the increase of whose government and peace there shall be no end; who sits upon the throne of David, and upon his kingdom, to order it, and establish it with judgment and justice, from henceforth even for ever; having all power given unto him in heaven and earth by the Father, who raised him from the dead, and set him at his own right hand, far above all principality and power, and might, and dominion, and every name that is named, not only in this world, but also in that which is to come: and put all things under his feet, and gave him to be head over all things to the church, which is his body, the fullness of him that filleth all in all: he being ascended up far above all heavens, that he might fill all things, received gifts for his church, and gave all Officers necessary for the edification of his church, and perfecting of his saints.

The practice of the London divines was to meet as a presbytery every Monday to consider means for enlarging the kingdom. Based on the Company of Pastors in Geneva (the presbytery in Calvin's time), the province of London was subdivided into 12 presbyteries, each with a weekly meeting. Each was to have approximately 12-15 churches, and as far as governmental structure, was nearly identical to the presbyteries we have today. The main exception was in terms of the ratio between ministers and Ruling Elders. In this British system of Presbyterianism, each of the London presbyteries were to be composed of 12 ministers and 24 Ruling Elders, with ruling Elders holding twice the proportional representation as ministers. After the Westminster Assembly and until 1659, these functioning presbyteries met twice a week (Monday and Thursday) and sought ways to reform the church and spread the kingdom.

A biblical study of these truths, primarily in the 15th chapter of Acts, would yield great biblical support for the Presbyterian form of government as incorporated in the Westminster Standards. God's society is no slipshod organization. It is an organism yes; but it is also the best organization in the world. He made it, and it is his church. Thus it should be implemented his way, too. God loved this church very much. Not only did he give his Son for her, but further he gave her a continuing government and method of problem solving, which is exhibited in Scripture.

The first Pastoral Letter in church history (recorded in Acts 15:23-29) is addressed from "the apostles and Elders" "to the Gentile believers in Antioch, Syria, and Cilicia." Those locales tell us that the drafters of this document did not envision themselves making decisions for only one locale on a case-by-case basis. The church headed by Jesus Christ was not designed to be a society which had different doctrines tailored to the fickle tastes of individuals. She was one body and this decision was for the entire church in all locations. The underlying view is that Christians everywhere would want to heed the wisdom of this decree. Strangely absent from this record is the thought that each church would do just as it pleased on this question. These were standards by the whole church for the whole society. It was one unified spiritual society with the same beliefs and practices, not just a consortium of loosely affiliated churches. The decision of the Assembly of Jerusalem was for all churches.

Sometimes, even in Reformed churches, it looks as though a spirit of Independency is run amok. Busy presbyters are quick to dismiss some proposal that does not reflect their own concern as unimportant, and calls for each church to act as it sees fit are heard more often than we wish to admit. Some have even, over time and by default, come to view the higher courts as advisory only, in effect believing that Independency is best. In strong contrast to this are two key aspects of NT church life: (1) how quick leaders were to submit to others, and (2) how unified the church was in doctrine.

The standards of the church were the same. In both doctrine (cf. Jude 3 "the faith handed down once and for all to all the saints") and in practice, the standards on major issues were to be the same. The church was One, Holy and Universal Church. It was not a series of diverse franchises, each of which pursued its own ends, programs, or impulses. It was one society. Hence, when this pastoral letter was sent out, the presbyters intended it to be received by all Christians and heeded for its instructions.

The unity of the church lends itself to these kinds of common decisions. Only if the church has an underlying one-ness does any kind of letter or formal action like this make sense at all. If each church was strictly independent and unrelated, this letter would quickly be disposed of or else considered "advisory" only. This was not reckoned as "advice only," but was received as the settled, deliberated standard of the church, and the Christians submitted to its wisdom. It was for the whole church, not just some parts.

As hallmarks of this inter-connectedness, the biblical church will seek to have a keen eye out for accountability and checks-and-balances. The fibers that hold us together are mutual fellowship. One manifestation of this mutual fellowship is that we care enough to discipline, rebuke, even interrupt, when we know the other will not automatically welcome our rebuke. Still, we have learned from Scripture and history that if any one is left alone and unaccountable, then eventually even the best of saints may fall.

Earlier (1641), the Scotsman Alexander Henderson had summarized Presbyterianism in this fashion: "In the authority of these assemblies, parochial, presbyterial, provincial, and national, and in the subordination of the lesser unto the greater, or of the more particular Elderships to the larger and general Eldership, doth consist the order, strength, and steadfastness of the Church of Scotland . . . *Here is a superiority without tyranny*, for no minister hath a papal or monarchical jurisdiction over his own flock, far less over other pastors and over the congregations of a large diocese. *Here there is parity without confusion and disorder* . . . Every particular church is subordinate to the presbytery, the presbytery to the synod, and the synod to the national assembly . . . *here there is a subjection without slavery.*" (italics added)

Finally a word as to motive is important. It would be remiss to ignore that the driving motive for the Westminster Assembly's views on government was to preserve the integrity of the gospel, to help build up the flock of Christ, and to propagate the good news of Jesus. They saw all of these governmental provisions as means to that end, and their sole motive in laying these out was to exalt Christ and further the work of God's society. The main mark on cultures has come through this society and its individuals.

The poet John Donne was a contemporary with some of these divines. In an Easter Sermon (XXIII), Donne spoke of the church as our school: "The place then where we take our degrees in this knowledge of God, our Academy, our University for that, is the Church . . . the ordinary place for Degrees is the University, and the ordinary place for Illumination in the knowledge of God, is the Church . . . the Church is our Academy, there we must be bred." Thankful for God's society, let's not only remember it but also recommit ourselves to it. As the hymn expresses,

> "I Love the church, O God: Her walls before thee stand,
> Dear as the apple of thine eye, And graven on thy hand.
> For her my tears shall fall, For her my prayers ascend;
> To her my cares and toils be giv'n, Til toils and cares shall end."

Assignment: Read from one of the following on Reformed Theology or Presbyterian Government:
1. *The Deacons Handbook* – Berghoef & DeKoster pp. 53-93 or Part V or skim
2. *The Growing Local Church* – MacNair (chaps. 1, 6, 8 – for Deacons)
3. *The Growing Local Church* – MacNair (chaps. 1, 6, 7 – for Elders)
4. *The Elders Handbook* – Berghoef & DeKoster (chaps. 2, 10, 16-18)
5. *Introduction to the Reformed Tradition* – John Leith (chaps. 2, 4 or 5)
6. *What is the Reformed Faith* – J. R. deWitt
7. *The Westminster Assembly and Its Work* – B. B. Warfield (any chapter)
8. *Calvin: Theological Treatises* – W. K. S. Reid – *Passim* Part I
9. *The Institutes* – Calvin (Vol. II, Book IV, chaps. 3-7 or 11-14)
10. *The Humanness of John Calvin* – R. Stauffer

11. *Calvin on Scripture and Divine Sovereignty* – John Murray
12. *The Church: A Believing Fellowship* – Leith/Ramsay (chaps. 6, 8 & 9)
13. *A Cloud of Witnesses* – Smylie (chaps. 1, 2, 3, 5)
14. *Studies in Southern Presbyterian Theology* – Morton Smith (chap. 1 or skim)
15. *Watchman, tell it true* – Otto Whitaker (pp. 343-452; esp. chap. 32)
16. *Biblical Church Discipline* – Daniel Wray

Our Constitution: The Book of Church Order

The presbyterian polity confessed above is firmly rooted in biblical interpretation and pastoral practice. Before we overview our Book of Church Order (hereafter BCO), the principles of biblical polity should be clearly enunciated. These, after all, are what the Officer vows to uphold.

Principles of Presbyterian Government

A. From Thomas Witherow's *The Apostolic Church: Which is it?*

The Issue: There are Six Great NT Principles below (In the margin, mark Y (Yes) or N (No) under the columns headed as follows: "H" for hierarchical, "C" for congregational, or "P" for Presbyterian for the following principles. Each may have more than one letter.)

H   C   P

a. Office-bearers are chosen by the people (Acts 1:23; Acts 14:23; Acts 6:5-6) but based on qualified calling not popularity (i.e., it is confirmatory).
b. The office of bishop and Elder is identical (Acts 20:17, 28; Titus 1:5-7; 1 Timothy 3:1-7; 1 Peter 5:1-4).
c. There is to be a plurality of Elders in each church (Acts 14:23; Acts 20:17; Phil. 1:1).
d. Ordination is the act of a presbytery, that is, of a plurality of Elders (Acts 6:6; Acts 13:1-3; Acts 14:23; 1 Tim. 4:14 and 5:22; 2 Tim. 1:6; Tit. 1:5).
e. There is the privilege of appeal to the assembly of Elders; and the power of government is exercised by them jointly (Acts 15).
f. The only Head of the Church is the Lord Jesus Christ (Eph. 1:20-23; Eph. 5:23; Col. 1:18).

The Question: *Which form of government best fits these principles?*

B. Principles of biblical polity from Louis Berkhof's *Systematic Theology*
   a. Christ is the Head of the Church and the source of all its authority.
   b. Christ exercises his authority by means of his Royal Word.
   c. Christ as King has endowed the Church with power.
   d. Christ provided for the specific exercise of this power by representative organs.
   e. The power of the Church resides primarily in the governing body of the local church.

From the two examples above, one can see how essential it is to have our practical polity based on biblical principle. Some churches do not have a constitution of any kind. Invariably that leaves the members in a tenuous position of one kind or another. If Officers and members have no set procedures, they will either have to spend an inordinate amount of time re-inventing the wheels of protocol, or else they will find themselves subject to the whims or excesses of strong or charismatic leaders. The better way is to have certain fixed procedures that safeguard the interests of the many. Our BCO, while far from perfect and thus amendable (see chapter 26), is similar in form to the previous Presbyterian books of order and thus reflects that definite history. Most of the PCA BCO was drafted quickly and under the duress of formation in 1973. Therefore, for expediency sake, the drafting committee, primarily accepted an earlier edition of the PCUS BCO and modified it (only about 10% of the total wording was changed) in the attempt to avoid the abuses that had recently been experienced. Thus, if one were to compare this in structure and content to Presbyterian books of order prior to the 1960s, he would notice much similarity.

Below, we summarize the points that we think are essential for every Officer to understand.16

Our Preface I provides a Christological definition of the church, and eight "Preliminary Principles" are enunciated in Preface II. These were derived from the first American Presbyterian General Assembly in 1788, and they set helpful parameters for church government. These principles affirm that God alone controls our conscience and that churches should conform to his Word. It is perfectly acceptable (II:2) for churches to declare their own standards and how they wish to qualify leaders. That is not an infringement on conscience, although it may be too strict or too lax. Moreover, in an early version of "ideas have consequences" thought, our BCO notes that "Godliness is founded on truth" and "there is an inseparable connection between faith and practice" and truth and duty (II:4). Teachers are to be sound in the faith, and church discipline will be needed. The church, as distinct from the civil government, cannot create her own laws or bind the conscience (II:7); that is the meaning of all church power being "only ministerial and declarative."17

The Constitution of the PCA is defined in Preface III (and again in BCO 26-1). The Constitution, obviously subordinate to the inerrant Word of God, is the doctrinal standards of the Westminster Confession of Faith and both Catechisms and the Book of Church Order.

Following the Preface, our Book of Church Order has three main divisions:
1. The Form of Government (sometimes aptly abbreviated FOG);
2. The Rules of Discipline (sometimes aptly abbreviated ROD);
3. The Directory for Worship (which is almost the DOW, surely a Freudian slip).

An Outline of the F.O.G. is given in chapter 1. The chapters in parenthesis are keyed to that topic.
1. The Church (2-5)
2. Its Members (6)
3. Its Officers (7-9)
4. Its Courts (10-15)
5. Its Orders (16-26 — Note especially chapter 24)

---

16 Morton Smith, the first stated Clerk of the PCA, has published a *Commentary on the Book of Church Order* (Greenville, SC: Greenville Seminary Press, 1990). It contains fuller discussions of each section than we do here. It may be ordered from Greenville Theological Seminary. Cf. also our eBCO (capo.org), which has links from current sections to historic precedents that provide helpful context on those sections.
17 One of the successors to James H. Thornwell, Thomas Peck, understood the historical background of this phrase better than many contemporaries. Peck noted that "ministerial and declarative" is in contrast to the force of the secular governor, whose power is magisterial and legislative. Cf. my *Savior or Servant*, 368-369, for more discussion on this topic, which is frequently lost on many modern Presbyterians.

The categorization of the Church as visible and invisible is carried over from the WCF. It consists of all who profess the faith and their children (2-1). Practical division into separate congregations or denominations does not fracture the unity of the church (2-2). Church power is defined in chapter 3 as spiritual. This spiritual power is exercised individually (3-2) by Officers in their several acts, while it is also exercised jointly in the power of jurisdiction whenever the Elders meet jointly. BCO 3-4 makes it clear that the government of the church is not to be confused with the civil sphere of government. Just as the church is free from and expects no hindrance from the political government, so the civil government should be allowed to perform its task without hindrance from the church. However, that does not mean that the church should be muzzled on moral issues; only that it not intrude itself into the civil as its primary calling. The church, after all, has its own Officers and courts (3-5), and its authority is conjoined with divine authority when it conforms to the law of Christ. For more on the original meaning of the concept of church power and how it is exclusively spiritual, see the notes and study below ("The Case for Presbyterianism: Biblical, Doctrinal, and Practical")

The particular Church is described in chapter 4 as consisting of professing Christians and their children, who have gathered together under the authority of Christ's rule for worship and godly living. The only biblical Officers assigned are Elders and Deacons. The Session, comprised exclusively of Elders (including any pastors), is the authoritative agent of power in the Presbyterian Church. The duties assigned to the church, as unique and separate from any other sphere of government, are chartered in BCO 4-4. Since chapter 5 refers to mission churches and how they are formed and organized, the Officer should read this chapter.

Chapter 6 defines who the members are of the church and states the privileges of communing and non-Communing members.

Much will be said about the duties of Officers later; in fact, we will return to discuss chapters 8, 9, and 12 in our final session. However, chapter 7 affirms that there are two general types of Officers for Christ's church in Scripture: extraordinary (apostles, prophets, and bearers of revelation) and ordinary (Elders and Deacons). Only the ordinary Officers are perpetual, and within the office of Elders, our BCO recognizes two classes: Teaching Elders (ministers or pastors) and Ruling Elders (those with some other full-time vocation). These Elders work together to provide spiritual oversight for the church (7-2), and the Deacons are called to serve the needs of the people. Both of these offices require male leadership as the biblical qualifications indicate and require men who are trained and gifted for these callings.

These Elders meet in courts—an old but dignified term that refers not only to legal hearings but moreover to regal diplomacy, such as the "court of King Henry 8th"—in regular gradation. All of these are presbyteries, and the notion of "gradation" indicates that these are properly submissive to one another. The courts/presbyteries in our denominations are the Session, the Presbytery, and the General Assembly (10-2). The moderator is normally the Pastor (10-3), whose position is not above the other Elders but largely functional, i.e., to process the business in an orderly fashion just like a "president" originally meant "the presider." Each presbytery also elects its own clerk, who is to function as a secretary for the presbytery and record and convey official communications. Each court meeting is to begin and end with prayer, an aspect of our government that should not be minimized.

Chapter 11 further amplifies the type of jurisdiction our church courts possess. It is reiterated again in 11-1 that our assemblies have no political authority and obviously cannot mete out physical or temporal punishments. When the BCO discusses jurisdiction as "only ministerial and declarative," that concept is explained in the very context of BCO 11-2. Those words mean that the church is to tend to "the doctrines and precepts of Christ" and ecclesiastical matters—not seek to perform the tasks of the secular jurisdiction. Specifically, presbyteries may adopt doctrinal and moral positions derived from Scripture, but they are not legislatively to create new laws to bind the conscience. Accordingly, God gives them all the power and authority necessary to enact those biblical principles in the life of the church.

Our church courts are inter-related and one in nature (11-3), and our courts are not "separate and independent tribunals, but they have a mutual relation, and every act of jurisdiction is the act of the whole church performed by it through the appropriate organ" (11-4). Later, BCO 14-7 will affirm accordingly that the actions of the General Assembly should be "given due and serious consideration" by the lower courts of the church, and judicial decisions, in "subsequent similar cases," should be appealed to. Notwithstanding, each sphere is to mind its own business: the Session oversees a single church, the Presbytery oversees the churches and ministers in a geographical region, and the General Assembly oversees matters that pertain to the national church. Importantly, "the jurisdiction of these courts is limited by the express provisions of the Constitution" (11-4). If that principle is maintained, hierarchicalism seldom results.

The duties of the Session in BCO 12 will be discussed below in our final session. Chapters 13 and 14 discuss the role and tasks of Presbytery and General Assembly. Technical matters, such as quorums, formula for representation, procedures for the reception of transferring ministers (for Presbyteries), committee structure of General Assembly, and the tasks of Presbytery and General Assembly are contained in these chapters.

A commission differs from a committee according to our constitution (15-1). Committees are designed to serve an appointing body and return with information and recommendations. However, committees do not authoritatively finalize actions; they prepare matters for the delegating court. A Commission, on the other hand, or a small sub-set of the presbytery, may *finalize* the action in keeping with its commission. Originally, a commission was designed by expedience to act for the whole presbytery—although early Presbyterianism was always, in view of their acceptance of human depravity, leery of handing unchecked power to any individual or subset of a court. Commissions, thus, were seen as the presbytery *in minimus*, meeting but clothed with full power. These commissions entrusted with routine tasks were not originally exclusive bodies, but any member of the appointing court could join with the commission to execute its assigned task if he was able. Frequently, matters such as installing a minister, judicial hearings, and other important matters may be assigned to a commission. No commission, however, according to our constitution, has secular force, and commissions can neither impose their will on local churches nor seize their property. The Standing Judicial Commission (SJC) of the PCA was first created in 1989; its work is chartered in chapter 15.[18]

---

18 Prior to that time, the PCA appointed judicial commissions at each General Assembly. Among the rationales for the creation of the SJC were to provide quicker decisions, save expenses by regional panels, and to deal with a huge number of complaints (during the 1980s, the General Assembly averaged less than 10 judicial cases per year). The 2002 Assembly had 41cases before it, and over $58,000 was needed for expenses for the non-regional SJC; moreover, few cases were finalized within a 12-month period.

Chapters 16 and 17 depict the PCA's understanding of calling and ordination. These are very important chapters, and a superb approach to calling is articulated in BCO 16-1. That section specifies three needed aspects for a calling to serve the church: (1) a clear conscience that one may serve in that office, along with an interest in so serving; (2) a clear approval ("manifest approbation") by God's people that a man is called and gifted; and (3) a formal concurrence by a supervising court of the church. This tri-partite requirement serves the church well to:

- Ensure that men do not serve without an inward call;
- Protect the church from self-willed individuals who think they are called but do not have the clear approbation of the church;
- Draw upon the wider judgment of other Elders to ascertain a valid calling.

In many cases, an individual may be retiring in demeanor and not thrust himself into the limelight. Under this definition of calling, others may encourage him that they see his gifts. Also, the judgment of calling is not left up to one person. One of the fundamental principles of biblical Presbyterianism (see study below), in contrast to the Episcopal form, is that "no man can be placed over a church without the election, or at least the consent of that church."

Ordination is the solemn setting apart of called persons (17-2). This is done by the court and in keeping with biblical instruction, "no man shall be ordained unless . . . to the performance of a definite work." (17-3) The next several chapters pertain to interests and processes leading to ordained ministry.

Chapters 18-19 treat the process by which candidates enter the ministry, licensure, and internship. Officers should acquaint themselves with these aspects of the church's ministry—for some of them may eventually pursue ordination as pastors, and it is hoped that they will also be able to help sons of the church toward ordination with familiarization of these steps.

Chapter 20 details the process of electing pastors. Each church is to follow the constitutional aspects here, but there is ample freedom also for each church to tend to its own affairs. For those churches that are unfamiliar with this process or who rarely use it, this chapter contains immense practical wisdom.

The next chapter similarly depicts how ministers are ordained and installed. The presbytery, of course, is responsible for a very thorough examination (see the individual aspects of BCO 21-4), and the ordination vows, to which we will return below, are listed in BCO 21-5. Also contained in this chapter are the questions that the congregation swears. The various pastoral relations are stated in chapter 22; and the process of dissolution of those is provided for in chapter 23. We return to chapter 24 in the final session, and chapter 25 discusses procedures employed in congregational meetings.

The process by which our standards may be amended is given in chapter 26. Large super-majorities are required—and cause courts to slow down and avoid hastiness in view of this process—and that is as it should be in any constitutional society.

For More Study: Read the article below for a modern, principled, and practical defense of presbyterianism.

The Case for Presbyterianism: Biblical, Doctrinal, and Practical
David W. Hall19

Many adequate defenses of biblical presbyterianism are made on historical, sociological, or experiential grounds. Indeed, historic reviews of comparative forms of church government—such as those by Calvin, Knox, Beza, Cartwright, the Westminster divines, Turretin, Samuel Miller, Thomas Smyth, and others20—argue convincingly for presbyterianism even without appealing exclusively to biblical foundations.

Numerous appeals for presbyterianism are also supported on experiential grounds. The case for presbyterianism is often defended for protecting against hierarchical encroachment; at other times, it is argued that presbyterianism enhances the distribution of charismatic gifts or balances form and freedom. Occasionally, a theology of human nature is presented to buttress the claims of presbyterianism. Moreover, various reactionary appeals are proffered.

While all these historic, psychological, and practical arguments have merit, nonetheless, presbyterianism cannot stand as a trans-temporal ecclesiology unless it best supports biblical and doctrinal teachings. The argument below maintains that not only is presbyterianism founded upon the best of biblical interpretation and the surest of doctrinal matrixes, but additionally it affords the safest and most caring government in all ages.

The Westminster divines21 shared that opinion regarding the value of government: "The Presbyterian Government . . . is not in Nature any invention of man, but an Ordinance of Christ; nor is the execution of it to be stated by the will of man, but only by the . . . Sacred Scriptures. . . . This Government allows no execution of any part . . . except according to the particular, or at least, the general Rules of Scripture." According to these perceptive scholars, the church could thus avoid tyranny, arbitrariness, and abuse—providing an enduring form of church order that would bring unity and qualified ministers, heal divisions, secure order, and support orthodoxy. Moreover, they believed that this scriptural form was "a better and safer Provision against all Arbitrary Government in the Church than all the Ordinances, Decrees, and Statutes" of man, tradition, or style. This government, according to these Pastors, was "only destructive to corruption which is deadly and destructive to the soul." Their sole goal, in other words, was to present a structure that was God's own choice and for the betterment of his flock.

Similarly, my case for presbyterianism is that it most accords with the biblical and doctrinal teachings of Scripture; also, in keeping with the supreme wisdom of its Creator, it best cares

---

19 "Presbyterianism" in *Always Reformed: A Dialogue of Differences within the Reformed Tradition*, David G. Hagopian, ed. (Phillipsburg, NJ: Presbyterian & Reformed Publishing Co., forthcoming). Used with permission.
20 I have included a number of summaries in *Paradigms in Polity* (Oak Ridge, TN: Covenant Foundation, 1994), pp. 55-102. Cf. also my "The Patristic Testimony to Presbyterianism" in *Holding Fast to Creation* (Kindle e-book).
21 Although many sources and eras could be drawn on for this argument, this presentation seeks to use the quintessentially original exponents of Westminster presbyterianism for its argument. Thus, I primarily cite the 1646 production by those Westminster divines, *Jus Divinum Regiminis Ecclesiastici*, David W. Hall, ed, (Dallas, TX: Naphtali, 1995). The following quotation appears on pp. iv-v of that volume; hereafter, *Jus Divinum*.

for the practical needs of the churches. If the convergence of biblical, doctrinal, historical, and practical theology is considered, those who follow scriptural implications in their local and national churches will discover what was unearthed centuries ago: whenever the Scripture is studied (not prejudiced by an extant traditional form of government) for an answer to this question, "What institutions and forms has God given to the church for its own structure in all ages?", students gravitate toward functional presbyterianism, whether under that name or some other. That was the ecclesiastical rediscovery of Knox and Melville; that is how "Scottish" ecclesiology triumphed in Puritan England (1553-1662); that was the form behind the expansion of American colonial presbyterianism; and that is the discovery awaiting many new churches in the 21st century.

Biblically Founded Ecclesiology

Presbyterianism is more ancient than the New Testament. It was a form of ordering created and employed by God thousands of years before the New Testament. All who value God's covenantal dealings and who do not see a radical divide in the history of redemption between the testaments discover that, long before priests and centuries before synagogues, God ordered his people by the rule and leadership of presbyters.22

Moreover, Exodus 18 provides a divine structure for both church and state. This form in its mediated aspects is so filled with divine excellence that it works in numerous spheres of organization. Exponents of rival forms of ecclesiology seldom boast that the form of government employed by the church works in the civil government. Yet, the federal structure revealed in Exodus 18 succeeds in the civil realm as well. John Knox, who applied the truths of Genevan Calvinism to the church, and the Colonial founders of America were similarly convinced of the divine sagacity of this plan.

Many theorists, ranging from Aquinas and Machiavelli to Althusius and Thielicke, see Jethro's advice as a pristine example of federalism or republicanism. Calvin commented: "Hence it more plainly appears that those who were to preside in judgment were not appointed only by the will of Moses, but elected by the votes of the people. And this is the most desirable kind of liberty, that we should not be compelled to obey every person who may be tyrannically put over our heads; but which allows of election, so that no one should rule except he be approved by us. And this is further confirmed in the next verse, wherein Moses recounts that he awaited the consent of the people, and that nothing was attempted which did not please them all." Thus, Calvin viewed this as a representative republican form. Later Thomas Smyth would call it "Ecclesiastical Republicanism," linking the federal nature of both civil and church government.

The heart of this form is its provision of an orderly system of appeals and rule. Qualified Elders make decisions, but not so authoritatively as to be beyond appeal.23 Graded levels of

---

22 The Septuagint, written long before partisan contests over ecclesiology, exhibits numerous instances of *presbuteroi* before the Temple and prior to the NT. Presbyters predate the Exodus (Ex. 3:16, 4:29), and are already operative at Mt. Sinai (Ex. 19:7) when the Law was given. They were involved in communal correction (Lev. 4:15), and protected the purity of worship (Num. 16:25) Although the priesthood is developed as a distinct order alongside of the presbyters, Elders are present to inaugurate the priesthood (Lev. 9:1). Presbyters participated in key aspects of Joshua's ministry (Josh. 24:1), and were well-established into the period of the Judges (Jud. 8:14). Elders continued a leadership function late into the OT period (Ruth 4:2; Prov. 31:23; Ez. 8:11). See also Num. 11:26, Ex. 4:30, Dt. 19:12, among other verses, for OT usage of *presbuteroi*, which is customarily a plurality.

courts allow those closest to the issues to make proper determinations; but abuses may be corrected by appeal to a higher level, much like the original judiciary in the USA. If republicanism is contrasted with monarchism or autonomy in civil government, it is fairly contrasted with episcopacy and congregationalism in church government.

Presbyters continued to the end of the OT and obviously existed between the testaments. Between the testaments, the institution grew, and synagogue worship enhanced the office.

The NT finds Elders in the time of Jesus. Despite the fact that many *presbuteroi* (Mt. 15:2) were corrupt at the time of Jesus' ministry, he nowhere condemns the office *per se*. While scribes, hypocrites, and teachers of the law are severely criticized in Matthew 23, *presbuteroi* are not similarly rebuked. Most interpreters understand Jesus' teaching on church discipline (Mt. 18: 15-18) to assume the office of Elders, who had previously been charged with that duty.

After Christ's resurrection, the *Book of Acts* exhibits the continuing office of *presbyter* in the earliest NT ecclesiology. While the apostles and prophets were extraordinary charismatic offices, the ordinary offices of Elder and Deacon appear in numerous missionary congregations in the early NT. Elders, as the ordinary successors to the apostles, are to devote themselves to prayer and the ministry of the word (Acts 6:2), while the Deacons are instituted in the NT to minister to other needs (Acts. 6:1-6). To the Elders is given the function of ordination by laying on of hands (Acts 6:6, 14:23, 1 Tim. 4:14, 5:22).

While there were prophets and teachers (Acts 13:1) and *presbuteroi* and *diakonoi* in the NT church, there is no separate priestly office as in the OT. As soon as new churches were established in the NT, the apostles appointed or had elected *presbyters* "in each church" (Acts 14:23). Apparently, Paul and others did not desire to leave new converts without mature leadership and proven structure.

The Synod of Jerusalem, moreover, is a pristine example of the broader church making decisions by its presbyterial representatives. Although "brothers" are present for parts of this assembly, the key speakers and decision-makers were "the apostles and Elders"—a phrase used five times in Acts 15 alone. The "apostles and Elders" met to consider the question (v. 6), made the decision (v. 22), and authorized the communication (v. 23). This functioning presbyterial court manifests the following characteristics: (1) It resolved a genuinely doctrinal dispute; (2) It served as a forum for debate and resolution; (3) A plurality of *presbyters* spoke and deliberated; (4) The decision was based on the Scriptures instead of tradition or experience; (5) The decision was intended for all churches; (6) When the decision was circulated to outlying areas, it was received joyfully—not perceived as an inhibition of self-rule. The fact that other NT epistles were intended for regional churches further corroborates that presbyterianism existed before the end of the canon.

---

23 A hierarchalism of final instance, not first instance, is what is denied by presbyterianism. In presbyterianism there is always opportunity for authoritative correction; in formal episcopacy, there is not. Lowerarchicalism, on the other hand, begins and ends with the congregation. This, too, differs from original presbyterianism.

The qualifications for this office (which also indicate that Elder and overseer are the same office by a comparison of the qualifications) are explicitly revealed in 1 Timothy 3 and Titus 1. Such revealed specificity indicates that this office is neither temporary nor trivial.

The exegetical conclusion stands that the offices of bishop and Elder are functionally equivalent (cf. also Titus 1:5-7 for synonymous use of the two terms). The office of presbyter is functionally the same as that of overseer according to Paul (cf. Acts 20:17 with 20:28) and Peter (cf. 1 Pet. 5:1-5). Peter also portrayed himself as a co-presbyter (1 Pet. 5:1), and Paul never elevates himself over the abiding office of Elder. The Apostle John, at the end of the canon, also depicts the office of presbyter as a function that will continue into heaven (Rev. 4:10, 5:8). The end of the canon does not envision the abolition of the office of Elder, as a study of the ecclesiology of Revelation will show.24

Indeed, it appears that there is no time in recorded religious history that God does not employ *presbuteroi*. God used Elders to stabilize and cultivate mission churches (Acts 14:23), to practice church discipline (1 Cor. 5), to ordain subsequent generations of ministers (1 Tim. 4:14, 5:22), to evangelize (2 Tim. 4:5), to teach and oversee the doctrinal values of the church (1 Tim. 3:2), to resolve doctrinal disputes for the larger church (Acts 15), and to govern the affairs of the church (1 Tim. 5:17). The office is not replaced by any other office in the church and is to continue until Christ comes again (Rev. 4:10), a claim that is not easily substantiated by ecclesiologies with other Officers.

Rather than hierarchical structures or strictly democratic polities (lowerarchicalism), Presbyterian republicanism appears as a balanced form from beginning to end of the canon. It is the preferred model of Scripture.

Doctrinal Consistency between Theology and Practice
Presbyterianism also best fits with the major doctrinal teachings of Scripture. It is vital to treat church government holistically and integrate it into the rest of the theological corpus. Views of church polity are not neutral, any more than scientific theories or political programs are. A particular theology, in fact, lays the foundation for polity. The discerning Christian will be quick to reject any polity advertised as value-neutral or non-theological. No theology or philosophy is founded in an ideological vacuum; neither are polities. It is less naive to recognize polity's theological foundations from the outset. Thus any polity may be evaluated not merely in terms of pragmatic efficiency, but also in terms of the validity of its theological presuppositions. However, in no case should the organic connection between theology and polity be ignored or minimized. Church government is organically connected to the theology, which bears it. For Calvinists who hold supremely to certain biblical doctrines, the best government will be the one that fits with the best theology. Presbyterianism best preserves the following theological factors.

Biblical Authority; Presbyterianism is fundamentally Scripture-driven. That is to say, it has no original authority of its own; only derived authority (which is what Elders apply). To the extent that presbyters follow the revealed will of God, that form of government has divine authority. Should they deviate from scriptural teaching, however, their rule is nullified by

---

24 Cf. James Ramsey's commentary on *The Book of Revelation* (Edinburgh: Banner of Truth, 1977), pp. 78-94.

higher authority. Presbyters are always *sub verbum* (under the Word), never masters over it. Their task is to steward the Word and apply it to the flock. When doing so, they have authority. Scripture is the rule; Elders follow and enact those decrees. In contrast, other major forms of government fail to provide the right kind of authoritative rule. Rule by a democratic congregation (lowerarchicalism) is not the same as rule by Scripture, and prelatical decisions that are beyond correction (hierarchicalism) may err in application of authority. Neither popular will nor human authority trumps Scripture in well-ordered presbyterianism. Only Scripture is inerrant; neither congregations nor bishops are entrusted biblically with such authority.

The Bible's instruction on matters of government is as much the revealed mind of God as the Bible is the revealed mind of God on salvation, social responsibility, prayer, or providence. James H. Thornwell helpfully pointed out that while issues of government might be "mere trifles compared with" the Gospel scheme of salvation, nevertheless they were not trivial matters, nor of "no value." Merely, he argued, because government "is not the great thing, it does not follow that it is nothing. We are as far removed from latitudinarianism as from bigotry. We wish to study the whole will of God (Acts 20:28), and we wish to give everything precisely that prominence which he designs that it should occupy in his own Divine economy." Similarly, Thomas Witherow warned against distinguishing between essentials and nonessentials as setting "at nought" parts of God's Word and "mutilat[ing] the Bible, stigmatiz[ing] much of it as trivial." To hold that large sections of the Bible are unimportant is "to assert a principle, the application of which would make havoc of our Christianity . . . Every divine truth is important, though it may be that all divine truths are not of equal importance."

Presbyterians stubbornly refuse to act as editors or evaluators who seek to prioritize canons within canons of Holy Writ. *All* scripture is inspired and profitable—even the verses that inform about church administration or government. Evidently God did not think these subjects to be below the scope of revelation. Hence we benefit from the Bible's revealed organizational corpus, as well as from its revealed soteriological corpus. Both have the same divine Origin.

The heart of biblical order is the belief that sinful minds, apart from the special revelation of God, will not derive correct structures. Hence, God as an act of his mercy, much like his revelation in the Law, gives to his people that which they would not contrive on their own. In his mercy, he spares us not only eternal lostness, but also some measure of temporal lostness by sparing us endless organizational searches. Instead of Sisyphusean futility, God reveals the basic pattern of government for his people. The regular life and ordering of the church is far too important, at least to God, to leave either to caprice, to the shifting sands of corporate culture, or to human ingenuity. Such revelations from God on organizational matters are tokens of God's grace, wisdom, and providence. Presbyterianism is a servant to Scripture; even reason, experience, and tradition must bow to that authoritative Word.

Covenantal Incorporation of the People of God: Presbyterianism is more community-oriented than independent polities. The Westminster divines weighed the relative merits of such approaches and found them wanting. Not only did they wish to avoid a hierarchicalism like they saw in England, equally, there was another horn of dilemma to avoid (lowerarchicalism), as they disclaimed: "Nor the *coetus fidelium* or the body of the people, as prebyterated, or unpresbyterated"25 is the seat of power. Hence, this presbyterianism avoided these two extremes by affirming real power (not advisory alone as held by the independents) wielded by non-statist agencies (over against the Erastians).

These presbyterian authors recognized a distinct danger in the more democratic congregational polities. One key fault-point on the part of the independents was their lodging of power with the congregation, instead of Christ's own Officers. The 1646 *Jus Divinum* queried: "When was any such power derived from Christ to the multitude of the faithful?" One answer to this rhetorical question (answered in the negative) was: "Not the first [century church], for then the Apostles themselves should have derived their power from the Fraternity or Community of the faithful."26 Related to the very essence of church power is the source, whether *a humano* or *a divino*. The original intent of the majority of divines at Westminster was that church power was *a divino*, donated by God to his Officers, not commissioned conditionally upon the consent of the governed, as desirable as it ordinarily is to pursue consent.

The presbyterian divines in the Westminster era did not hesitate to oppose a *sola dicta* (verbal counsel alone) brand of ecclesiology, even if sincerely held by other esteemed Calvinistic separatists. Accordingly, this scheme of "Presbytery and Presbyterial Government is for a rule to the Churches of Christ in all after ages."27 Classical presbyteries are necessary and invented by divine right. The kind of power they maintain, negatively and positively, was described: "Now in these and such like cases, suppose both parties be resolute and willful, and will not yield to any bare moral *suasion* or advice, without some superior *authority*, what healing is left in such cases, without the assistance of an *authoritative presbytery*, wherein the whole has power to regulate all the parts?"28 Thus authoritative presbyteries are necessary for healing; and their therapy cannot be fully efficacious with merely advisory power. A surgical scalpel, as opposed to the civil sword, is given to and necessary for the church.

As keen exegetes, the authors of *Jus Divinum* based this on Acts 15-16, in part, particularly noting that the conclusions of the Synod of Jerusalem are described in the original as *dogma* (Acts 16:4)—far from "advice" or left up to concurrence by the majority as if by democratic referendum.

The Calvinistic divines, who maintained a healthy distrust of humanly-wielded power, made sundry diatribes against the overly-democratic notion that church power is merely advisory. They intended subordination in practice, not counsel alone, to preserve the frail unity of the church. Thus we can understand why in the Preface to *Jus Divinum*, these self-same authors claimed that independency could remedy no case, which presbyterianism could not; they even believed that presbyterianism could improve some situations. With greater heuristic explanatory power as a theory, it was so widely embraced because it was seen as an *advance* in theory and remedy in practice, especially as a protective device against the libertine sects and the enthusiastic subjective tendencies of the sectaries who were pollinating at the time. Congregationalism could work in cases of "perfect submission, all is at rest." However, wherever willfulness or unbending conviction dominates, independency is insufficient for

---

25 *Jus Divinum*, p. 72. Note these terms refer to the views of the independents at the Assembly and the Brownists outside the Assembly.
26 *Jus Divinum*, p. 95. This is reiterated again on p. 179.
27 *Jus Divinum*, p. 213.
28 *Jus Divinum*, p. 189.

remedy. Independentism's advisory force might cure a few minor illnesses in other words, but if surgery was needed, *sola dicta* would not heal.

Several divines criticized the merely advisory role for higher courts as being deficient in ecclesiastical authority. While esteemed Puritan, Thomas Goodwin, was reluctant to embrace the presbyterians' term "subordination,"29 he was a minority. The majority position, however, was exemplified by Charles Herle, who stated: "An argument against a coercive power is to argue against our Assembly, and the ordinance by which we sit. So government, and what government can there be without coercive power, a power proper to that government? . . . If there be no government, it is not *regnum* but *tumultus* . . ."30

While Goodwin was arguing that church authority was given "electively" by the people to their Officers, he also begged for criticism by saying, "As in democraticall government the power is in the people; the charge of an Officer is an act of authority, it is the power of the keys . . . When Christ chose 12 this is an act of power; why not soe when done by the people?"31 Surely the reference to "democraticall" caught the ears of the presbyterians, leading Charles Herle to respond in tones similar to the assertions of the 1646 *Jus Divinum* that Christ gave his power directly to the Officers, not the company of the (democratic) faithful: "If the power is not first in the church then the Officers cannot represent the church; otherwise how will any of those rules that the Officers shall make bind the church?"32 It is clear that Herle and the presbyterians understood power as "binding," and not necessarily dependent upon the consent of the congregation. The majoritarian view of the London presbyterians was clearly opposed to an advisory-only scheme of church power.

None of the ideas above confer on higher courts any more authority than they should. They, and all presbyters, are bound by the same standard of Christ: Not to be domineering lords as the gentile rulers, but to be servants (Mt. 20:25-26). This doctrine can be, and has been, abused. However, an abuse of a proper power, Calvinists have always agreed, does not nullify the right use. In lieu of lowerarchicalism,33 presbyterianism stresses community harnessed by covenantal structure.

The Sovereignty of God: The rule by Elders with authority imitates the decrees of God. God sovereignly rules. He does not ask permission, seek referenda, nor submit his decisions to the counsel of the people or the *coetas fidelium*. He examines, deliberates, and decides. Once his counsel is revealed, it is to be followed. As noted, Acts 16:4 uses *dogma*, a biblical word, which is not exclusively the property of hierarchies. The apostolic church was not reluctant to speak of dogma and the sovereignty of God.

The sovereignty of God is at the heart of Reformed theology. This sovereignty of God reminds all creatures that they are not their own masters. No man or group is permitted to rule. God alone rules, and his creatures are to carry out his commands. Neither does God rule by permission of his creatures nor at their vote or referendum. He is, by definition, the sovereign.

---

29 Ibid.
30 Minutes, Feb. 13, 1645. Cited by Robert S. Paul, *The Assembly of the Lord* (Edinburgh: T & T Clark, 1985), p. 435.
31 Cited in Paul, op. cit., p. 151.
32 Ibid.

This frustrates the strong-willed and the fortitude-challenged alike. The ultimate decisions about the church are not delegated to men or even to presbyters. They are already made for us by the Sovereign; human office is simply "executive"—merely to execute or carry out his decisions or directives. Thus, Elders cannot be too innovative, nor are they charged with the duty of modernizing the church or conforming it either to contemporary managerial trends or to regnant civil polities. God is sovereign, and he sets up his church as he wishes. We are not so much to recommend what, in our opinion, works or what our culture has practiced. We are, instead, to mold our church to his divinely-revealed patterns and permit his sovereignty to dictate, even if it opposes an existing tradition. It is no accident that Calvin's strong rediscovery of the sovereignty of God also stimulated Knox and others to rediscover a parallel sovereignty of God in ecclesiology. The best ecclesiology fits the best theology.

The sovereignty of man, tradition, trend, mood, or other relative, culture-bound, or subjective factors is obviated by presbyterianism.

Man's Depravity: Some forms of government appear to trust the ability, intuition, managerial competence, or spirituality of humans more than the collegial style of biblical rule. Just as Acton said, "power corrupts, and absolute power corrupts absolutely," equally it can also be said that if even the finest spiritual people are entrusted with unchecked rule, things will eventually go astray. Presbyterianism, in a number of ways, limits some of the effects of depravity. Its checks and balances do this in a way that few other forms can boast.

All government is necessitated by human depravity and the Fall, and as such, is necessarily a mechanism of response to that fallen condition. Both civil and ecclesiastical forms of government are necessitated by the Fall and depravity. Although ordering is inherent within the Trinity and in creation, government as given by God is purposefully erected to restrain sinners and protect the righteous. If we in some state of nature were able to act "upon our honor" as it were, then government would not be needed. James Madison, reflective of his education under a Knoxian paradigm, commented: "If men were angels, no government would be necessary." Presbyterians have applied that idea even to the sanctified within the church.

If sin were not operative, or if uninterrupted progress could produce a depravity-free species, there would be no need for coercive government. If perfectionistic schemes of sanctification were correct, then we would be compelled to agree with the polity so often suggested by gnostic theologians. However, even optimistic orthodox views of sanctification do not lead us to expect that the church militant will achieve any such hamartiology. We expect people to be sinners, and thus we seek to construct the best possible form of government that will at least limit, although not eradicate, such ill-effects of sin.

Since God gave governments to restrain willfulness, it is helpful to stress regular and thoughtful means of accountability. To best facilitate this, most evangelicals have acknowledged the necessity of constitutions following the faithful patterns of God. Such constitutions serve to delimit unbridled subjectivity and will-reign, exhibiting our firm belief in the need to limit the power of any individual. As Abraham Kuyper surmised, Calvin knew "that even kings are sinners, who yield to temptation perhaps more readily than their subjects, inasmuch as their temptations are greater. . . . he knows equally well that the self-same sin moves the masses, and that, hence resistance, insurrection, and mutinies will not end, unless a righteous constitution bridles the abuse of authority, marks off its boundaries, and offers the people a natural protection against despotism and ambitious schemes."

Hence, constitutionalism is a restraint on sin. It is sin, however, in either civil or ecclesiastical government that demands a certain form. Our theology of sin and our anthropology are the values that shape our subsequent church government. Theology thus forms polity.

Opposes Gnosticism and Fits Christology: Some evangelicals lapse into unintentional gnosticism in several areas, but one area routinely shows more gnostic tendencies than others. Bible-believers are virtually always too preoccupied with other spiritual concerns than to "bother" with church government. Despite the failure to appreciate this area of faith—to our own detriment—no realm of government should be left solely to human discretion. The Christ of Gnosticism would only remedy a narrow range of intangible ills. Similarly, the Christ who was only Divine could neither sympathize with our weaknesses, nor provide an equal sacrifice for us. In place of that, the best Calvinistic theology presents Christ who is a prophet, priest, and king. These offices are all provided for within presbyterianism. The Savior matches perfectly the design of the church and the condition of man, where frequently other forms do not do sufficient justice to these key theological aspects. Church government is part of biblical theology and not an area to abandon to gnosticism, individual experience, secular management theory, or psychological group dynamics.

Modern Christians will want to be equally biblical in ecclesiastical government as they are in the practice of civil government or any other biblical issue. It would be a striking theological irony if modern evangelicals, better instructed of late on the cultural mandate along with its accompanying need to witness in government, became adroit at secular involvement or civil governance while remaining incompetent in ecclesiastical government. If we can be meaningful participants in secular government, then all the more so, we should have some measure of maturity in ecclesiastical governance. Governmental activism is not restricted to the realm of civil government alone. Nor is ecclesiastical negligence much more than gnosticism.

Honors and Preserves Form and Freedom: Presbyterianism does justice to both the proper authority of an individual congregation and to the catholicity of the church. It provides principles of form that are valid in all cultures and ages. It also supplies sufficient structure, while at the same time it does not strangle due discretion. It preserves both form and freedom. It honors unity and diversity simultaneously, a feat managed only by divine origin.

Appreciates Economy of Effort: Unfortunately many people often utter things like, "God wouldn't waste his time putting such petty matters as church discipline and order in the Bible"; or "All of the church's operations, since it is a human government, are to be left up to, and determined by the local society, however, they see best." Such comments seem to err in two directions: (1) They overestimate human managerial ability, and (2) They underestimate God's revealed plan for his church.

There is actually much information in the Bible about how God wants to run his church. The key is to remember that it is *his* church, hence not ours to design. We follow his commands in the areas of the government and administration of the church, just like we follow his commands in any other area of life. God has not left believers isolated to fend for themselves.

Contrary to the prevailing American *ethos*, those who are not connected to the body of Christ and those who are not flourishing with one another are depicted as "cut off from the head" (Col. 2:19). Unrelatedness is neither a virtue in the NT nor the OT. The Bible is squarely against individualism as an infrastructure for a form of government. The Scriptures are consistently opposed to the modern rights-oriented societies of the western world. When problems arise, our Father has loved us enough to give us other counselors, godly Elders, and the infallible Bible which reveals to us who God is and what he wants. For our own good, God has put together an organized form for settling controversies. God gave the greater counsel (Pr. 15:22) and the Assembly to his church. That is part of God's problem-solving method (Acts 15).

God's church is no slipshod organization. It is an organism yes; but it is also the best organization in the world. He designed it, and it is his church. Thus it should be implemented his way, too. God loved this church very much. Not only did he give his Son for her (Acts 20:28); furthermore, he gave her a continuing government and method of problem-solving that is exhibited in Scripture.

Restrains Against Domineering Willfulness. In our own times, we are often chagrined at how intensely Christians strive for autonomy. It was not the expressed desire of the NT church to "do its own thing." The churches felt a strong bond. The Scripture corrects and rebukes us when we want to say: "Each church can do anything it wishes." That is difficult to reconcile with the NT. Consider, e.g., how often the NT speaks of a uniform standard among its churches. Not only was a decision reached for all the churches in Acts 15, but elsewhere in the NT a uniform approach was adopted (1 Cor. 7:17; 11:16; and 14:33-38).

There is no regular case in the NT in which a church or fellowship dwelling in the same region disregards the other Christians or their counsel. There is a definite inter-connection between doctrinal orthodoxy and the implementation of it. To the degree that the church holds to biblical truth, it will find itself dissatisfied with provincialism and isolation from others in the Body. Biblical orthodoxy is catholic, and true fellowship of spirit yearns to be connectional. If the church is catholic, then it will be unified and apostolic. Often the modern church is too easily satisfied to settle for non-catholicity. Our American context lends itself to an Enlightenment 'democratization' and a distinctively Lockean view of voluntaryism, tending toward privatization or consumerism. Yet the biblical testimony corrects those urges, and values inter-related fellowship as a goal of its ministry both to (1) moderate some of the effects of unchecked sin, and (2) edify the saints by such connectedness. Simultaneously, a theology of government will devalue isolation in its multiple forms.

As hallmarks of this inter-connectedness, the biblical church will seek to have a keen eye out for accountability and checks-and-balances. Those who value the authority of Scripture, the sovereignty of God, the continuity of the Covenant, human nature effected by depravity, an epistemology founded on divine revelation, economy of effort, balance between form and freedom, and other crucial theological verities will find that presbyterianism best preserves, supports, and conforms to those same theological principles.

A Theology of Government: Practically Demanded

Presbyterianism seeks to govern the church according to the principles of government taught in the Holy Scriptures. We are neither free to add to nor detract from those. Our sole goal, like any topic in theology, is to put forth what the Bible says. There is no reason to treat polity by different standards than other theological *loci*. To paraphrase a C. S. Lewis title (*Mere Christianity*), we should seek *Mere Polity*. Such biblical polity has long been recognized by movements of reformation in pursuit of a return to scriptural Christianity. If we but have ears to hear, we can learn from this already charted biblical consensus rather than attempting to imitate an organization that is *semper reinventus*.

Polity is a part of revealed doctrine, not an unrelated appendage to the heart of biblical living. There is one consistent form of government that fits the underlying theology of the church, and it must be a government that (1) honors God's Word as the revealed law and mind of our Creator, (2) accounts for depravity in our nature and action, (3) seeks to reinforce by checks and balances the limitation of such depravity and finally (4) seeks to give glory and honor to Christ, the sovereign Head and King of the Church and not the human agents. That form which is biblical and primitive should be the love of every disciple. The form of government that is consistent with these theological values is one that is less dependent on man's ability and ingenuity than on the sovereign administrative power of God.

It is no accident, therefore, that many evangelicals have little or no appreciation for biblical government. Normally, any government at all is left up to individuals. Accordingly, it is the role and right of the saints to govern to the best of their ability. The redeemed individual has made an individual, personalistic decision for Christ. From that moment, he will follow that personal decision and continue to make individual polity decisions, preferably unhindered by tradition, law, creed, or structure of man-made denominations. To formulate government in this fashion is entirely consistent with corresponding views of sin, anthropology, and sovereignty.

Usually, in these traditions, either some form of natural law or spiritual spontaneity is determinative for the polity of that body. Freedom from law (viewed as inherently prohibitive) or sometimes even a reckless form of grace—which looks very similar to anti-nomianism—discourages such believers from being confined by form or structure. Structure is inherently disdainful to many. This individual-centered (as contrasted with community-centered) set of polity commitments values freedom over form. Moreover, it is consistent with the majoritarian polity of modern evangelicalism stemming from its democratic *ethos*. As a result, there is a diminished role for checks and balances. Uninhibited spontaneity and the human will reign, in these forms of government, rather than proven polity.

For now, suffice it to note that polity is in accord with a biblical theology. A theology's distinctive views of sin, grace, God and man are inescapably mirrored in its companion polity. Like liturgy, it is not so much a question "Will we have one?" for all do, either by design or by default, but "Which theological principles will shape your liturgy?" So with polity; it is not "Will we have a polity?" but "Which polity will we have, as structure is assuredly based on theological principles?" We argue for coherence between reformed doctrine and practice.

The organic principle, therefore, uniting the best of theology, sacramentology, and polity is the Divine Definition. This Divine Definition is consequently applied to each sphere, such that government is *jure divino* (or by divinely defined rule). Sacramentology is divinely defined as "that which is immediately instituted by Christ himself" (*WCF* 27:1), or divinely defined. Theological truth, likewise, is that which is revealed or defined by God as being true. Accordingly, biblical worship is prescribed by divine definition. Thus the organic and radical principle of the revealed faith, be it in government or other theological *loci,* is that such views are all to arise from divine definitions, revealed from the God of grace to wayward men who would otherwise not discover such definitions.

It is not accidental, therefore that those who hold to the special revelation of God, find themselves—almost inescapably—thrust toward a view of church government and worship that may be described as regulative in both spheres. In neither are we free to innovate or conjure. Instead, we are bound to follow our Creator. This may be despised by some as an inhibition of our human creativity, but this also safeguards and exalts our Creator and Redeemer rather than the redeemed. He is sufficient, and as Sovereign Governor he regulates all areas of life. Government would have to be proven either to be an area of non-significance for this life or else an area over which God has no business in order for it to escape his rule.

Above I have argued that presbyterianism best approximates the biblical teachings on church structure and also comports best with the reformed theology of Scripture. Indeed, it is difficult, as many have discovered, to remain reformed apart from presbyterian order. Finally, to suggest its efficacy, below, I will note some of the practical benefits of presbyterian church government.

(1) It is a loving thing to have a well-ordered church, governed by the biblical norms. Church government or structure is not inherently inimical to loving pastoral care and sensitivity. Such opinion views shepherding and structure as mutually exclusive.

On the contrary in many instances, the most loving thing pastors can do is provide loving, supportive church government and structure. We are not so gnostic as to presuppose that spirit contradicts body. Likewise, we do not accept a dichotomy between loving action and structural support. Both form and love cohabitate in God's government for his church. In fact, a lack of love spawns chaos, not order. It is not loving to fail to provide guidelines, leaving each individual to an autonomy of their own judgment. Frequently a clear authoritative resolution is the kindest thing for a church.

Pastors who leave governing solely up to the impulse of the whims of the moment are not loving hosts for the flock. Like good structures, good pastoral government aids in the walk along a level spiritual highway. Good church government is a distinct help to the normal Christian. In fact, to default in church government is an unloving and irresponsible act. It is patently uncaring to desert the flock to a pasture without corral or provender. Pastors and Elders must rediscover polity, as its etymological origin implies, as politeness. Part of the original meaning of "polite" was its reference to advanced culture or refined manners. Neophytes were not polite. Those who were sophisticated or characterized by civility were polite. Do we owe our parishioners any less than this kind of polite treatment? Well-developed polity is but the mature or organized practice of civility toward one another. A helter-skelter approach to polity is systematic ignorance of concerns of the body politic. It is also a violation of the Golden Rule. Hence well-formed polity is helpful for edification and a servant to impartiality.

(2) Church government is a gift of the Holy Spirit. Romans 12 dignifies the image of church government by listing *kubernesis* (governing) as one of the charismatic gifts of the Holy Spirit (12:8); thus exonerating this gift from the sinister overtones often associated with corrupt civil governments. As the Scriptures depict government in such fair light, the church (and its ministers) would do well to embrace government as a grace-gift. Never in Scripture is church government described with negative overtones. Rather, it is a positive gift of God to his church, betokening the grace, care, and love of the Savior for his church.

Church government in its ordered form is not a contradiction of the Holy Spirit's leading. On the contrary, the Holy Spirit may work in certain patterns, developing channels of norms. Such historic channels of response gradually evolve into structure. Such structures, deduced from revelation, are normative guides for the church in all ages and cultures. It is not too much to claim that the Holy Spirit works through revealed structures. The Christian has no more to fear from revealed order than from revealed Law. While it is true that we exhibit an historic and mammoth antinomian tendency in the modern church, such failure should be recognized for the error it is. Law and Grace are not mortal enemies. Neither is presbyterian government in its ordered form a contradiction of the Holy Spirit's leading.

(3) Presbyterianism is time-tested and spares endless organizational reinventions. For those who value organizational progress, we can urge, "Don't re-invent the wheel." The biblical aspects of government need not be ignored by each successive generation nor rediscovered by the alternating generations. We could profit much by studying the "old paths" (Jer. 6:16, 18:15), and attempting to mold our inchoate governments after the progress of our spiritual ancestors. Far from being a pharisaic expression of traditionalism, that is the better part of wisdom as we seek to rule out those inefficacious modes of governing. History has value in eliminating erroneous dead-end paths. Church polity—which spans several theological variables, none of which have changed drastically over time—has not changed in its major principles. The proven paradigms from the history of polity have great pedagogical value for the future.

Earlier theological giants were leaders not only in academic theology but in ecclesiology as well. Their greatness would not be esteemed today, if their theologies contained only arid philosophical matters incapable of *praxis* in the local church. To the contrary, part of the enduring legacy of these divines is their contribution to polity. Indeed, a case can be made that Protestant theology at its apex also had an inherent (and healthy) preoccupation for the church to be governed by the very systematic principles of theology it maintained.

Few of the great and enduring theologians have failed to articulate their system in polity form. The historical concurrence between great theology and great polity is too frequent to ignore. The best theologians seem also to be the best students of polity. Thus, if the church is to reclaim superior theology, it should be expected that she will also reclaim and exhibit superior polity.

Theology, for the past 500 years, has seen great contribution from its leading lights to the field of polity. It was not beneath Knox, Beza, Calvin, or Luther to speak of ecclesiastical polity. They did not change garbs as the classroom changed from Christology to ecclesiology. With the same reverence, the same tools, and the same theology (and even urgency), theology and practice went hand in hand. These were not ivory-towered Gnostics. Many were pastors; it is unthinkable that Calvin and others would divorce practice from doctrine. That is why Calvin devoted nearly one-fifth of *The Institutes* to ecclesiology, with large sections devoted to polity matters. In fact, Calvin devoted more space to church government than he did to discussing the knowledge of God, Scripture, Trinity, the Decalogue, Christology, Election, or Sacraments.

No change in the universe or in the church since his time, suggests that we should be inclined otherwise today. Our case for presbyterianism, therefore is founded on biblical, doctrinal, and practical reasons.

Thus it is hoped that the Church will be biblical not only in doctrine, not only in Sanctification, and not only in our view of Providence and the guidance of the Holy Spirit. We will strive to apply the whole counsel to the whole person—not their individual soul only. The body, too, needs the divine order. Furthermore, it is hoped that we will see the Holy Spirit guiding us and impelling us toward a view of government, which honors God as much in our day-to-day government as we do in our Doxology. To do so is not only theologically sound but also pastorally advantageous. To do less is to be gnostic in one form or the other.

For More Study: See a companion article, "The Pastoral and Theological Significance of Church Government," in *Paradigms in Polity* (pp. 12-34)

Also, see the abridgement of Thomas Witherow's *The Apostolic Church: Which is It?* in *Paradigms in Polity*, pp. 37-51. This summary of Witherow serves to reinforce the basic principles of scriptural government. ***It should be required reading for all officers.***

Session #5a

Church Discipline: A painful and necessary expression of love and respect

Now we turn our attention to the Rules of Discipline. Church discipline is *the loving attempt to reclaim a professing Christian by word and deed in keeping with the commands of Scripture.* The fact that it is so seldom practiced in many churches today no more lessens its need than does the fact that many churches today seldom pray as they ought. Our Confession of Faith summarizes its usefulness in chapter 30, "Of Church Censures." That first paragraph reminds us that the government within the church is, at Christ's own appointment, distinct and different from the civil government. Christ's church is not ruled by politicians, presidents, or CEOs; instead the Officers that Christ has given to the church and who exercise church discipline are the ordained Elders.

The second paragraph of WCF 30 further underscores that these "keys of the kingdom" (see Mt. 18:17-18) are exclusively given to the Officers of Christ's church, and this delegated power authorizes them to retain or remit sins, to exclude from the visible church those that do not repent, and to absolve (or declare forgiveness for) those who do sincerely repent.

Scripture, Confession, and Constitution on Discipline

Our Book of Church Order contains a second major division in chapters 27-46, the Rules of Discipline. Chapter 27 of the BCO enunciates the essential foundations for biblical church discipline in keeping with the purposes contained in WCF 30:3. The purposes of biblical church discipline as stated in our Confession are:

(1) to reclaim and gain offending brothers (or professing members of the church; see Mt. 18:15-17; Gal. 6:1; 1 Cor. 5:5; 2 Thess. 3:15);

(2) to deter others from like offenses (1 Tim. 5:20)—the consistent practice of church discipline signals to our youth and the outside world that we take the moral commands of Christ seriously and will not wink at sin;

(3) to purge out the leaven that could affect the body (1 Cor. 5:6-8);

(4) to vindicate the honor of Christ and the holiness of the church (1 Cor. 11:27; 2 Cor. 2:9, 17; Titus 1:13, 2:15, and 3:10);

(5) to prevent the wrath of God that might visit the church that does not police itself (Rev. 2:14-25).

Similarly, our BCO states the goals of church discipline (27-3) as useful for maintaining:

      (a) the glory of God;

      (b) the purity of his Church;

      (c) the keeping and reclaiming of disobedient sinners.

The goals associated with these virtues are "the rebuke of offenses, the removal of scandal, the vindication of the honor of Christ, the promotion of the purity and general edification of the church, and the spiritual good of offenders themselves." (BCO 27-3)

Other Reformation confessions clearly identified church discipline as one of the marks of the true church (e.g., the 1560 *Scots Confession*, ch. 18; the 1561 *Belgic Confession*, ch. 19, etc.). In his *Institutes of the Christian Religion*, John Calvin noted: "But because some persons, in their hatred of discipline, recoil from its very nature, let them understand this: if no society, indeed, no house which has even a small family, can be kept in proper condition without discipline, it is much more necessary in the church, whose condition should be as ordered as possible. Accordingly, as the saving doctrine of Christ is the soul of the church, so does discipline serve as its sinews . . . Therefore, all who desire to remove discipline or to hinder its restoration, whether they do this deliberately or out of ignorance, are surely contributing to the ultimate dissolution of the church. For what will happen if each is allowed to do what he pleases? Yet that would happen, if to the preaching of doctrine there were not added private admonitions, corrections, and other aids of the sort that sustain doctrine and do not let it remain idle." (Book IV, ch. 12, section 1)

This power given to the church is spiritual and declarative in contrast to the coercive, physical (or financial) power assigned to the civil government (BCO 27-4), and the Officers of the church are to practice these measures, instruct the church in these matters, and seek to practice it as the Scriptures teach. According to our constitution, "Scriptural law is the basis of all discipline because it is the revelation of God's Holy will." (BCO 27-5). The steps of church discipline, according to BCO 27-5 are:

(1) First, to preach the Word; every time the living, active Word of God (Heb. 4:12-13) is preached, it cuts, convicts, challenges, and reveals God's holy will, which is the first part of discipline.
(2) Then, if needed, private admonition (Mt. 18:15), calling the sinner to repent; if that happens, formal discipline is forestalled.
(3) If, however, the private admonition is spurned, then additional witnesses, normally involving the most trusted agents of the church—the Elders—are called to verify either sin or repentance.
(4) Finally, if not heeded, the Church acts through her ordained agents in a joint capacity to admonish, suspend, excommunicate, or depose from office (in the case of an Officer).

WCF 30:4 also outlines the modes of discipline ("for the better attaining of these [30:3] ends") as:

(1)   admonition or verbal rebuke (the NT word for admonition means "to put into mind," indicating that activity of reciting biblical truths with the purpose of calling Christians back to God's standards);
(2)   suspension from the sacraments—a painful step to deny a person one of God's means of grace;
(3)   excommunication, the authoritative pronouncement that a person is not recognized by the church as a Christian and removal from privileges associated with church membership;

Our standards, thus, are uniform in these principles. Officers of the church must understand the biblical foundation of these disciplinary steps. Distinctions are made in our BCO between types of offense. An offense is "anything in the doctrines of practice of a church member professing faith in Christ which is contrary to the Word of God." (BCO 29-1). From the outset, we must remember that an offense is not something that is contrary to my wish for another person, or contrary to preference or taste, but it must be a clear violation of Scriptural teaching to be considered valid for church discipline. Such offenses or scandals can rarely be hidden indefinitely, so the Officers of the church need not become over-zealous in this task. Sin will make itself very clear in the congregation. Offenses, however, may be more or less limited in their scope or publicity. Some are private and personal, and others are general and public (BCO 29-2). Our constitution defines these (BCO 29-3 and 29-4), and notice should be taken of this as an initial diagnosis of need.

The Scriptures teach much on this subject and give us the principles to follow. The Officer should be acquainted with a variety of Scriptures that address this subject. One objection should be cleared away from the beginning. Some people misinterpret Jesus' teaching in Matthew 7:1-6 and think that it forbids the making of any moral judgment. Officers must be clear about this: that passage in the Sermon on the Mount does not prohibit the Officers in Christ's church from making and pronouncing moral judgments or making church disciplinary steps. A proper understanding of those verses include the following:

(1) A type of judgmentalism is rejected, specifically a hypocritical judgmentalism. If one continues to read on to verse 2 of this chapter, our Lord denounces the wrong kind of judging, i.e., judging by a double standard. If we judge, we are to be willing to apply the identical standards to our own lives. Thus, before the Officers proceed in church discipline, they should review their own practice and willingness to live by the uniform standards of Scriptural morality. It is wrong for an Officer to judge another member, if he is not willing to be judged by the same measures (Mt. 7:2). However, sound interpretation of this passage does not warrant the absence of church discipline.

(2) Those who exercise church discipline must examine themselves first (see also Gal. 6:1) to see if they have a beam in their own eyes. Officers must not be blatantly immoral and simultaneously seek to address relatively small defects of other church members.

(3) Jesus himself, within the very context, pronounces those who reject biblical teaching as "dogs" or "swine" if they trample on the pearls of scriptural wisdom; that is certainly a judgment, which is not contradicted by Jesus' teaching in Matthew 7:1. Thus, Jesus does not prohibit the right exercise of judging and church discipline.

Once this is understood, we can recall Jesus' own (red letters!) teaching on the steps of church discipline. In Matthew 18:15, the first step called for by our Lord is that if a brother (a professing Christian or church member) sins, an individual should go to him privately and inquire about the activity to see if it violates Scripture. If it does not violate Scripture, but is a matter of taste, ignorance, or something that the offender resolves to correct, then the formal discipline may stop. This first step is admonition, and if the individual acknowledges his sin or carries out repentance, then Jesus views this as winning over our brother—we have reclaimed the offender, and due process halts.

If, however, the sinner persists—assuming again that the activity is clearly sinful and that the first step has been followed—then the person who initially approached the sinner should not stop loving and caring, but should solicit other witnesses in keeping with the OT standard that every matter must be established by two or three witnesses. So, the second step is to take additional witnesses, normally Elders at this stage, who can further verify if (a) the activity has truly occurred; (b) if the activity is clearly a violation of Scripture; and (c) if the person repents or persists in this sin. If the activity has not happened (if things were misunderstood or based on rumor), then discipline does not proceed, although even in that case the Elders may wish to give verbal warnings to be careful not to come close to sin. Moreover, if the activity is not clearly deemed to be sin, then neither should discipline proceed. If, on the other hand, the activity has happened and it is sin, then the sinner must repent or else a next step is mandated by Christ.

That third step, if necessary, is to "tell it to the church." This means to involve additional Christian friends and church members, all in the attempt to bring the sinner back into the fold. The NT belief was that church membership was so vital, especially in an age when people could not "church-hop," that any true Christian would forsake his sin—even if painful—in order to avoid losing the precious fellowship of other Christians. All steps are designed to re-integrate the sinner into the moral and spiritual norms of Christ.

However, some persons love their sin more than the righteousness of the Christian community. After the repeated entreaties above, if the person still will not repent, then according to Jesus, he is to be treated as an unbeliever (a pagan or a tax-collector). That is the act of cutting off from the church, or disfellowshiping, or excommunicating. Protestants need to understand that excommunication does not belong to the Roman Catholic Church alone. Our Lord himself taught this, and we must practice this if we hope to (a) remain obedient to him, and (b) act as loving and committed as possible to our Christian brothers. To fail, then, to practice this passage is to (a) disobey Christ's explicit teachings; (b) believe that we know better than his Word; and (c) fail to act in love toward our spiritual family.

Many other Scriptures address this same practice. In 1 Corinthians 5, the apostle Paul rebukes the Corinthian church for not policing its own morals. In that case, notorious sexual immorality was known and the church did not treat the church member by the same moral norms as Scripture maintains. Paul indicated that he had already passed judgment on this case, even though not physically present (note the robust connectionalism of the early church). He advised the Corinthians to hand this person over to Satan for the destruction of the flesh so that his soul might be saved. Although some interpreters fail to see the symbolism of this passage, it should not be thought of as the church beseeching Satan to have his way with the impenitent person. Instead, the early church viewed the world as divided into two realms: (1) the realm of Satan and the world or (2) the realm of God and the church. Thus, to turn a person over to the realm of Satan was to excommunicate him from the realm of the church and treat him, just as Jesus said in Matthew 18, as a pagan. Such church discipline is necessary for the purity of the church, the honor of Christ, the deterrence of others, and the possible repentance of the sinner.

Later, in 1 Corinthians 5, Paul clarifies that the church cannot police those outside its membership. We are not called on to authoritatively judge those outside the church. To do that, or to avoid associating with unbelievers, would force us to remove ourselves from the world totally. That is not God's design. However, we are entrusted with the practices of the church, and we are called on simply to judge those within the church, those who profess to be brothers. We are not to associate with those within the church who persist in sexual immorality or other violations of Scripture. To avoid them assumes that they have been cut off from the church. Furthermore, the opening verses of the next chapter (1 Cor. 6) exhibit that God calls us to judge; in the end, believers will even be used to judge angels. Once again, the prohibition against proper judging does not exist.

Severe measures are indicated further in the NT. In Titus 3:10, the Scripture orders us to warn a divisive person once, then a second time, and after that to have nothing to do with a person who is dividing the church. The person who persists in dividing the congregation is warped and self-condemned.34 Other NT passages such as Revelation 2:14-25 and 2 Thessalonians 3:6, 14-15 should be studied as well for preparation for this duty belonging to the Elders.

Our Book of Church Order in chapters 30-39 contains many aspects of due process. Officers, especially the Elders to whom this function is assigned, should familiarize themselves with these specifics and keep the Index of the BCO handy for future reference related to these matters. Below is an overview (and there is no substitute for a complete reading of these chapters) of the contents of those chapters:

- Chapter 30 defines the censures inflicted by church courts. In this chapter, the censures of admonition (30-2), suspension (30-3), excommunication (30-4), and deposition (30-5) are defined.
- Chapter 31 explains who the parties are in any case and provides the steps to begin due process.
- General principles, including details about citation, charges, the official record of the case, statutes of limitation, etc., that apply to all cases are exhibited in chapter 32.
- Chapter 35, then, details what evidence is admissible and provides necessary information on evidentiary value.
- Chapter 33 addresses basic matters that apply to any case before a session, whereas Chapter 34 addresses a case that is particularly related to judicial process against a Minister.
- Chapter 36 discusses how to apply the censures and displays the necessary wording for respective censures. The companion chapter 37 provides guidance for how to remove the censures upon repentance.
- Special rules that apply to cases not needing process (such as a free confession) are contained in chapter 39.

One of the best, short studies on church discipline is Daniel Wray's *Biblical Church Discipline* (1978; available from the Banner of Truth Trust). We highly recommend it. He notes, "It is necessary in our hardened and apostate age for the church to be called back to the NT doctrine of church discipline." The church has become far too tolerant of error and immorality, thereby risking God's wrath. We cannot ignore, minimize, or grow indifferent to God's call for the

---

34 In fact, it might be helpful for church Officers to inform members and the congregation that the sinner has "excommunicated himself" (by his own choice), when such act is completed. That active-voice phraseology more correctly represents the entire process than to allow it to appear that the Officers have initiated the action as if the person "was excommunicated (passive-voice) by the Elders."

church to practice what she preaches. The church's tendency, writes Wray, to "be more concerned about what is expedient than right, has robbed the church of biblical integrity and power." And although may rationales to neglect church discipline exist, such as that to discipline is to lack love or that abuses in this area have occurred, we can no more call ourselves loving if we fail to practice this toward our brothers than we could call ourselves loving if we knowingly let a grandchild walk toward a landmine.

Let me conclude with a final section of Q&A on the **Five Biggest Questions about Church Discipline** (already covered, of course, are possible objections that: Jesus ordered us not to ever judge, discipline is inherently unloving, and the goal of church discipline is repentance and restoration). The five biggest objections to practicing church discipline in my experience are:

(1) If we practice discipline won't this cause either divisions or prevent the church from growing? *Answer*: The prospect of persons not liking what the church stands for should not prevent her from practicing the commands of Christ, who himself was a stone that causes stumbling (Luke 2:34). Whenever the Word of God is preached with force and clarity, it is possible that sinners will not like that, preferring instead to have their ears tickled, but that does not legitimate the avoidance of the Word. If mature Elders follow due process, they can show their work to other members unashamedly, and divisiveness may actually be pre-empted if faithful and loving discipline is exercised early and consistently. We also, as human servants of the Sovereign Lord, ought not elevate our own expectations for numerical growth over the revealed call to act in obedience to this charge.

(2) If all people are sinful, how can even the best Elders condemn? *Answer*: The issue is not sinfulness but repentance. Elders and church members alike are called to the same standards; Elders do not make up the laws of Christ—they simply follow the Scriptures. The condemnatory aspect of church discipline is but an echo of what God has already said. Thus, the church can and must pronounce what is sinful. Moreover, if a sinner wants to have church discipline removed or absolved, all he has to do is comply with the commands of Christ. Furthermore, if the church fails to make necessary moral condemnations, we confuse our children and members, encouraging them to think that evil is good (Is. 5:20).

(3) Should we exercise church discipline, even if we know that the offender will simply 'drop out' of church or join another one down the street—isn't it in vain? *Answer*: Regardless of outcome, we—especially those Officers who have sworn to uphold the law of Christ—have an obligation to be faithful to what Scripture clearly calls us to do. We should be more concerned to please Christ than to retain members, especially if they love their sin more than their church membership. The Officers of the church also have an obligation—actually, it is an extension of the Golden Rule—to treat another church as they would want to be treated. If a known child molester were coming to your youth picnic, wouldn't you want to be forewarned? Similarly, in cases of notorious scandal or immorality, we should communicate with the other church, not to hurt the impenitent but to protect the innocent in that flock.

(4) Can we ever tell if repentance is sincere? *Answer*: It is certainly true that a person may exhibit or experience temporary repentance. Equally true, no Elder can read the heart; we can only judge action or behavior as consistent or inconsistent with scriptural teaching. Our Confession speaks of true repentance as occurring when a person sees his sin as

"filthy and odious" and hates that sin. The Officers of the church probably should use as much care in judging the fruit of repentance (Mt. 3:9-12) as they do in judging sin in the first place. They should look after the interests of the person harmed (if present in the case), they should factor in the person's history and seek to limit manipulativeness, and they should design some stringent tests to prove the person's seriousness. A truly repentant person will do almost anything—study the Prodigal son in Luke 15 or Zaccheus in Luke 19 to see exemplary attitudes—in order to be received back into the fold. Then, when true repentance occurs, the person should be forgiven and grace applied. Even after that, especially in cases where the scandal has been public or notorious, the sinner should be surrounded with oversight, accountability, and removed from known temptations as much as possible. The Officers of the church must deal circumspectly with all these factors in restoring (Gal. 6:1) a person to full fellowship.

(5) What if we practice church discipline and see no immediate fruit? *Answer*: Church discipline is like many other commandments (to pray, to tithe, to evangelize, to nurture discipline) in that believers are called on to act and trust God to produce fruit. It is more important for children of the heavenly Father to obey him than to see the results. I can think of cases of discipline in which persons wrote me *ten years after* the discipline to express their thanks or appreciation; others may not take as long. Since the Bible itself tells us that no discipline is enjoyable (Heb. 12:1-8), the Officers of the church should expect that in many cases, the impenitent will not embrace correction. The main thing for Officers to do is to examine their own motives and make sure that they are merely following the Scriptures—and that to fail to do so will force them to be disobedient—and then act deliberately, lovingly, and faithful to Scriptures. Then, in good time, fruit will be seen in many areas, even if the sinner under discipline never repents. Of course, in cases where repentance is rapid (assuming that it is sincere—and this is where undershepherds must know their sheep), the Officers of the church may provide gracious salve and restore the offender.

Finally, some are sincerely concerned that the practice of church discipline will give the faithful congregation a bad reputation. While it might in some communities, those who know what has transpired should defend the honorable reputation and also teach what is at stake if we fail to act decisively toward moral evil. It is also possible, when done properly, for church discipline to be seen as a level of love and accountability, as well as moral seriousness, that few churches offer. It can, in other words, help distinguish a congregation from other churches in the area; and it can provide enormous and visible object lessons for all involved to observe that the church takes the Bible with the utmost seriousness and is even willing to endure unpopularity in a community in order to receive the blessing of Christ.

I also advise Officers (and some newer or younger Officers are tempted in this area) that they need not become vigilantes in order to carry out this aspect of church life. We do not need Elders invading privacy or looking for fault at every turn; that would be an abuse in this area. Nor should motives be questioned. Instead, Officers can rest assured in this biblical promise: "Be sure that your sin will find you out." (Num. 32:23). That is to say, since sin can never remain in neutral, it will either be fertilized or mortified. The kind of sin that warrants church discipline will present itself to the Elders or else it will become a part of our regular conversations, such that the Elders don't have to go looking for sin. It will find us, and Officers must already know the biblical principles and Rules of Discipline so that when a case arises they can serve the Head of the Church and seek to protect the flock, attempting all the while to regain the offender.

Discipline in Due Process

All of these matters above refer to discipline in the technical sense. Another aspect of church unity and inspection is how higher courts are accessed or take a supervisory role over the lower courts. The modes by which a matter may come under the supervision of the higher courts are spelled out in chapter 39. They are (and a succeeding chapter is devoted to each):

(1) Review and Control35;
(2) Reference;
(3) Appeal; and
(4) Complaint.

Each court submits is official minutes to the higher court at least once a year for review. Chapter 40 records the provisions that apply to that factor, which is so important (albeit quite detailed) for the unity and purity of our church. Sessions submit their minutes to the Presbytery, and Presbyteries submit their minutes to the General Assembly, and each is open to the correction of the wider body of reference. If mistakes are made—and we should be eager for brotherly correction—the higher court records the violations, which are sometimes minute (such as typographical errors) and at other times substantive (which merit quick attention and redress). The costs of neglecting this inspection are discussed in 40-4, and the assumption throughout is that the church courts desire to operate in unity and with consistency.

Another manner in which a matter may come before the higher court is by Reference (BCO 41). A Reference is a formal request (41-1) by a lower court for the higher court to give its advice on a matter that divides the presbytery or that carries wide ramifications (see 41-2).

An Appeal (chapter 42) is only available to those who have submitted to a trial (42-2). This Appeal permits the appellant seek relief from a higher court, if he believes his trial was unfair or impartial in some way (42-1). The specific procedures used in an Appeal are provided in this chapter.

Chapter 43 discusses a parallel procedure—Complaints—by which any "act or decision of a court" is complained against and redress sought.

Chapter 45 then discusses other manners to bring to the attention of the higher court some perceived mistake or disorder. One may dissent to a decision of the court (45-1) if he voted on the issue, or one may protest (45-3), or one may lodge an objection (45-4), even if he was not part of the court. In each instance, reasons may be supplied as a witness for posterity, the

---

35 An earlier attempt to amend out of the BCO the words "and control" from this chapter heading failed to be approved by the requisite number of presbyteries; thus the long-standing language is preserved in our BCO (cf. also p. 210 below). However, a subordinate set of protocols, "The Rules of Assembly Operations," which govern only the meeting of the annual Assembly, were successfully amended at this point and now refer to this function as "the Review of Presbytery Records." Despite the inconsistent practice in this area, the fingerprint of the former practice, which allowed more corrective authority to the higher courts, is still visible.

language must be temperate and respectful (45-5), and a court may, if it wishes, record a response to the dissent, protest, or objection.

The Rules of Discipline section is completed with chapter 46 on "Jurisdiction."

The Directory for Worship

The third and final part of the BCO is the Directory for the Worship of God. Our denomination has given full, constitutional authority only to chapters 56-58, those sections that contain membership vows (BCO 57) and the important procedures governing the two sacraments, Baptism (BCO 56) and the Lord's Supper (BCO 58). It is not that the other matters are insignificant at all, but in keeping with the wisdom of our tradition, Worship is governed by the regulative principle, but it has never been our intention to prescribe an exact and entire liturgy. Thus, the Directory for worship is "an approved guide and should be taken seriously as the mind of the Church agreeable to the Standards."

Thus, we recommend that every Officer read these chapters and understand them. They are not difficult, and they contain pious advice, drawn from Scripture. Accordingly, we will merely outline the topics addressed and suggest that Officers read other selected works (see below on this) on these subjects as their interests and necessities demand.

- Chapter 47 informs us about the general principles of worship; much of this is assumed to be known already from a study of WCF 24.
- Chapter 48 reviews the keeping of the Lord's Day.
- Chapter 49 contains basic principles for ordering the public worship.
- Chapter 50 explains how the Scriptures should be read in public worship.
- Chapter 51 covers the subject of music and the manner of singing.
- Chapter 52 addresses corporate prayer, and it provides helpful guidelines for how the minister leads worship and integrates prayer with the sermon.
- Chapter 53, then, discusses preaching.
- Chapter 54 sets forth principles concerning the giving of offerings in worship.
- Chapter 55 states that it is proper to use great creeds (the Apostles', the Nicene, or excerpts from the WCF) in worship.
- Chapter 56 treats the subject of Baptism, and Chapter 58 exhibits the proper aspects of celebrating the Lord's Supper.
- Chapter 57 contains our membership vows and information on how to receive members.
- Specialized services of worship are covered in chapters 59-62, including: Weddings (59), visitation of the sick (60), Funerals (61), Services of Fasting or Thanksgiving (62), and Family worship (63) [Note: the Appendixes contain sample forms and liturgies for these occasions, along with forms for certain disciplinary specifications]. Of course, each of these topics deserve full treatment, and we recommend that Officers interested in studying specific aspects request guidance and suggestions from their pastors or other Elders on these topics.

****

For More Study: On the topics of worship, prayer, and the Sabbath, the Rev. Carl Robbins (Woodruff Road PCA in Simpsonville, SC) has recommended the following as very helpful for his Officer training (also ranked in terms of technical difficulty; most available from Amazon.com or the PCA Bookstore).

On Worship
- (Easiest, 60 pp.) Terry L. Johnson, *Reformed Worship*;
- (More in-depth) Robert Rayburn, *O Come Let Us Worship*;
- (More in-depth) Daryl Hart and John Muether, *With Reverence and Awe*;
- (Difficult) Carlos Eire, *War Against the Idols*.

On Prayer
- (Easiest) J. C. Ryle, *Prayer*;
- (More in-depth) Douglas Kelly, *If God Already Knows, Why Pray?*;
- (Longer but not difficult) Matthew Henry, *A Method for Prayer*.

On the Sabbath
- (Easiest) A. A. Hodge, "The Day Changed and the Sabbath Preserved"'
- (More in-depth) Walter Chantry, *Call the Sabbath a Delight*.
- (Longer but not difficult) Joseph Pipa, *The Lord's Day*.

Session #6: The PCA: Its Origins, Realities, and Prospects

A Brief History of the PCA

Like any social organization, the story of the origin of the PCA is part personal testimony, part myth, part motivation, and much reaction; and not all reaction is bad. After 30 years of unfolding, more than anything, the PCA seems to have been formed to provide and nurture a socially conservative and theologically evangelical community. Along the way, the PCA has acquired some commitments to the Reformed confessionalism of the Westminster Standards. How many of the founding fathers were consciously committed to that is still a matter of debate, even among the remaining founding fathers. One thing, however, is clear: when formed the PCA churches did not opt for independency and they strongly desired to avoid the liberalism of the mainline Presbyterian Church. In the early days, PCA founders might have unified around these initials: ABL (Anything But Liberal). Such hodgepodge of motives, not always capable of sorting out while under duress, should both be appreciated and should be a call to Officers to lend a hand in clearing up the best and most biblical identity for the future. Below is a short history of what led to the formation of the PCA in 1973.

Officers and members should remember that there were two antecedent denominational strains: (1) the Southern Presbyterian tradition, exhibited by the (then) PCUS (Presbyterian Church in the United States); and (2) more Reformed, smaller denominations, such as the OPC (Orthodox Presbyterian Church), ARP (Associate Presbyterian Church, with direct ties to Scotland and originally separate from American Presbyterianism), and the RPCES (Reformed Presbyterian Church, Evangelical Synod—which would merge with the PCA in 1983).[36] All of these denominations professed some level of allegiance to Scripture and Confession, with the second strain demonstrating considerably stronger adherence to the Westminster Standards by 1973 than the PCUS.

Several early dissenting groups began to surface after WWII. A small number of Presbyterian congregations left the mainline church between 1948-1968 (e.g., Hull Memorial in Savannah and Westminster [formerly pastored by Peter Marshall] in Atlanta).

Four groups that would later contribute to the first Steering Committee for formation of the PCA formed in the post-WWII period. They were:

1. **The Presbyterian Journal**. This publication (which later became *World* Magazine) was founded when a returning medical missionary, Dr. L. Nelson Bell (father-in-law to Billy Graham), returned from a life of missionary work in China. Upon his return, he found that the church of his childhood had drastically changed. He and a few others based their work near Asheville, NC, and provided a journalistic voice of dissent and criticism of the mainline Presbyterian denomination. Along with him, G. Aiken Taylor and others would help fuel the beginning of the PCA.
2. **Presbyterian Evangelistic Fellowship**. This attempt to re-evangelize southern Presbyterian congregations was begun in 1958 by the Rev. Bill Hill, an evangelists as

---

36 The accompanying chart in Appendix T at the end of this manual traces the genealogy of the various Presbyterian churches in this nation. See the chart styled, "Timeline and Presby-Roots of the PCA."

fiery in spirit as short in physical stature. Rev. Hill and others formed a network of evangelists within the PCUS, who consistently opposed liberalism. Other key associates in PEF (which continues to the present) were Ben Wilkinson and Kennedy Smartt.

3. **Concerned Presbyterians**. One of the extraordinary aspects of the PCA's origin was the presence of a determined cadre of Ruling Elders and laymen, who refused to allow their churches to drift leftward. Kenneth Keyes (a realtor in Miami), Jack Williamson (an attorney in Greenville, Alabama), and others united non-Ministers together to oppose the liberalism of the PCUS. These dedicated Christians brought a corporate and business sense to the table and continued to be a strong voice in the formation of the PCA.

4. **Presbyterian Churchmen United**. This ministerial counterpart to the Concerned Presbyterians was formed in the late 1960s to preserve a traditional remnant in the PCA and to oppose specific measures at the presbytery and General Assembly level.

These four groups helped publicize the weaknesses of progressive Presbyterianism and organize southerners to oppose the modernism of the PCUS. Clearly, this denomination was formed as much in opposition as it was around a positive message.

Numerous specifics gave rise to the formation of the PCA in the 1970s. Among the causes for Dissatisfaction prior to 1973 were the following:

1. **Plan of Union** (1954). This first attempt to unite the northern and southern branches of mainline Presbyterianism (the same year as the infamous *Brown v. Board of Education* ruling on desegregation) failed but worried the more conservative southerners.

2. **Ordination of Women Elders**. This change was approved in 1964 and was viewed as an attempt either to modernize the ancient church's practice or to prepare the PCUS for eventual union with the UPCUSA (the Northern Presbyterians).

3. **View of Scripture**. In both the seminaries and in official publications, it became increasingly clear that the mainline church did not value Scripture as "the only infallible rule of faith and practice." Scripture was not treated as the sole authority for the declining mainline church.

4. **Weakening of Ordination Vows**. As the view of Scripture changed in reality, naturally the official position of the church changed as well. Eventually, the PCUS changed their codified ordination vow on Scripture from "the only infallible rule of faith and practice" to Scripture "contains the Word of God" [and parts *might not* contain God's Word as Neo-Orthodoxy suggested].

5. **Second Plan for Reunion** (1969). Denominational progressives rarely give up after one successful attempt. A second plan for reuniting the northern and southern branches of mainline Presbyterianism was attempted and ever-so-narrowly defeated in 1969. Nonetheless, the gains in support clearly indicated the near-inevitability of reunion (which would eventually be accomplished in 1983). Even the defeat of this, however, led to more encroachment of traditional Presbyterianism in the south as the next two items indicate.

6. **Restructuring of General Assembly** (1970). The major boards and committees of the Southern PCUS were restructured by 1970; most conservative and traditionalist elements were minimized or reorganized toward the sidelines.

7. **Union Synods and Union Presbyteries**. Also following the 1969 defeat of Reunion, the constitutions of both northern and southern Presbyterian denominations permitted courts

that were geographically contiguous to a court of the other denomination to declare themselves "union" courts. Accordingly, a *de facto* union around the borders of the erstwhile confederacy took place, giving voting rights to each court in the other's affairs. This both further shrunk the territories where conservatives were in the majority and added to the forces of Reunion.

8. **Book of Confessions**. Following the UPCUSA practice, the southern Presbyterians eventually adopted a pluralistic approach to confessions, allowing ordinands to profess their adherence to a number of confessions (at least one of them inspired by Karl Barth) instead of holding to the single standard of Westminster. This act made it clear that the denomination of the future could not possibly have a unified doctrinal posture.

9. **Leftist Social Pronouncements**. During the unrest of the 1960s, many of the liberal clergy began to make left-leaning statements (on abortion, homosexuality, economics, Vietnam, nuclear arms, etc.); galling to some members was the involvement of clergymen in public protests and marches, particularly when those causes rankled the beliefs and traditional views of southern evangelicals. Some Officers viewed the clergy as more involved in social activism than in preaching the Word.

10. **Ecumenical Involvement**. The PCUS, in lock-step with the UPCUSA, became increasingly involved in ecumenical organizations (e.g., the World and National Council of Churches, COCU [Churches of Christ Uniting]). Conservatives clearly saw this as yielding a diluted witness and a threat to Presbyterian government, if Bishops were routine.

From a review of these and other causes, one can sense that the founders of the PCA had substantial concerns and reasons to fear that their faith would not be permitted or propagated in the liberal Presbyterianism, which was only beginning. From the vantage point of the early 21st century, they were clearly correct, and the mainline church—which united in 1983, a date by which the earlier differences between northern and southern branches had largely disappeared—has only accelerated and continued in those liberal directions. Furthermore, during the 1970-2000 generation, that mainline communion lost over one-third of its communicant members, only a fraction of which gravitated to the PCA.

The Organization of the PCA

Beginning in 1969, southern Presbyterian evangelicals took more and more steps toward separation. A Declaration of Commitment—which was published as a full-page ad in select secular newspapers across the South—was signed by over 500 ministers in 1969. In this Declaration, these Protestants testified that regardless of liberalizing trends, they would hold firmly to Scripture and Confession. The Concerned Presbyterians and Presbyterian Churchmen United would soon cooperate in additional efforts.

The conservatives, who had long been working from within and in keeping with the constitutional measures afforded, saw the 1971 General Assembly as their last stand. They were unsuccessful in electing a moderator (D. James Kennedy of Fort Lauderdale, FL, was nominated), unsuccessful in halting the liberal slide, and viewed themselves, resultingly, as a minority, which might not be tolerated. Following the Assembly defeats, plans were made to erect a Steering Committee for a Continuing Presbyterian Church.

The *Presbyterian Journal* sponsored an annual conference in the mountains of Western North Carolina over Labor Day weekend. Following the 1971 Assembly's handwriting on the wall, three representatives from each of the four dissenting groups above (Presbyterian Journal, PEF, Concerned Presbyterians, and Presbyterian Churchmen United) formed the Steering Committee. They committed themselves to two immediate goals: (1) avoidance of separation from the PCUS, except as a last resort; and (2) attempts to negotiate an "escape clause" (by which a congregation could constitutionally withdraw from the PCUS with their property) during the ongoing discussions of mainline Reunion. As a token, unionists promised these conservatives—in an attempt to garner southern support for Reunion—an escape clause. However, following the 1972 General Assembly, it became clear that an escape clause would not be forthcoming, despite earlier assurances. Thus, in February 1973 the Steering Committee of 12 called for a Convocation of Sessions to be held in Atlanta (Westminster Presbyterian church) in May of 1973. Growing out of that meeting, a 40-man committee was appointed to plan for the new denomination, should things not be turned around at the June 1973 General Assembly. Needless to say, things were not turned around.

Then an Advisory Convention was held in August at Asheville, NC, to hear the reports of the 40-man committee, which had presented structural and constitutional provisions. Following that Advisory Convention, the announcement was made that the First General Assembly of the National Presbyterian Church (the original name of the PCA, which was used only one year and then changed to the PCA in response to the threat of litigation from a mainline church) would meet on December 4, 1973 (the anniversary date of the founding of the Presbyterian Church in the Confederate States of America) at the Briarwood Presbyterian Church in Birmingham, AL.

The PCA thus commenced with 260 churches and 55,000 communicant members, a significant beginning and one that immediately surpassed the size and membership of other longer-standing conservative denominations. At that first General Assembly the church adopted the WCF and an amended BCO. Moreover, four permanent committees were appointed, drawing on the previous work of earlier dissenting groups, as follows:

1. Committee on Administration;
2. Christian Education and Publications;
3. Mission to the World;
4. Mission to the United States (now MNA).

PEF donated its evangelistic work to MUS and its foreign missionaries to MTW, thus giving the infant church a jumpstart on missions.

Following the formation of the PCA in 1973, several other large PCUS churches left the southern church to link arms with the PCA in the late 1970s and early 1980s. As these large, evangelical churches entered the PCA stream, they were determined to keep alive the ministries of evangelism and missions.

For nearly a decade, the PCA continued to attract a small stream of dissenting mainline congregations. They also explored union—not the type experienced in the PCUS but a union based on strong confessional and biblical commonalities—with the OPC and the RPCES. One of the early advisors to the PCA was Dr. Francis Schaeffer, who suggested that—in view of the tendency to splinter among small churches and in light of the sincere agreements on matters with the OPC and RPCES—the PCA should discuss honest, not coerced, union with these other churches, who also shared a rejection of the modernizing trend. Accordingly, in the early 1980s, following lengthy and spirited discussions, votes were taken on whether or not to unite with the OPC and the RPCES (this was called Joining and Receiving to indicate that matters of Confession and government were not being negotiated but accepted *en toto*). The PCA did not vote to J&R with the OPC but did with the RPCES, which also approved. Accordingly, in 1982 the PCA Joined and Received the RPCES. Another invitation was made to the OPC in 1984, but this attempt failed to receive the requisite number of PCA presbyteries.

Thus in 1983, the PCA was enlarged by non-southern churches and had a more national presence. Growth continued during the 1980s, and by the early 1990s, the PCA had over 1,000 churches and membership had grown nearly four-fold. In 1998, the PCA celebrated a quarter-century of development, and by the end of 2001, the PCA had 1,227 churches, 3,082 ministers, and 247,556 communicant members.

Along with growth in national terms, it also had a large foreign mission force, a college (in Chattanooga) and seminary (in St. Louis), an impressive campus ministry (RUF), and denominational headquarters in suburban Atlanta. Of course, along with these accomplishments, there were also matters of ministry and faith that were controversial and potentially divisive. Vigorous debate and strong differences of opinion during the 1990s illustrated that the PCA was far from unified on a number of issues, ranging from gender roles, matters of public morality, the degree of adherence to the WCF, and missions strategy. These debates had the potential of further splitting the PCA but also were opportunities to apply biblical principles to matters of ministry.

One other thing was clear: even if the debates were intense and heated at General Assemblies, those forums did not always dictate or represent what each congregation did in its own local context. Normally, when one could measure the PCA by its grass roots, it was a strong church.

Bibliography on the PCA: Officer candidates should familiarize themselves with the development and history of the PCA. Among the books to consult are:

- Otto Whittaker, *Watchman, Tell it True* (a book that focuses on the life and role of the Rev. Bill Hill and his struggles with liberalism).
- Kennedy Smartt, *I Am Reminded* (an anecdotal account by one of the founders of the PCA).
- Frank Smith, *The History of the Presbyterian Church in America* (a full and historical collection on the founding of the PCA).
- John Edwards Richards, *The Historical Birth of the Presbyterian Church in America.*
- Paul Settle, *To God All Praise and Glory* (a pictorial and brief history of the PCA by one of its founders, commissioned for the 25th anniversary).
- Morton Smith, *How the Gold Has Become Dim* (a studious apology for why the formation of the PCA was necessary and a testimony from one of its founding fathers and first Stated Clerk).

For additional study; as a type of ecclesiastical vaccination, it might be helpful for Officers to read the short analysis below about the tactics by which liberals have made inroads.

HOW PRESBYTERIANS LOST THE BATTLE

By Gary North

About 23 years ago,37 I began a project which, if things go well, I will complete early next year. I haven't worked full time on it. In fact, I let it sit for about 21 years. But it has fascinated me the whole time. It is a study of how the modernists (theological liberals) took over the northern Presbyterian Church.

After a detailed study of the theology, strategy, and tactics of the modernists, I have come to some preliminary conclusions about how they did it. More than this: I think I have been able to discover a strategy which they successfully used to capture not only the northern Presbyterians but virtually all the mainline denominations except the Missouri Synod Lutherans.

Someday, I hope to supervise the publication of a series of detailed volumes devoted to a denomination-by-denomination account of how and when the modernists captured each one. I realize that the market for this series will be limited, but it needs to be produced, not only for historical reasons, but also for reasons of institutional self-defense in the future. We need to see to it that when revival comes, and God's churches grow, that we do not experience a repetition of these events. We may make new institutional mistakes, but I pray we will not make the old ones.

I have analyzed the modernists' program of conquest for the Presbyterian Church U.S.A. (northern Presbyterians) from 1869 until 1936. The liberals adopted a strategy which was consistent with their worldview, and then they adopted tactics that were consistent with their strategy. It is important to understand that this program was consistent. It was not devised in some back room (so far as I know), but it had a logic of its own. This logic was a development of the theology of liberalism-modernism.

The conservatives in the Presbyterian Church, U.S.A. did not see what their opponents were doing after 1895. They did not devise a counter-strategy. The old rule of politics governed the development within the Church: you can't fight something with nothing. The consistency of the modernists was based on their willingness to work out the implications of their worldview within the context of the denomination. It is my contention that a majority of the evangelicals also were consistent to their theology, and this is why they surrendered until 1923 without a major fight, and why, when they began to resist in 1923 they had in principle lost the battle by 1926.

Let us consider the theology of modernism and its implications. I can do no more than summarize very briefly the basic position. In my forthcoming book on the capture of the Church, *Rotten Wood*, I will fill in the historical details and provide the documentation.

Presuppositions

There is no permanent plan of God which provides coherence to the universe.
There is no inerrant and permanent verbal revelation of God to man.
There must therefore be an inerrant word of man in order to provide coherence in the universe.

---

37 This article, which I believe was subsequently developed into a book-length monograph, originally appeared in *Christian Reconstruction*, Vol. IX, No. 5 (Sept./Oct., 1985).

This inerrant word is evolving: "dynamic," "progressive," "process-oriented," "dialectical," and therefore relative over time.

Creeds are men's verbal representations of a symbolic (zero fixed content) representation of God, rather than men's verbal approximations of God's permanent word.

The essence of the church's ministry is concern for mankind rather than the defense of the integrity of God's word.

The unity of God must be reflected in the unity of man.

The unity of man must be reflected in the unity of man's institutions.

Creeds divide mankind.

Any institutional disunity must be smoothed over dialectically, until such time as the forces of unity can purge out the pro-creedal elements.

Strategy

The goal is the attainment of institutional control of as large an organization as possible.

Seminaries are targeted first: the recruiting of the next generation, plus your enemies pay your salary. Also, an educational institution is inherently cooperative: financing and recruiting.

Denominational colleges are targeted (same reasons).

Emphasis on certification by establishment humanist institutions of higher learning as the preferred (later, required) criteria for service in denominational institutions of higher learning.

Emphasis on educational credentials for highest church positions. (liberal and ecumenical ethos dominates formal education generally, as does the doctrine of "academic freedom," which can be transferred to other institutions.)

Centralized agencies within the church are targeted: your enemies pay your salary. Also, a denominational institution is inherently cooperative: financing and recruiting.

Personal recruiting of bright or popular young people.

Recruiting of wealthy or powerful laymen with offers of prestige positions or the promise of future influence.

Infiltration of the church's publishing outlets.

Creation of new publishing outlets within the church.

Institutional confrontations are initially avoided.

Cooperation with other churches or ecclesiastical groups is fostered (ecumenicists inside all groups support each other).

Reliance on other people's money at every stage, if possible.

Tactics

The Bible's language is adopted to advance the cause of the unification of man.

Calls for creedal discipline are resisted in the name of toleration ("pluralism").

Emphasis is placed on practical religion: emotional benefits, feeding the hungry, etc.

Shared concern for mankind is placed on a par (and then above) "divisive" concern for creeds or doctrines.

Pleas for peace are repeated whenever the creedalists begin to organize their forces.

Implementation of all procedural protections against false charges of heresy, and the issuing of warnings concerning the high costs of such a fight, and the institutional sanctions to be imposed on people who bring unprovable accusations.

All battles against enemies are conducted in terms of institutional criteria, not creeds: toleration, peace, and (in the final stages) obedience to hierarchical authority.

Mastery of the church's bureaucratic machinery. Placement of allied forces in these permanent bureaucratic positions.

Strengths and Weaknesses

The great strength of the Presbyterian Church was its commitment to scholarship. It withstood the inroads of higher criticism for many decades. Eventually, these assaults had to be met, but after the successful heresy trial of Prof. Charles Briggs in 1893, the orthodox forces never again mounted a successful heresy trial. This gave the modernists a "free ride." The seminaries, Princeton excepted, suffered greatly as a result. Modernism, especially anti-biblical textual criticism, eroded the theological foundations, while Darwinism was beating down the gates. The compromises with Darwinsim made by President McCosh of Princeton University and even by B. B. Warfield made it very difficult for those who followed to shore up the defenses.

Once Darwinian categories got into the thinking of Presbyterian college and seminary professors, they were willing to draw the relevant conclusions. Their Darwinism was not fully self-consistent. It had to be sold to the faithful, so it could not be presented in an unvarnished form. But the basic presuppositions were adhered to: denial of six-day creation, denial of a short history for mankind, denial of a clear-cut distinction between saved and lost. Eventually, the more liberal conclusions took root: unity of man, necessity of environmental transformation in order to "save" man, and the elevation of civil government to the position of saving institution. This did not take place immediately or widely; it was limited prior to 1936 primarily to the New York Presbytery and the graduates of Union Theological Seminary in New York City and Auburn Theological Seminary in upstate New Your. But the conservatives found it too expensive or institutionally impossible to dislodge the heretics in New York.

The modernists within the Church had formidable intellectual opponents, unlike the liberals in other denominations. These conservative scholars, most notably Warfield, the Hodges, and later, J. Gresham Machen, were not fooled by textual criticism, and they recognized that the liberals were promoting a rival religion. Nevertheless, the forthright stand taken by Machen after 1922 was insufficient to rally the troops. There was a very good reason for this: the troops had compromised with weak theology as early as 1869, and they grew weary of fighting "mere theological" battles in an age which was consummately pragmatic. The conservatives wanted peace above all, and results secondarily. They wanted successful churches and effective mission programs, and contention over the "fine points of theology" were viewed as detracting from the "real work of the Church," namely, growth. It was this implicit pacifism and pragmatism of the conservatives that the modernists successfully exploited.

The Modernists' Advantages

They had many. First, their leaders had considerable and growing protection in numerous seminaries. So did the conservatives; academic leaders, but the latter group was not cutting against the Church's grain. The modernists' leaders needed this protection early in the conflict. They needed money which would come despite the contrast between the laymen and the professors. Laymen could feel more secure about mounting an attack against a liberal preacher, or even easier, against an as-yet un-ordained man. They could never feel secure in an attack on an entrenched intellectual, whose argumentative skills were great, and whose institutional protection was greater.

Next, the modernists had the spirit of the age with them. The spread of Darwinism, the acceptance of political pluralism, the rhetoric of democracy, and the rise of Progressivism and liberalism all combined to give the modernists outside support. They could raise money from such sources, and for their opponents to fight them, they would have to challenge the spirit of the age. It was not random that Presbyterian fundamentalist William Jennings Bryan's overwhelming public relations defeat by Clarence Darrow at the Scopes' trial in 1925 was followed the next year by the defeat of conservatives in the Presbyterian Church and also by major setbacks for conservatives in the Northern Baptist Church. Embarrassment gutted the conservatives; it took over 50 years for them to begin to recover.

Conclusion

The modernists steadily gained ground in the Presbyterian Church because few men stood their ground and refused to let the modernists take it. The modernists did not have anything like a majority until after 1936. They had a plurality, however, because the creedal Presbyterians did not have the dedicated support of the conservatives. The seekers of power joined forces with the seekers of peace. Thus it has always been. The result was the capture of the Presbyterian Church, U.S.A. by those who did not believe in the creeds of the Church, but who did not attempt to change this creed until 1967. They bided their time, mobilized their troops, and won on the battlefield. Should we do any less?

****

Officers should also ask their pastors or the teacher of this course for information about their own regional presbytery.

****

Officers Duties

Earlier as we perused the BCO, we skipped over a few chapters, reserving them for this final session. We now return to summarize BCO chapters 8-9 and 12 on the duties of Officers. The duties of Elders are charted in chapters 8 and 12; the duties of Deacons are set forth in BCO 9.

Elders' Duties

The various biblical titles for Elders are reviewed in BCO 8-1 to define further the work, which is "one of dignity and usefulness." The qualifications, which summarize but do not exactly reproduce those in Timothy and Titus, are contained in 8-2.

A variety of duties are listed in BCO 8-3 for the office of Elder. The following are important aspects of this office. The Elder as an undershepherd serving Christ is to:
- Watch over the flock entrusted to their care; this task indicates that Elders should view themselves as shepherds and care for the overall health and nurture of the sheep.
- Guard against corruptions of doctrine or morals that might root in the church; they must know what is being taught and be able to separate truth from error.

- Serve, participate in, and take oversight of the spiritual interests in their own church as well as in the larger church through presbytery and General Assembly.
- Visit people in their homes; this shepherding task does not belong to the pastor alone.
- Visit the sick; ministry by Elders in hospitals is important although frequently ignored.
- Instruct those who are lacking in biblical knowledge.
- Comfort the grieving—the Elders have a vital role when there is a death in the church.
- Care for the overall spiritual development of the children of the church.
- Pray with and for people—an Elder should be comfortable praying with members.
- Assist the Minister of the Word in seeking fruit that blooms from the preaching of the Word.

In addition, an Elder is to set an example among the flock in several ways. *First*, he is to model exemplary character in the church. *Second*, he is to embody and practice the normal duties, which are expected from non-ordained and growing Christians. *Third*, he is to be a leader in evangelizing.

Moreover, certain joint aspects of the office of Elder are given in BCO 12, and the companion chapter (13) discusses the presbytery. Chapter 12 specifies that the Minister(s), along with the ruling Elders, comprise the Session. Its quorum is at least half of the ruling Elders or three (12-1), if the session has more than five Elders. The pastor is normally the moderator (12-2) unless an emergency or conflict-of-interest is present. BCO 12-5, then, enumerates other duties of the office of Elder, and this set of duties emphasizes Elders acting in corporate capacity. They are uniquely to:

- Examine and receive persons for membership into the church;
- Discipline or admonish members who are delinquent;
- Make sure that parents present their children for baptism (hence, it would be hypocritical and impossible for a man to serve as Elder who does not practice what he preaches in this area);
- Dismiss members to other churches and provide letters authenticating their good standing;
- Examine, ordain, and install additional Officers who are elected by the church;
- Review the proceedings of the Deacons;
- Approve and adopt the budget;
- Approve, subject to BCO 25, matters affecting the property of the church;
- Call congregational meetings when necessary;
- Oversee and establish all Bible classes which meet in the church, including Sunday schools, the WIC, the MIC, and other special Bible studies;
- Promote world missions and emphasize the importance of the Great Commission;
- Call for offerings for special purposes;
- Oversee the worship and preaching, as well as all services hosted by the church;
- Lead worship if the Minister is not present;
- Determine the best ways to minister and allocate the church's resources;
- Serve as commissioners to the higher courts; and
- Carry out the lawful injunctions of the higher courts.

The session normally meets monthly but is required to meet at least quarterly. Minutes are kept of the meetings (which are opened and closed with prayer), and the Session is to keep a record of baptisms, deaths, and dismission of members (BCO 12-8).

BCO 8-4 distinguishes two orders of Elders: (a) Teaching Elders and (b) Ruling Elders. The duties and accountability of the Teaching Elder is described in 8-4 through 7. Ruling Elders, who date back to the time of the OT, are appointed by God to govern and assist (8-8) the Teaching Elders. Our constitution is also clear that both classes of Elders (teaching and ruling) have the same authority.

Deacons' Duties

The office of Deacons is "ordinary and perpetual," (BCO 9-1) and it is designed to express sympathy and service of Christianity as well as the communion of saints, following the example of Christ. The duties of Deacons are set forth in BCO 9-2, including the following:

- Minister to those in need, to the sick, the lonely, and those in distress—Deacons are to take the initiative and look for these needs in the church;
- Develop good stewardship ("the grace of liberality") and plan the most effective ways of collecting the offerings—we make sure that this task, however, does not require Deacons to avoid public worship;
- Disburse the church's offerings to the causes budgeted or stipulated;
- Care for the property of the church—not only the church plant but any other properties (Manse? School? Other buildings? BCO 9-2 also makes it clear that Deacons cannot exchange church property, though, without approval of the Session and consent of the congregation)—and keep things in suitable repair;
- Submit to the supervision and authority of the Elders in the discharge of these duties.

This office is so important that should there, for any reason, be a shortage of servants, the tasks shall devolve to the session.

The qualifications for the office of Deacon are given in BCO 9-3. Other organizational matters for the diaconate are provided in BCO 9. The pastor is an advisory member of the Diaconate. The Board of Deacons elects its own Chairman, Secretary, and a treasurer (who may or may not be a member of the Board but is always accountable to it). Their minutes are kept by the Secretary, and they are presented to the Session for review. Since these two offices are to work together closely, it is wise for them to meet together periodically to discuss common matters. Godly women may be appointed by the Session as diaconal assistants (not ordained; 9-7)

Over the years, we have also found it helpful, in this final session of the training course, to inform the candidates about the practical organization of the local church. Among the topics we discuss are:

- The unique history of the particular church;
- Meeting times for the boards;
- The committees of each board;
- Types of service to expect if installed;

- Particular difficulties or warnings;
- Where to find other resources.

****

Officer Examinations

One of the final aspects of Officer training is to prepare candidates to take their vows meaningfully and to prepare them for the process that leads to that. The process leading to election, ordination, and installation is set forth in BCO 24. Each church (24-1) is to follow this procedure, which begins with the requirement to publicize the date of election at least one month in advance. Much, of course, has to be done prior to that. The Session shall remind the congregation of the biblical qualifications and invite their suggestions (which are not formally nominations, because the Session must make sure that only properly qualified candidates are nominated). A training period is assumed, and after some appropriate training and before the congregational election, each "prospective Officer shall be examined in his Christian experience, his knowledge of the system of doctrine, government, discipline contained in the Standards, the duties" of his office, and "his willingness to give assent to the questions required for ordination." (24-1) The Session, then, shall examine the prospective candidates and "then report to the congregation before election day those eligible for election." In keeping with our government as depicted above, it is only the Session that can properly examine and determine fitness for office. The Elders are the ones entrusted by Christ with the oversight, recruitment, and training of new Officers, and only those who have first been tested (1 Tim. 3:9-13) should be recommended to the congregation.

After the training period—which should adequately prepare the candidate in all the areas of examination as per BCO 24-1—the Session should examine the candidates. We have included several sample examinations that our church has used below (See Appendix E). The Session may ask the candidate to write out or orally give his testimony (see Session 1 above); moreover, the Session may also examine a candidate in writing or orally over the duties of his office, the qualifications of his office, and his adherence to our doctrinal and governmental standards. This is one of the most important functions of Elders, and they should remember that they are to guard the deposit (2 Tim. 1:14) and the future faithfulness of the church by this process. They may, accordingly, approve or disapprove of candidates or request that they study certain areas more before a re-examination.

After the Elders approve the examinations of candidates, they may then either recommend them all or only certain ones to the congregation. All recommended candidates must be announced a week before the actual election. On the day of election, the moderator proposes a question to the congregation (24-4: "Are you now ready to proceed to the election of additional Ruling Elders (or Deacons) from the slate presented?"). If the congregation approves, they may proceed to voting by private ballot without additional nominations. If a member of the congregation wishes to nominate a man who has been approved for office by the Session—but not one who has not been examined and approved—that member may nominate a candidate for election. The Session may also make its recommendation of candidates if floor nominees are made. After hearing the Session's report on candidates, a church member may move at any time that the nominations be closed and that the church proceed to the elections. All nominees must receive a majority of the votes cast (24-1), and after the conclusion of the election, the Session shall set a date for a service of ordination or installation following a worship service (24-5). At that time, the Officers-elect are to publicly affirm their vows contained in BCO 24-5. Accordingly, the issue of doctrinal faithfulness (subscription) should have been studied in the training class.

Officer Vows and Confessional Integrity.

Each Officer is asked to answer vows for his respective office meaningfully. The first ordination vow commits us to be guided by Scripture as our only infallible rule of faith and practice. This requires that the Officer have the strongest possible loyalty to the Bible, not only as his own spiritual lifeline but also as the guidebook for his office. The second vow (see below) asks him to commit to the Westminster standards as containing the truths the church is to maintain. Accordingly, if he changes his views or did not understand these standards in the first place, he is to take the initiative, as an act of submission, to notify the court to which he submits (local church Officers notify the session, ministers notify their presbyteries). Since there is much misunderstanding and debate about the meaning, history, and application of this second ordination vow, crucial historical and biblical information is supplied below.[38]

> The Adopting Act: An Adequate Model
>
> One of the hotly contested issues in confessional Presbyterian churches is just how does one maintain doctrinal orthodoxy. Most Calvinist churches have struggled with the best method to accomplish this over the years. For a good introduction to the subject in general, Officers might wish to order or consult *The Practice of Confessional Subscription* (1995, rpr. 2001), available The Covenant Foundation, 648 Goldenwood Court, Powder Springs, GA 30127.
>
> American Presbyterians sought to balance the oppressiveness of a rigid hierarchical church with the anarchy of a lowerarchical libertinism. One method to do so was her subscription (literally "to sign under or to agree by signing one's name" to a written instrument). What the American Presbyterian Church intended initially may be seen in the 1729 Adopting Act, a posture that was reinforced at numerous times over the next century.
>
> By this important and official act in 1729, the Presbyterian Church announced her determination to be an explicitly confessional church. In this historic act, she clearly delineated the requirements of orthodoxy and orthopraxy. Although there has been considerable debate, the records themselves are clear that the intent was to establish a doctrinal integrity. If we allow the record to speak for itself, that approach and conclusion is clear.
>
> The canon of interpretation for constitutional law, or Presbyterian history for that matter, is to give preferential weighting to the official acts, unless explicitly indicated to the contrary. In seeking a consensus, a framework for discussion, which would later become known as the preliminary act, was adopted. The preliminary act is certainly *preliminary*. And it is definitely

---

38 The other vows are fairly straightforward. In the third vow, Officers are to "approve" the principles of biblical polity in the BCO (note the contrast between mere approval of polity principles with the high requirement to "believe" the Scriptures and secondarily to "receive and adopt" the Westminster standards in the earlier vows). Officers are also to pledge to support their office with a godly example, regardless of opposition or temptation, and they are to submit to their brothers in the same office. This means that Officers vow to work for the purity and unity of the church, and sometimes they must—for the good of that purity and unity—follow the advice of their other brothers.

important. However, it is not more important than the *final* act. To reverse such weighting is to impose a later will on our forefathers 250 years after the fact and disallow them a rebuttal. To interpret the preliminary act as preeminent, moreover, is to fail to take into account the changes of mind, the refining of opinions, and the role of deliberative reflection in this assembly. Instead, it would be the better course to accord the actual Adopting Act the priority in our interpretation. It was, after all, the Act adopted by the 1729 Assembly. Short of explicit (not inferential) proof that these did not mean what they said, we must remain satisfied with their act.

The Adopting Act did not leave the definition of "essential and necessary articles" up to the individual nor up to future posterity. It was precisely that "posterity" earlier mentioned, which they hoped to protect by this Adopting Act. The Adopting Act took care of the definition of "essential and necessary articles" by explicitly stating them in the immediate context. To paraphrase the scriptural hermeneutical canon of "Scripture interprets Scripture," in this case "Minute interprets Minute." The immediate act itself and the succeeding minutes define for us the answer to this much-inflated problem.

This discussion below is an attempt to clarify some misunderstanding of the Adopting Act. In this documentary witness we have the authors' own clarification. In God's own providence their own explication of their intent is displayed. There are few cases in all of history, which provide so clear a contemporaneous account of original intent. Every Elder would do well to be acquainted with this historic and courageous act.

The sources (with page references supplied in parentheses) are from Guy Klett's *Minutes of the Presbyterian Church in the United States of America, 1706-1788* (Philadelphia, PA: Presbyterian Historical Society, 1965) and the *Minutes* of General Assemblies (Vol. I spanning the years 1789-1820 and Vol. II from 1821-1837.) Contained below is as little commentary as possible, with as much of the actual record being given as it originally appears on the subject in the Minutes.

Certainly, some moderns may wish to disagree with or depart from these ancient guideposts, but before doing so, they might recall the wisdom of G. K. Chesterton, who one said, "Before you pull any fence down, always pause long enough to find out why it was put there in the first place." The collection below of early Presbytery/Synod/General Assembly actions on this subject is intended to, at least, permit Officer candidates to view the reason for the usefulness of this fence.

The Adopting Act: A Documentary Witness39

By 1728, the overture that would lead to the Adopting Act reached the attention of the Synod. The overture was as follows: "There being an overture presented to the Synod in writing having Reference to the Subscribing of the Confession of Faith &c. The Synod judging this to be a very important Affair unanimously concluded to defer ye Consideration of it till the next Synod." (p. 98) The 1729 Adopting Act is recorded for Presbyterian posterity in these words: The Committee brought in an Overture upon the Affair of the Confession, which after long debating upon it, was agreed upon *in haec verba.*

---

39 Reprinted from David W. Hall and Joseph H. Hall, *Paradigms in Polity*, Copyright, The Covenant Foundation, Oak Ridge, TN, pp. 348-364; used with permission.

Altho' the Synod do not claim or pretend to any Authority of imposing our faith upon other men's Consciences, but do profess our just Dissatisfaction with and Abhorrence of such Impositions, and do utterly disclaim all Legislative Power and Authority in the Church, being willing to receive one another, as Christ has received us to the Glory of God, and admit to fellowship in sacred ordinances all such as we have Grounds to believe Christ will at last admit to the Kingdom of Heaven; yet we are undoubtedly obliged to take Care that the faith once delivered to the Saints be kept pure and incorrupt among Us, and so handed down to our Posterity. And do therefore agree, yt all the Ministers of this Synod, or that shall hereafter be admitted into this Synod, shall declare their agreement in and approbation of the Confession of Faith with the larger and shorter Catechisms of the assembly of Divines at Westminster, as being in all the essential and necessary Articles, good Forms of sound words and systems of Christian Doctrine; and do also adopt the said Confession and Catechisms as the Confession of our Faith. And we do also agree, yt all the Presbyteries within our Bounds shall always take Care not to admit any Candidate of the Ministry into the Exercise of the sacred Function, but what declares his Agreement in opinion with all the Essential and Necessary Articles of said Confession, either by subscribing the said Confession of Faith and Catechisms, or by a verbal Declaration of their assent thereto, as such Minister or Candidate shall think best. And in Case any Minister of this Synod or any Candidate for the Ministry shall have any Scruple with respect to any Article or Articles of sd. Confession or Catechisms, he shall at the Time of his making sd. Declaration declare his Sentiments to the Presbytery or Synod, who shall notwithstanding admit him to ye Exercise of the Ministry within our Bounds and to Ministerial Communion if the Synod or Presbytery shall judge his scruple or mistake to be only about articles not Essential and necessary in Doctrine, Worship or Government. But if the Synod or Presbytery shall judge such Ministers or Candidates erroneous in Essential and necessary Articles of Faith, the Synod or Presbytery shall declare them incapable of Communion with them. And the Synod do solemnly agree, that none of us will traduce or use any opprobrious Terms of those yt differ from us in these extra-essential and not-necessary points of Doctrine, but treat them with the same friendship, kindness and brotherly Love, as if they had not differed from us in such Sentiments.

At 3 o Clock P.M. all the Ministers of this Synod now present except one yt declared himself not prepared viz. After proposing all the Scruples yt any of them had to make against any Articles and Expressions in the Confession of Faith and larger and shorter Catechisms of the Assembly of Divines at Westminster, have unanimously agreed in the solution of those Scruples, and in declaring the sd. Confession and Catechisms to be the Confession of their faith, excepting only some Clauses in ye 20. and 23. Chapters, concerning which Clauses, the Synod do unanimously declare, yt they do not receive those Articles in any such sense as to suppose the civil Magistrate hath a controlling Power over Synods with Respect to the Exercise of their ministerial Authority; or Power to persecute any for their Religion, or in any sense contrary to the Protestant succession to the Throne of Great Britain.

The Synod observing that Unanimity, Peace and Unity which appeared in all their Consultations and Determinations relating to the Affair of the Confession did unanimously agree in giving Thanks to God in solemn Prayer and Praises. (pp. 103-104)

In subsequent years, the church sought to make sure of the intent of this act. So, as early as the very next year, there is both an indirect reference as well as a direct reference to the previous year's act (1729) and its implication for the young church. In 1730, a candidate was examined and his scruples to the Confession were considered. The records state,

Mr. David Evans having proposed all the Scruples he had to make about any articles of the Confession and Catechisms & c: to the Satisfaction of the Synod, and declared his adopting the Westminster Confession of faith and Catechisms agreeable to the last years adopting Act, he was unanimously received in as a Member again. Whereas some Persons have been dissatisfied at the Manner of wording our last years Agreement about the Confession & c: supposing some Expressions not sufficiently obligatory upon Intrants; overtured yt the Synod do now declare, that they understand those Clauses that respect the Admission of Intrants or Candidates in such a sense as to oblige them to receive and adopt the Confession and Catechisms at their Admission in the same Manner and as fully as the Members of the Synod did that were then present. Which overture was unanimously agreed to by the Synod. (p. 108)

The future implementation of the Adopting Act was to be based on the "same manner and as fully as the members of Synod did that were present" in 1729. Again this 1730 decision was unanimous. The first challenge to the act of 1729 is affirmed in the same direction and even to the same manner and fullness. The subsequent clarification in no way lessens the required adherence. The decision stands.

Later, the next year, in 1731, the official and original intent is expressed in the Minutes, as can be seen from the following. "Enquiry being made of Mr. Robert Cross as to his opinion relating to the Synod's Agreement with Reference to the Westminster Confession of Faith & c: The said Mr. Cross did declare his hearty Concurrence with what the Synod had done in yt Affair, and that he did accept of and adopt the said Confession of faith and Catechisms as the Confession of his faith." (p. 111) Thus the synod corroborated once again the earlier decision. There seems to be little disagreement with enforcement, and the presbyters were unanimous and clear themselves.

The Minutes from 1734 record:

Ordered yt the Synod make a particular Enquiry during the Time of their Meeting every Year, whether such Ministers as have been received as Members since the foregoing Meeting of the Synod have adopted, or have been required by the Synod, or by the Respective Presbrys to adopt the Westminster Confession and Catechisms with the Directory, according to the Acts of ye Synod made some Years since for yt Purpose, and yt also the Report made to the Synod in Answer to sd. Enquiry be recorded in our Minutes.

    Mr. Saml. Pumrey, Mr. James Martin, Mr. Robert Jamison and Mr. Saml. Hemphill declared for and adopted the Westminster Confession Catechisms and Directory commonly annexed, the former as the Confession of their faith and the latter as the Guide of their Practice in Matters of Discipline as far as may be agreeable to the Rules of Prudence & c: as in the adopting Acts of this Synod is directed.

    Mr. Willm. Tennent Jr. Mr. Andrew Archbold ordained; and Mr. Saml. Blair licensed, did each and every of them declare their Assent and Consent to the Westminster Confession and Catechisms and Directory annexed, according to the Intent of ye Act of Synod in yt Case made and provided. (p. 121)

Also the Minutes of 1735 continue the same testimony of clear understanding not only of the *extent* of adherence required by the Adopting Act but further even the *intent*.

Enquiry being made according to the order of last Synod, whether those admitted into any of our Presbrys since last Synod have adopted ye Westminster Confession of faith & Catechisms & c: according to ye adopting Act of the Synod, it was reported, yt Messrs, Isaac Chalker, Simon Horton and Saml. Blair ordained by the Presbry of East-Jersey, and Mr. Hugh Carlisle admitted into New-Castle Presbry have done it in the several Presbrys according to the order aforesaid. And Mrs. Isaac Chalker and Hugh Carlisle not having seen the adopting Act, have now had the same read to them, and do now concur in their assent to the Terms of the Adopting Act. Ordered yt each Presbry have the whole adopting Act inserted in their Presbry Book. (pp. 127-128)

Further, toward the end of the 1735 Synod, the Synod again endorsed the Adopting Act as follows.

Synod to make an order to the following Purpose.

First, That no Minister or Probationer coming in among us from Europe be allowed to preach in vacant Congregations until first his Credentials and Recommendations be seen and approved by the Pry unto which such Congregation doth most properly belong, and until he preach w̄ith approbation before sd. Pry and subscribe or adopt the westminster. Confessn. of Faith & Catechisms before said Pry in Manner and Form as they have done; and yt no Minister employ such to preach in his Pulpit until he see his Credentials and be satisfied, as far as may be, of his firm Attachment to sd. Confession & c: in opposition to the new upstart Doctrines & Schemes, particularly such as we condemned in Mr. H—ll's Sermons. (p. 132)

This persistent view is further exhibited in 1739, as the Synod continues to require adoption of the standards as earlier ordered: "Messrs. Zanchy, Alexander were after the usual Tryals ordained since the last Synod, and yt they did all of them adopt ye Westminster. Confession & c. according to ye order. of ye Synod in yt case provided." (p. 160)

The church was quite consistent on this matter as its earliest records uniformly reveal. If the study is confined to the official records of the church, the voice of the church is not ambiguous.

In 1736 the best confirmation of the adherence view is expressed. To the objective historian, this self-clarification from the original authors amidst the original records should be decisive for the interpretative question as to the intent of the Adopting Act's relevance. In answer to some questions arising from the churches in Paxton and Derry, the Synod's affirmation should be heard as a whole:

Ordered yt ye Minutes of ye last sedt. be read. The acct. of ye Fund not yet brought in.

The members appointed to draw up an overture on Mr. Hunter's affair report yt they have not done any Thing in yt affair on acct. yet they did not agree in their Judgments. The further Consideration of yt affair deferred till afterwards.

An overture of the Committee upon the Supplicatn. of ye People of Paxton and Derry was brought in and is a [s] followeth. That the Synod do declare, yt inasmuch as we understand yt many Persons of our Perswasion both more lately and formerly have been offended with some Expressions or Distinctions in the first or preliminary act of our Synod, contained in the printed Paper, relating to our receiving or adopting the westminster Confession & Catechisms & c: That in order to remove said offence and all jealousies yt have arisen or may arise in any of our

People's minds on occasion of sd. Distinctions and Expressions, the Synod doth declare, yt the Synod have adopted and still do adhere to the westminster. Confession Catechisms and Directory without the least variation or alteration, and without any Regard to sd. Distinctions. And we do further declare yt this was our meaning and true Intent in our first adopting of sd. Confession, as may particularly appear by our adopting act which is as followeth. All ye ministrs. of ye Synod now present (which were 18 in number except one yt declared himself not prepared) after proposing all the Scruples any of them had to make against any articles and Expressions in the Confession of faith and larger and shorter Catechisms of the Assembly of Divines at westminster have unanimously agreed in the solution of these Scruples and in declaring the said Confession and Catechisms to be the Confession of their Faith, Except only some Clauses in the 20th. and 23rd. Chapters; concerning which Clauses the Synod do unanimously declare that they do not receive these articles in any such sense as to suppose the civil Magistrate hath a controlling Power over Synods with respect to the Exercise of their ministerial Authority, or Power to persecute any for their Religion, or in any sense contrary to the Protestant Succession to the Throne of Great Britain.

And we hope and desire that this our Synodical Declaration and Explication may satisfy all our People as to our firm attachment to our good old received Doctrines contained in sd. Confession without the least variation or alteration, and that they will lay aside their Jealousies, yt have been entertained through occasion of the above hinted Expressions and Declarations as groundless. This overture approved *Nem. Contradicente* (without a negative vote). (pp. 141-142)

This declaration is an attempt to respond to some misunderstanding of the Adopting Act, providing for us here the author's own clarification. They wish to clarify what they intended in that 1729 Act. Would that we would heed it without the fetters of biased reconstructions. They use these words to make their positions well known and definitive: ". . . the Synod have adopted and *still do adhere* (emphasis added) to the westminster. Confession Catechisms and Directory *without the least variation or alteration* (emphasis added), and without any Regard to sd. Distinctions. And we do *further declare yt this was our meaning and true Intent* (emphasis added) in our first adopting of sd. Confession, as may particularly appear by our adopting act which is as followeth . . ." Then follows the extract from the original act. This subsequent Synod is granting for all history a certain clarification of the original intent of the Adopting Act. There are few cases in all of history which provide so clear a contemporaneous account of original intent. Its almost, as if anticipating later questions, these presbyters give a proleptic answer.

Further, this act once again states both the unanimity ("*Nemine Contradiction*" is the Latin for "without negative vote") and the desire for these Pastors to have their intent fully understood as adhering with "firm attachment" to the old form of confessional adherence "without the least variation or alteration." Listen to these authors themselves: "And we hope and desire that this our Synodical Declaration and Explication may satisfy all our People as to our firm attachment to our good old received Doctrines contained in sd. Confession without the least variation or alteration, and that they will lay aside their Jealousies, yt have been entertained through occasion of the above hinted Expressions and Declarations as groundless. This overture approved *Nem. Contradicente*." (p. 142)

The battle between the Old Side and the New Side has bearing on this matter beginning in 1743. In those Minutes from Synod, we find this protest expressing the Old Side sentiments.

1. We protest that it is the indispensable Duty of this Synod, to maintain and stand by the Principles of Doctrine, Worship and Government of the Church of Christ, as the same are summed up in the Confession of Faith, Catechisms and Directory composed by the Westminster Assembly, as being agreeable to the word of God, and which this Synod have owned, acknowledged and adopted; as may appear by our Synodical Records of the years 1729, 1729 [sic], 1736, which we desire to be read publickly.
2. We protest yt no Person, Minister or Elder should be allowed to sit and vote in this Synod, who hath not received, adopted, or subscribed the said Confessions, Catechisms and Directory, as our Presbyteries respectively do, according to our last Explication of the adopting Act. (p. 187)

The emphasized portions once again bear testimony to the intent of the Synod in regard to the Adopting Act. A few pages later, the Minutes of that same 1743 Synod express, "Again, Is not ye Continuance of Union with our protesting Brethren very absurd, when it is so notorious that both their Doctrine and Practice are so directly contrary to the adopting Act, whereby both They and we have adopted the Confession of Faith, Catechisms and Directory composed by the Westminster Assembly? In sum, a continued Union, in our Judgment, is most absurd and inconsistent, when it is so notorious, yt our Doctrine and Principles of Church Government, in many Points are not only diverse but directly opposite: For how can two walk together, except they be agreed?" (p. 190)

In 1745 after the division had begun, the Synod declared,

Every Person that is or has been a Member shall now voluntarily subscribe the Essential Agreements on wch. our Synod formerly was established and which are the general approved Agreements of our Churches. And as we think yt a subscription of these Articles will be a Renouncing Disorder and divisive Practice, and will when obtained lay a Foundation for Maintaining Peace, Truth and good Order, which was wt was desired in the Protest, by wch. the Brunswick Brethren stand excluded. We therefore in Compliance with the Request of these Brethren and in order to remove all Scruples propose that all yt are now or ever have been Member of this Synod shall subscribe the following fundamental articles and Agreements, as their Acts, and all who will do so shall be Members of this Synod. (p. 205)

By 1751 the quarreling sides began to pursue re-union. As they did the Old side was careful to record their previous agreements to the Confession of Faith publicly and officially, as well as to re-affirm the Adopting Act. Evidently the Adopting Act cut a large path across the collective memory of these American Presbyterians. They did not wish to forget this. Nor did they want their posterity to forget their consistent adherence to objective standards. The whole act may be read below, but special attention is drawn to the emphasized and pertinent words.

And tho we retain ye Same Sentiments of ye Work of God which we formerly did, Yet we esteem mutual Forbearance our Duty, Since We all profess ye Same Confession of Faith, & Directory of Worship; We wou'd therefor humbly propose to our Brethren of ye Synod of Philadelphia, yt all our former Differences be buried in perpetual Oblivion, & that for the Time to come both Synods be united in one; & thenceforth there be no Contention among us, but to carry it towards each other in ye most peaceable & brotherly Manner, wch. We are perswaded will be for ye Honour of our Master, the Credit of our Profession, & ye Edification of the Churches committed to our Care: Accordingly we appoint the Revd. Messrs. John Pearson, Gilbert Tennant, Ebenezer Pemberton, & Aaron Burr to be our Delegates to wait upon ye Synod of Philadelphia wt these Proposals, & if they Shall See meet to join wt us in this desireable Design, We think it wou'd be best to appoint a Commission of both the Synods to meet at such Time & Place as they shall choose And finally to determine this Affair And to preserve the Common Peace we wou'd desire that all Names of Distinction which have been made use of in ye later Times be for ever abolished, *that every Member give his Consent to the Westminster Confession of Faith & Directory, according to the Plan formerly agreed to by the Synod of Philadelphia in ye Year 1729* (emphasis added). Further yt every Member promise that after any Question has been determined by a Major Vote, he will actively concur or passively submit to the Judgment of ye Body, but if his Conscience permit him to comply wt neither of these, that then he shall be obliged peaceably to withdraw from our Synodical Communion without any Attempt to make a Schism or Division among us. This is not intended to extend to any Cases but those wch. ye Synod judge essential to ye maintaining of Doctrine Discipline & Worship; that all our present Congregations be acknowledged as Congregations belonging to ye Synod, but to belong to ye same Presbytery as they now do, till a favourable Opportunity presents for an advantageous Alteration. That we all agree to esteem & treat it as a culpable Evil to accuse any of our Members of Error in Doctrine or Immorality in Conversation any otherwise than by private Reproof, till ye Accusation has been brought before a regular Judicature & issued according to the known Rules of our Discipline. Signed P[per{ Order of the Synod.} (p. 229)

One scant year later (1752), in an official minute, this same suggestion is affirmed in these irenic words:"3dly: You have formerly declared that, tho' your Sentiments of what ye Esteem A Work of God Continued the same, yt ye judged mutual forbearance your Duty since we all profess the same Confession of Faith & Directory for Worship." (p. 235) Also any who desired to reunite were invited to re-affirm the previous intent of the Adopting Act.

As the committee laboring for re-union (from 1752-1758) met, they affirmed two indisputable pillars, which are pertinent to the study of the manner of confessional adherence in this controversial period. The first pillar is the mutual adherence by both Old Side and New Side to the WCF. The second pillar is the binding relevance of the Adopting Act as a precondition for ministerial fellowship. The intent and extent of the Adopting Act as defined in 1736 was still maintained. Later in 1752:

The Ministers & Elders before-mentioned first considered & agreed upon the following Articles as the Plan & Foundation of their Synodical Union.

   1.   They agree that the Westminster Confession of Faith, with the larger & shorter Catechisms be the publick Confession of their Faith *in such Manner as was agreed* (emphasis added) unto by the Synod of Philadelphia in the Year 1729 & to be Inserted in the latter End of this Book. And they declare their Approbation of the Directory of the Assembly of Divines at Westminster as the general Plan of Worship & Discipline" (p. 263).

These presbyters even desired to perpetuate their decision by including the Adopting Act of 1729 with the official papers of the Synod for posterity. Any hermeneutical canons that discount the conscious intent to leave behind an adopted definition of the body's own sentiments under question must be treated as suspect rather than revered.

One year later, in this same period of negotiation, in 1753, the Synod said, "3. Our professing, that mutual Forbearance as to different Sentiments, respecting, the late religious Appearances, was our Duty, Since *we all profess the Same Confession* (emphasis added) of Faith & Directory for Worship, And our desiring & hoping for a joynt Testimony to the late glorious Work of God, are not inconsistent, in as much as the Manner, in which we have proposed this particular is different from that of the others," (p. 286) once again affirming the common adherence to the WCF by both Synods.

In 1756 the Synod further clarified what orthopractical purpose the confessional standards would play in the reunited church. It was intended and affirmed that the WCF should serve as a "test of orthodoxy" in keeping with the "constitutional Act," which is clearly a reference to the 1729 Adopting Act: "We therefore Inform them, that *by Adopting the Westminster Confession, we only Intend Receiving it as a Test of Orthodoxy in this* (emphasis added) Ch[church]; & it is the Order of this Synod, that all who are licensed to preach the Gospel; or become Members of any Presbytery in our Bounds, Shall receive the Same, as the Confession of their Faith, according to our constituting Act, which we see no Reason to repeal." (p. 311)

In keeping with this consistent record, the 1758 Synod, the final one prior to reunion in 1759, stated the doctrinal conditions requisite for reunion, "2. That every Member give his Consent to the Westminster Confession of Faith & Directory according to the Plan agreed on in our Synod & that no Acts be made but concerning Matters that appear to be plain Duty or concerning Opinions that we believe relate to the great Truths of Religion, & that all publick and fundamental Agreements of this Synod Stand safe." (p. 323)

A little later in that same 1758 Synod, it was once again affirmed that both Old Side and New Side agreed on doctrinal adherence in theory. "3. You have formerly declared that tho your Sentiments of what you esteemed the Work of God continued the same yet you Judged mutual Forbearance your Duty, Since we all profess the same Confession of Faith & Directory for Worship. But now you Seem to Insist on a Joint Testimony for Such a glorious Work of God in the late religious Appearances as a Term of Union, by making it one of your Proposals for Peace & Union." (p. 325)

Also the 1758 Synod wrote the final version of the statement, which would spell out their self-understanding of the doctrinal basis of reunion. To disagree with their own, so deliberately crafted and worded self-definition, one would have to prove severe character flaw, ignorance, or malice concerning these men. In 1758 the final minute before reunion expressed the equation of the WCF as "an Orthodox and excellent system of christian [sic] doctrine" in these words:

1. Both Synods having always approved and Received the Westminster Confession of Faith, larger & shorter Catechisms, as an orthodox & excellent System of Christian Doctrine, founded on the Word of God; we do Still receive the same as the Confession of our Faith, and also

adhere to the Plan of Worship Government & Discipline contained in the Westminster Directory, strictly enjoining it on all our Members & probationers for the Ministry, that they preach & teach according to the form of Sound Words in sd. Confession & Catechisms, & avoid & oppose all Errors contrary thereto. (p. 334)

Moreover, an excerpt from a pastoral letter in 1797 reveals the attitude of early American Presbyterianism toward the WCF: "We take present occasion of declaring our uniform adherence to the doctrines contained in our Confession of Faith, in their present plain and intelligible form; and our fixed determination to maintain them against all innovations. We earnestly wish that nothing subversive of these doctrines may be suffered to exist, or to be circulated . . ." (p. 129)

It should be noticed once again that there was little ambiguity in this resolve. The General Assembly of 1797, if called to the witness stand, could only affirm: (1) their uniform adherence to the doctrines contained in the WCF, (2) that such uniform orthopraxis should be interpreted as referring to the "plain and intelligible form" of meaning and previous practice, (3) the Assembly's "fixed determination to maintain them against *all* innovations", and furthermore that (4) "nothing subversive of these doctrines may be suffered . . . or circulated among the churches." This was the tradition of the earliest polity.

In the year 1800 the Assembly cautioned, "That, on the other hand, the synod must be careful to ascertain that all the ministers and congregations belonging to the Presbytery do fully adopt, not only the doctrine, but the form of government and discipline of our Church." (p. 189) So careful were these Presbyterians that they even formally stated that lower courts must be zealous in requiring (not optional) that each congregation "fully adopt" (the terminology is not accidental) both the doctrine of the church as well as the forms of polity. By the year 1800, 71 years after the Adopting Act, the term "adopt" is still being perpetuated, and the attempt to hold to those original confessional standards is still required without the least variation or alteration.

In the 1804 "Narrative of Religion," the Assembly reiterated its orthopraxis in two places. The first declares the generic intent to keep the gates of the church up to shut out weakness and ignorance, thus allowing impurity: ". . . But if the gates of the church are opened to weakness and ignorance, she will soon be overflowed with errors, and with the wildest disorders. We shall bring the ministry into disgrace and contempt, which should be like the priesthood of Aaron, without blemish." (p. 300)

In the second revealing comment the Committee appointed to study whether to alter the Confession of Faith reported:

After a very serious attention to the subject committed to them, your committee have resolved to propose no alteration whatever, in the Confession of Faith and Catechisms of our church, and are clearly of opinion, that none ought to be attempted.

The creed of every church, as it ought to be derived immediately and wholly from the word of God, must be considered as standing on ground considerably different from that which supports the system of forms and regulations, by which worship shall be conducted and government administered. And if it be once rightly settled, can never be altered with propriety by any change of time, or external circumstances of the church.

Circumstances, indeed, may render it proper, in deducing a summary of faith from the Scripture, to dwell more largely and particularly on some points at one time than would be necessary at another; and every attentive and intelligent reader of our standards will probably remark, that the state of the church when our Confession and Catechisms were formed, was, in fact, the cause that its pious and learned authors expressed their sentiments on certain topics, especially such as relate to the controversies between Protestants and papists, more largely than would now be necessary, if the whole were to be formed anew. But still, as those sentiments are, we conceive, just in themselves, and as the particular delineation of them can do no harm, and will sometimes prove a guide both to the clergy and laity of our communion, we cannot wish to see any retrenchment made. It would give alarm to many of our people, who might suspect that this was but the introduction to innovations of more importance. And your committee will take the liberty to remark, that it is by no means to be considered as a vulgar or unfounded prejudice, when alarm is excited, by alterations and innovations in the creed of a Church. There are many reasons of the most weighty kind, that will dispose every man of sound judgment and accurate observation, to regard a spirit of change in this particular, as an evil pregnant with a host of mischiefs. It leads the infidel to say, and with apparent plausibility, that there can be no truth clearly revealed in Scripture; because not only its friends, of various sects, but of the same sect, pretend to see truths in it at one time, which, at another, they discover and declare to be falsehood. It hurts the minds of weak believers, by suggesting to them the same thought. It destroys the confidence of the people generally, in those who maintain a system which is liable to constant fluctuations. It violates settled and useful habits. It encourages those who are influenced by the vanity of attempting to improve what wise men have executed, or by mere love of novelty, to give constant disturbance to the church by their crude proposals of amendment. And it is actually found to open the door to lasting uneasiness, constant altercation, and finally, to the adoption of errors, a thousand fold more dangerous and hurtful than any that shall have been corrected. In a word, what was true when our Confession and Catechisms were formed, is now true. We believe that this truth has been most admirably and accurately drawn into view in these excellent performances. They have become venerable from their age. Our church has flourished under their influence; and we can see no reason to alter them. If there are a few things (and few they must be, and of less importance, if they exist at all) which it might be shown could be expressed more correctly, and in a manner less liable to objection, it is not proper, with a view to obtain this, to expose ourselves to the great inconveniences and injuries that have been specified. (p. 302)

A scant year later in the 1805 Assembly's "Narrative of Religion," we see more of the same, not less of the same as the Assembly confronted the tendency of the revivalists to diminish the role of creeds:

Consider, dear brethren, the pernicious tendency of their present disorganizing plan. Under the specious pretence of honouring the sacred Scriptures, they would persuade you to reject all written or printed creeds and forms of discipline, alleging that those who adopt such, substitute them for divine inspiration. But, dear brethren, we presume you need scarcely be informed of the absurdity of such insinuations. You know that we, you know that you yourselves, consider them differently. Confessions or creeds are only the doctrines which we believe to be revealed to us from heaven, collected from different parts of sacred Scripture, and brought into one view. Must not all who read their Bibles and believe them, form some opinion of what is taught therein? And where can be the criminality when they have thus searched and collected, to publish what they believe to be the truths of God? In so doing we act in open day, as children of the light, and do not leave the world to conjecture whether we be Pelagians, Semi-Pelagians, Catholics, Arminians, or Calvinists; or whether we differ essentially from them all. We do not leave those with whom we would unite in the most tender and endearing bonds, at a loss to know whether we believe or disbelieve what they esteem the essential doctrines of Christianity. Reject all written creeds! and why not with the same propriety all verbal ones? What must then follow? Those who believe our blessed Saviour to be no more than a mere man, and those who believe in his divine nature; those who believe that God will manifest an eternal displeasure against sin, and those who believe he will finally receive all wicked men and devils into his favour; in short, those who believe the truth, and those whose creed exhibits the most glaring errors and contradictions, may all unite together, enjoy the same privileges, and surround the same board of communion. Can light and darkness have fellowship together? Or can there be concord between Christ and Belial? Is there no necessity for a people, about to put themselves under the pastoral care of a shepherd, to know what kind of doctrines they are to be taught? Or is it perfectly indifferent which of the above contradictory systems they receive? But if we attend to their sentiments on church government and discipline, we will find them no less anti-scriptural, and subversive of all good order in Christ's kingdom. Their own declaration is, 'Christians have no power over one another to cut off, exclude, or unite.' (p. 327)

In the midst of this new tradition of disavowing creeds or confessions so characteristic of the revivalists, the Presbyterian Church did not agree. They labeled such efforts as "pernicious" and "subversive." This was no mild rebuke, but it was a scathing one. The Presbyterian General Assembly was adhering to confession as orthopraxis; and saw no "criminality" in that established and revered tradition. Still at this time, the weakening of the confessional adherence was not condoned.

Also from the 1806 "Narrative of Religion" (vis-a-vis the revivalists), the church proclaimed, "It should ever be recollected, that error in doctrine has a native tendency to produce immorality in practice; and therefore, that we should not be carried about by every wind of doctrine. . . . inasmuch as the church has been of late invaded by errors which strike at the very foundation of our faith and hope; such as the denial of the Godhead and atonement of the blessed Redeemer, the subjection of Holy Scripture to the most extravagant impulses of the heart of man. These, and other errors of a dangerous nature, have been industriously, and, alas! that the Assembly should be constrained to add, in some portions of our country, too successfully disseminated." (p. 357)

The 1812 "Narrative of Religion" declares the church to be "Warmly and firmly united to a strict adherence to the great doctrines of grace, our churches are living in harmony and brotherly affection, edified, and edifying one another" (p. 497), again defining for posterity the specific type of orthodoxy in mind.

A few years later (1822) the Presbyterian Church was still speaking in terms of the Adopting Act, by then nearly a century old. She did not seem to repudiate her past, stating: "The General Assembly can never hesitate, on any proper occasion, to recommend to those, who, at both their licensure and ordination, professed 'sincerely to receive and adopt the Confession of Faith of this Church, as containing the system of doctrine taught in the Holy Scriptures,' and to all other members of our Church, steadfastly to adhere to that 'form of sound words.'"(p. 50). Still this church, unless the opinions of moderns be imposed on her, viewed herself as continuing a presbyterial endorsement of those who "sincerely receive and adopt" the WCF as containing the system of doctrines taught in holy scriptures. This same body of divinity was thought to be the "form of sound words" (2 Tim. 1:3), which was to be adhered to. At this late date, confessional adherence still seems to be woven into the fabric of American Presbyterianism. Only one year earlier the Assembly was ordering a printing of its doctrinal standards (p. 20), hardly the act of a church that did not really intend to live by such.

One of the more overt clarifications of confessional adherence was given by the 1824 General Assembly. In this thoughtfully worded statement, the church both reiterated her confessional adherence as well as reissued a call to defend such as a veritable summary of the teachings of scripture. This church was not retreating from the Adopting Act. The modern reconstruction of this history cannot dismiss the clear intent of these self-consciously adopted words of the highest court of the Presbyterian church.

1. That, in the opinion of this Assembly, Confessions of Faith, containing formulas of doctrine, and rules for conducting the discipline and worship proper to be maintained in the house of God, are not only recognized as necessary and expedient, but as the character of human nature is continually aiming at innovation, absolutely requisite to the settled peace of the church, and to the happy and orderly existence of Christian communion. Within the limits of Christendom, few are to be found in the attitude of avowed hostility to Christianity. The name of Christian is claimed by all, and all are ready to profess their belief in the Holy Scriptures; too many reserving to themselves the right of putting upon them what construction they please. In such a state of things, without the aid of Confessions, Christian fellowship can exist only in a very limited degree, and the disorder of the Corinthian church, condemned by the Apostle, would be realized: 'I am of Paul, and I of Apollos.'

2. That though the Confession of Faith, and standards of our church, are of no original authority, independent of the Scriptures, yet we regard them as a summary of those divine truths which are diffused throughout the sacred volume.

   They, as a system of doctrines, therefore, cannot be abandoned in our opinion, without an abandonment of the word of God. They form a bond of fellowship in the faith of the gospel, and the General Assembly cannot but believe the precious immortals under their care, to be more safe in receiving the truth of God's holy word, as exhibited in the standards of our church, than in being subject to the guidance of any instructor, whoever he may be, who may have confidence enough to set up his own opinions in opposition to the system of doctrines, which men of sound learning, full of the Holy Ghost, and mighty in the Scriptures, have devised from the oracles of the living God. It should never be forgotten, that the church is solemnly cautioned against the danger of being carried about by every wind of doctrine.

3. This Confession of Faith, adopted by our church, contains a system of doctrines professedly believed by the people and the pastors under the care of the General Assembly, nor can it be traduced by any in the communion of our church, without subjecting the erring parties to that salutary discipline, which hath for its object the maintenance of the peace and purity of the church, under the government of her great Master.

Finally, the General Assembly recommend to all who are under their care, steadfastly to resist every temptation, however presented, which may have for its object the relaxation of those bonds of Christian fellowship, which have hitherto been so eminently blessed of God, for the order, edification, and extension of the Presbyterian church. (p. 114)

A year later (1825) a question of application of the adopted standards was put as follows:

The following question was presented by the committee of overtures, viz. "Is it consistent with the constitution of our church, and with its purity and peace, that persons who manifest a decided hostility to creeds, confessions and ecclesiastical formularies, as unscriptural and destructive to the rights of conscience, should be received as ministers of the gospel into the Presbyterian church?' The answer given by this assembly, reflecting the adherence to the confessions was adopted as follows. "1. That the Constitution, as is well known, expressly requires of all candidates for admission, a solemn declaration that they sincerely receive and adopt the Confession of Faith of this Church, as containing the system of doctrine taught in the Holy Scriptures. . . . 2. That the last Assembly, in a report of their committee, to be seen on the minutes, have so explicitly and fully declared the sentiments of this church in regard to her ecclesiastical standards, and all within her communion who may traduce them, that no further expression of our views on the subject is deemed necessary. (p. 145)

Thus, the official court actions of American Presbyterianism for a century indicate the consistency of the historic approach.

Charles Hodge presented the same case persuasively in his *Constitutional History of the Presbyterian Church*. He noted (and I think his quotation, since he was much closer to the original facts than we, should be heard in full):

When they say that they adopt the Westminster Confession of Faith and Catechisms as the confession of their faith, their language admits of but one interpretation. This was the very form in which the subscription was made in the strict Presbytery of New Castle. To make this mean that they adopted only so much of the Confession as is essential to the gospel, would be to suppose a use of language such as never before was made, at least by honest men. If a man says he adopts the *Thirty Nine Articles* of the church of England as the articles of his faith; is he ever understood to mean that he adopts those portions of them merely which are essential to the gospel? Or, if another says he adopts the Decrees of the Council of Trent, can he honestly mean that he adopts so much as is not inconsistent with the *Augsburg Confession*? Such a use of language would be inconsistent with the least confidence in the intercourse of life. It is not the meaning of the terms, and cannot honestly be made their meaning. Again, when the Synod say that every candidate must declare "his agreement in opinion with all the essential and necessary articles of the said confession," there is but one meaning that can be fairly put upon their language. The essential parts of a confession are those parts which are essential to its peculiar character. No man receives all the essential articles of a popish creed, who receives no more than is consistent with Protestantism. All such subscriptions are mockery and falsehood. If the Synod intended by the essential articles of the Confession the essential articles of the gospel, why mention the Confession at all? The Presbyteries, surely, could pick out the necessary doctrines of the gospel from the Bible, as easily as from the Confession. The interpretation, therefore, which would make the Synod mean by the expressions just quoted, that they adopted, and required others to adopt, those articles merely of the Confession which are essential to the gospel, is inconsistent with all just and honest use of language. Thus far then this act admits of but one interpretation consistent with candour and fair dealing on the part of its authors.

For more study on this topic, see *The Practice of Confessional Subscription* (order from the Covenant Foundation, 648 Goldenwood Court, Powder Springs, GA 30127).

G. K. Chesterton also spoke to this issue well:

We have remarked that one reason offered for being a progressive is that things naturally tend to grow better. But the only real reason for being a progressive is that things naturally tend to grow worse. The corruption in things is not only the best argument for being progressive; it is also the only argument against being conservative. The conservative theory would really be quite sweeping and unanswerable if it were not for this one fact. But all conservatism is based upon the idea that if you leave things alone you leave them as they are. But you do not. If you leave a thing alone you leave it to a torrent of change. If you leave a white post alone it will soon be a black post. If you particularly want it to be white you must be always painting it again; that is, you must be always having a revolution. Briefly, if you want the old white post you must have a new white post. But this which is true even of inanimate things is in a quite special and terrible sense true of all human things. An almost unnatural vigilance is really required of the citizen because of the horrible rapidity with which human institutions grow old. It is the custom in passing romance and journalism to talk of men suffering under old tyrannies. But, as a fact, men have almost always suffered under new tyrannies; under tyrannies that had been public liberties hardly twenty years before. (*Orthodoxy*, 210-211)

Appendix E: EXAM SAMPLES

Over the years, we have used different kinds of examination formats. Normally, at the final class session, we hand out (or mail later) a written exam like the samples below in order to save time. After each candidate completes the questions, he is given a time to meet with the Session. Copies of his answers are distributed (in advance if at all possible), and after a review of those instruments, the Elders may ask other questions and/or hear testimonies. Obviously, each church will want to develop and tailor its own exams. We offer these merely as beginning vehicles.

* * * * * * * * * * * * * * * *

EXAMINATION QUESTIONS (#1) FOR OFFICER CANDIDATES
COVENANT PRESBYTERIAN CHURCH, PCA

YES		I. STANDARD QUESTIONS (Please check Yes or No)
	1.	Do you believe that the Bible is inerrant and that it truly is the revealed Word of God?
	2.	Do you believe in Christ's Virgin Birth?. . . his sinlessness?. . . his miracles?. . . his bc resurrection?. . . his Second Coming?
	3.	Do you believe that all clauses of the Apostles' Creed are true, biblical and w defending?
	4.	Is it possible for a true Christian—a Born-Again believer—to lose his or her salva (Fall from Grace)?
	5.	Do you believe that evolution played any role in the original creation?
	6.	Do you believe that Man is totally depraved—unable to affect his own salvation in way except through God's saving grace?
	7.	Do you believe that God unconditionally chose some individuals for salvation—and s for condemnation—from before the foundations of the world?
	8.	Did Christ die to save only the Elect?
	9.	Can God's free and sovereign gift of grace be rejected by the exercise of Man's free v Can one refuse God's call?
	10.	Do you recognize the Presbyterian form of Church Government to be biblical?
	11.	Do you submit yourself to the Government and Discipline of the Church and promis study its peace and purity?
	12.	Should abortion be considered anything other than murder?
	13.	Do you believe in infant baptism?
	14.	Do you embrace the covenantal unity of God's plan of salvation, as well as the unit His Church in all ages?
	15.	Is there a "Second Baptism" of the Holy Spirit which occurs apart from conversion?

I attest these are my true and sincere beliefs,

_____ (Name)

II.   DISCUSSION QUESTIONS

     1.   What is the role of the Holy Spirit in the life of the Christian?

     2.   Are there distinctives of Presbyterianism, which are worthy of defending? Or should we be an Independent, Non-denominational Church?

     3.   What does Justification mean?

     4.   What is the Relationship of the Old Testament to the New Testament? What Role should Old Testament Law play in the life of today's Christian? Has the Church assumed Israel's place?

     5.   What did Christ's death accomplish?

     6.   What does the "Sovereignty of God" mean?

     7.   What are your Spiritual Gifts?

     8.   Is your home life in order?

     9.   What is the Christian's responsibility with regards to tithing?

     10.   Can you relate Circumcision to Baptism? Passover to the Lord's Supper?

     11.   Do you have any disagreements with the Westminster Confession of Faith, the Larger Catechism, or The Shorter Catechism? Are there things in those statements that you could not "Encourage and Defend?" (Titus 1:9).

     III.   OPEN QUESTIONS FROM THE FLOOR

The Session should excuse the candidates following completion of questions, so that a frank discussion and vote may be taken. Afterwards, the Session (or its committee) should notify the candidates of the results of the vote and notify them of any examined areas that need additional study.

EXAMINATION QUESTIONS (#2) FOR OFFICER CANDIDATES

A. Please check Yes or No:

Yes No

___ ___ 1.   Do you believe that man was created by a sovereign God, in his image and without sin?

___ ___ 2.   Do you believe that fallen man is able to contribute anything to his salvation?

___ ___ 3.   Do you believe that God in his good pleasure decreed before creation to select certain individuals for salvation and to bypass others?

___ ___ 4.   Do you believe Christ's Virgin Birth? Sinlessness? Miracles? Bodily Resurrection? Second Coming?

___ ___ 5.   Is it possible for a truly regenerated Christian to lose salvation (fall from grace)?

___ ___ 6.   Do you believe the Presbyterian form of church government to be biblical?

___ ___ 7.   Do you believe in Infant Baptism, both in principle and in personal practice?

___ ___ 8.   Do you embrace the covenantal unity of God's plan of salvation in both Testaments?

___ ___ 9.   Is there a "second baptism" of the Holy Spirit that occurs apart from conversion?

___ ___ 10.   Does God's prohibition of murder extend all the way from the unborn child to the terminally ill geriatric patient?

___ ___ 11.   Do you feel you meet the New Testament qualifications for office given by Paul?

___ ___ 12.   Do you submit to the government and discipline of the church and promise to study its peace and purity?

___ ___ 13.   Are there any doctrinal positions in the Apostles' Creed or Westminster Confession of Faith that you could not support?

Name:

B. Please underline the best answer(s) [*More than one* may be correct]:

1. The Bible [contains in selected sections; consists entirely of] the revealed Word of God.

2. As a result of Adam's original disobedience, all men without God's grace are [guilty before God's justice; as evil as possible in their actions; morally polluted in all parts of their personality].

3. Man [can; cannot] in his own power choose to follow God. On the other hand, man [can; cannot] refuse to follow God when called by Him.

4. The atoning work of Christ is "limited" in its [inherent perfection and sufficiency; extent of those for whom it was effected; neither].

5. The following are essential historical elements of the Reformed faith; [sovereignty of God; authority of tradition alongside Scripture; salvation based on a combination of the grace of God and the good works of men; justification by faith; priesthood of all believers; free will of man].

C. Please be prepared to discuss your sense of call to office and your view of your spiritual gifts.

D. Other possible topics for discussion, if members of Session request:

1. The special works ascribed to each Person of the Trinity.

2. The need for both Christ's divinity and humanity.

3. Christ's functions of Prophet, Priest, and King.

4. Elements of the process of salvation; regeneration; justification; conversion; sanctification; the roles of faith and grace.

5. The role in the Christian life of the Holy Spirit; the Law; the Sacraments; good works; prayer; giving.

6. The relation between the Passover and circumcision in the Old Testament and the Lord's Supper and Baptism in the New.

EXAMINATION QUESTIONS (#3) FOR OFFICER CANDIDATES

Name: Date:

A. Please check Yes or No: **Yes**   **No**

1. Do you believe that man was created by a sovereign God, in his image and without sin?   _____   _____

2. Do you believe that fallen man is able to contribute anything to his salvation?   _____   _____

3. Do you believe that God in his good pleasure decreed before creation to select certain individuals for salvation and to bypass others?   _____   _____

4. Do you believe Christ's Virgin Birth? Sinlessness? Miracles? Bodily Resurrection? Second Coming?   _____   _____

5. Is it possible for a truly regenerated Christian to lose salvation (fall from grace)?   _____   _____

6. Do you embrace the covenantal unity of God's plan of salvation in both Testaments?   _____   _____

7.. Is there a "second baptism" of the Holy Spirit that occurs apart from our regeneration and conversion and that is required for the full experience of the joys of salvation?   _____   _____

8. Does God's prohibition of murder include the unborn child and the terminally ill geriatric patient?   _____   _____

9. Do you believe the Presbyterian form of church government to be biblical?   _____   _____

10. Do you feel you meet the New Testament qualifications for office given by Paul?   _____   _____

11. Do you believe that the offices of Elder and Deacon are limited to males?   _____   _____

12. Are there any doctrinal positions in the Apostles' Creed or Westminster Confession of Faith that you could not support?   _____   _____

B. Please underline the best answer(s) [More than one may be correct]:

1. The Bible [contains in selected sections; consists entirely of] the revealed Word of God.

2. As a result of Adam's original disobedience, all men without God's grace are [guilty before God's justice; as evil as possible in their actions; morally polluted in all parts of their personality].

3. Man [can; cannot] in his own power choose to follow God. On the other hand, man [can; cannot] refuse to follow God when called by Him.

4. The atoning work of Christ is "limited" in its [inherent perfection and sufficiency to save from sin; the number of those for whom it was intended and effected; neither].

5. Appropriate elements for use in public worship are [any that are not specifically forbidden in Scripture; those that are specifically endorsed in Scripture].

6. Infant baptism is required because [it is explicitly commanded in the New Testament; it is the New Testament continuation of the Old Testament sacrament of circumcision; it is a critical step in God's covenantal dealings with his people; it is necessary for the regeneration of the recipient].

7. The gift of prophecy, defined as providing new revelation from God through the Spirit, [ceased with the end of the apostolic age; still continues on special occasions when God uses one of his people to provide authoritative new information; has been replaced with the completion of the canon of Scriptures]. As we study the Scriptures, the Holy Spirit provides [illumination; inspiration] to assist us in interpretation and understanding.

C. Give *brief* (2-3 sentences) answers to the following:

1. How has God made himself known to us?

2. What are the chief roles of each of the three persons of the Trinity?

3. Distinguish among regeneration, justification, and sanctification.

4. Why did Christ need to be both truly God (his divinity) and man (his humanity) to serve as our Savior?

5. Distinguish between the roles of faith and good works in our salvation. Are both needed? For what purpose(s)?

6. Theologians distinguish the moral, the civil, and the ceremonial laws given by God in the Old Testament. What subject area did each address? Which are still applicable after the completed atonement of Christ?

7. What are the purposes of church discipline?

D. Please be prepared to discuss your sense of call to office and your view of your spiritual gifts.

E. Match the letter of the items on the left with the appropriate number on the right:

#

a.	_____	Love, justice, omniscience	1.	Constitution of the PCA
b.	_____	Guilt and corruption	2.	Elements of God's providence
c.	_____	Abrahamic, Mosaic, Davidic, New	3.	Responsibility of the Session
d.	_____	Adoption of the church budget	4.	Attributes of God
e.	_____	Election of church Officers	5.	Signs of a true church
f.	_____	Westminster Confession of Faith, Larger and Shorter Catechisms, Book of Church Order	6.	"Pre-Reformation" Reformers
g.	_____	Preservation of creation, government of world	7.	Renewals of the Covenant of Grace
h.	_____	Preaching, sacraments, discipline	8.	Results of original sin
i.	_____	Waldo, Huss, Wycliffe	9.	Courts of the PCA
j.	_____	Session, Presbytery, General Assembly	10.	Responsibility of the Congregational Meeting

We are grateful to acknowledge the advances in these exams over time, which have been contributions by Dr. Marvin Poutsma of Oak Ridge, TN. Over the years, this faithful Clerk of Session has edited and refined many of these exams. This third one has greatly benefited from his careful improvements and insights.

Appendix S: The Importance of Shepherding

"Be shepherds of God's flock," the NT charges. This means that Elders seek to feed the sheep and care for their needs—not necessarily the same as their "wants." This also requires that shepherds stay close to and involved with the sheep. These offices are not like seats on a corporate board; they require a pastoral relationship. The article below makes that point well.

FOR THE CHURCH TO BE HEALTHY, IT NEEDS HEALTHY LEADERSHIP
Donald J. MacNair (as abridged by Richard Aeschliman)40

In many churches with "strong leadership," the church's Elders are perceived as a board of directors, as leaders who tell the people what to do. Such an attitude indicates to me that this church has failed to implement the Bible's commitment to the integrity of members' gifts. Often a church exhibits a double imbalance. On the one hand, it views its Elders as a board of directors, telling everybody what to do. On the other hand, incongruously, it believes that the congregation has a right to vote on everything—something near and dear to the hearts of Americans!

The Bible also clearly directs that a church's leaders are accountable to God for its members. "Obey your leaders and submit to their authority" (Heb. 13:17). The Elders oversee the church's life and ministry in order to give an account to God of the people he has entrusted to their care. Does that mean that the Elders are supposed to tell everybody else what to do and how to do it? I believe that Scripture in no way supports that interpretation. . . .

If the congregation perceives the Elders as dictators, it will perceive itself as those who are dictated to. If it perceives the leadership as nonexistent, it will perceive itself as on its own, probably bereft of focus and unity. If it perceives the Elders as shepherds along the lines of the biblical model, members will see themselves as sheep (in the best sense!): cared for, nurtured, following not by coercion but free to serve creatively in an orderly context. As Elders strive to develop a shepherding relationship with members, that church's infrastructure develops into one that both allows divine directives (use of members' gifts, Elders' orderly accounting) to be implemented and allows God to work through it.

Whatever else an Elder says or does, whatever jobs he carries out, whatever words he utters, programs he administers, visits he pays, or decisions he makes, the orientation of his life and the heart of his ministry before God consist in shepherding the people whom God has entrusted to his care. [W]hen sacrificial love and care motivate Elders to enable the saints to grow in Christ, not only do those Elders become in fuller measure the leaders God meant them to be, but also the congregation grows and serves in the way God meant them to.

Caring, loving, equipping—these three words express the essence of Christ's lesson about shepherding. A good shepherd is one whose care for the sheep drives him to equip them for doing what sheep do best, even at the cost of his own life. In the church, members should follow the lead of Elders, not because the Elders tell them what to do, but because the Elders have cared for them. What the members should feel is not compulsion but care. As they experience the depth of his commitment to them, they know him and trust him completely.

---

40 This abridgement is taken from *Equip for Ministry*, July/August 2002, 6-9. Used with permission.

It is important to see that all these wonderful benefits do not do for the sheep what the sheep are meant to do for themselves. Rather, they furnish an optimal environment in which the sheep can grow and flourish. Shepherds provide the safe environment. Secure sheep are sheep that produce wool, lambs, and meat. In other words, Elders nurture church life but cannot produce it. Their goal is the spiritual growth and ministry of their members, and this they can encourage and enhance but cannot program. . . .

Building this mind-set requires the same activities as maintaining it. This means that all Elders, at every stage of shepherd maturity, must be doing the same things. Simply stated they are to:

- Meditate, individually and as a session, on this model of Christ's.
- Pray, individually and as a session, for the Holy Spirit to actualize the shepherd model in all aspects of your life and ministry.
- Develop a strategy to hold one another accountable to think and minister like shepherds.
- Devise and implement plans that actualize this kind of mind-set and ministry. For example, devote regular meetings to these activities.
- Devise a way to assess your efforts. Your session must devise a practical way to listen regularly to the sheep for their testimony as to your shepherding them.

I have made my case that the shepherd model shapes the Elder's ministry from the roots of his being to the things he says and does and that the session should fashion an optimal environment for the congregation's spiritual growth and ministry. I utilize the acrostic G-O-E-S to help Elders identify and group their responsibilities as guardian, overseer, example, and shepherd.

- *Guarding* the sheep. Positively, the Elders ensure that members are growing in Christ. Negatively, the Elders discourage members from pursuing sinful practices. This coincides with church discipline.

- Being an Elder consists almost by definition of *overseeing*. Some Elders confuse power with authority. Being determined not to exercise "raw power," they avoid authoritative leadership, or at least fail to lead with any confidence. Others, determined to account properly to God for their charges, muscle them into obedience. The confusion between authority and power parallels the failure to distinguish between accountability and responsibility, which we discussed above.

- Possibly the most effective ministry an Elder can give to his church is his own [*example* of] Christ-likeness. A Christ-like Elder is one who shepherds according to Christ's model.

- *Shepherding* also refers to the concrete activity of looking after individual church members, monitoring their spiritual progress, and encouraging them on a person-to-person basis to grow in love and obedience to Christ.

Perhaps you feel overwhelmed by the task, especially by the prospect of shaping your whole life to fit the shepherd model on top of everything else you have to do! Of course, by now we can see that the shepherd's heart in principle is not an add-on but rather the fountainhead.

It is also important to develop procedures to insure that those who are chosen to be Elders do meet the biblical qualifications. I recommend the following plan to this end, which I have practiced in my own pastoral ministries:

- Have members nominate men to be Elders.
- For a period of several months, train these candidates, give them field experience, and pray together as a church for God's leading in the upcoming election.
- Conclude the training period with a gracious but careful evaluation by the session (which is the complete group of Elders currently installed to serve) of each candidate's qualifications and maturity. Offer for the congregation's approval only those candidates whom the session evaluates positively.
- The congregation, with no power to make additional nominations, elects Elders from among these trained and qualified candidates.
- This system effectively provides leadership that conforms to God's own qualifications.

Paul exhorts Timothy: "The Elders who direct the affairs of the church well are worthy of double honor, especially those whose work is preaching and teaching" (1 Timothy 5:17). His words indicate that God intends there to be a plurality of Elders, those officially entrusted with the spiritual oversight of the church, among whom are numbered Elders whose work is preaching and teaching. . . . Everything I say about Elders in these chapters applies without distinction to the pastor, who is an Elder among Elders. The pastor does not minister alone: he shepherds as part of a team, and he shepherds among a Spirit-gifted flock.

****

Welsh preacher Geoff Thomas noted this about how Elders shepherd the flock:

Think of that great description of the shepherd in Psalm 23. That man sees that his flock lack for nothing. He leads them to green pastures and still waters, that is, he makes sure that they are fed with the pure milk of the word of God. Then there are times when they get dejected, despondent and begin to wander away. He takes care of them and restores their souls. Then there are desolating experiences that they pass through, even walking through the valley of the shadow of death. They are in different species of anguish or in mental and spiritual agony. At those times he is always there with the members of the flock. The church has a vital ministry of consolation because it always has broken-hearted people. The minister especially takes care of them at those times. He also takes care of the lambs of the flock. 'He will gather the lambs in his bosom and lead gently those who are with young.'

To conclude, these are the basic qualifications God requires for those who would lead his church. So very often it is appointment to the office, and involvement in the work, that matures a man beyond his years and our expectations. Personal difficulty, struggle, loss and sorrow all have their place in preparing a man for gospel leadership. Our frequent lament is that there are not the leaders in the next generation to take our place. Every generation has said the same. One old Scottish minister was taking part in the ordination of elders, and as he looked at the group of men on whom he was about to lay his hands he clearly disdained the lot of them. He said outrageously, "Solomon built the Temple with gold and precious stones, but we are building today with the sods of clay and earth God has given us." Yes, we must build with the provisions that God donates to us now. There is nothing else. Latimer, Bunyan, Whitefield, Spurgeon and Lloyd-Jones no longer walk the lanes of 'England's green and pleasant land.' But we who are called by God to lead his church must seek with all our strength to be the kind of men God would have us be. We owe it to the church and we owe it to him. Then he may entrust greater blessings to us. (http://users.aber.ac.uk/emk/ap/sermons/1tim12.htm; See also the studies by Dr. Mark Ross in Session 1 above, which emphasize shepherding.)

Appendix F: A Caveat About Faddishness and Presbyters

Elders also need to be above trendiness; they need to develop a far-sighted approach and appreciate the contributions of earlier Christians to issues of importance today. Elsewhere, I have warned—and this is a product of nearly 20 years of ministry in the same church—of the acquired wariness that leaders, in general, should have about novel ideas and new ministry fads. Elders, in particular, should be vaccinated against the Athenian virus—the malady that causes one always to be seeking something new. In the local church, people need to be able to expect continuity, certainty, and fidelity. Most maturing Christians do not seek raw entertainment, nor should they expect a different stage with a different cast every week.

For Shakespeare, "The past is prologue." Many Christians are rediscovering that same truth concerning most issues of our day. The past is actually an excellent introduction to many current issues. Regrettably, many Christians stand upon the stage of history with virtually no idea of what has preceded. Besides being placed at a distinct disadvantage with such tardy stage entrance, Christians are finding that forsaking the best of prior thought is an extremely imprudent *modus operandi*. The seduction of the superiority of modernity blindfolds many to the past.41

Many act as though their chief desire is to run away from their spiritual predecessors as far and as fast as possible. Not only do many people forsake their spiritual parents, moreover, some contemporaries seem to suffer from repressed memories—a dubious syndrome that allows children to slander their parents *ex post facto;* all the while, such vilification denies these deceased ancestors the opportunity to speak for themselves. If they could speak, maybe Christians would find that their spiritual parents were not as barbaric as once suspected.

This Manual is offered in the hope that the next generation will be wiser in its admiration of history than recent generations have been. Specifically, I hope that future Christians will embrace the good from their spiritual forebears rather than despise it before they even become acquainted with it. When the apostle Paul spoke of "forgetting those things which lie behind," he certainly was not advocating that Christians should become mindless about the past. Yet, that is all too often the case.

One may wish to view this work as an apology for the usefulness of history and our spiritual grandparents (presbyters as the Bible might call them). Indeed, it is a defense of what has gone before. Perhaps as in the words of Woody Allen: "History has to repeat itself. For no one listens the first time." If the reiteration of some of the lessons of history will inform and equip present and future Christians, this writer will be pleased.

Another way to see this Manual is to view it as an attempt to vindicate some exemplary Christians who may have known and lived in far more conformity to God's will than many of us ever will. If they are our betters—despite massive maligning by modern skepticism—then it may be time to rehabilitate their reputations. I will be glad to be known as a vindicator of past saints as long as they were as exemplary as the ones discussed herein.

---

41 Part of this conclusion is an adaptation of the introduction to my *The Arrogance of the Modern* (Oak Ridge, TN: The Covenant Foundation, 1996); used with permission.

This work (among several others) is also a very lengthy footnote on a singular text with enormous epistemological ramification. Nearly every essay contained returns at some point to the *leitmotif* enunciated by Solomon: "There is nothing new under the sun." These sessions and discussions are many variations that support and elaborate upon that central theme. These lectures include some of my various meanderings to see if Solomon was accurate or not. Not to worry, his assertion remains unfalsified.

C. S. Lewis reflected a hearty perspective similar to the one in this work. In *God in the Dock*, he found himself highly skeptical of several modernistic notions. In "Dogma and the Universe," he spoke to a common scandal in the words below.

> It is a common reproach against Christianity that its dogmas are unchanging, while human knowledge is in continual growth. Hence, to unbelievers, we seem to be always engaged in the hopeless task of trying to force the new knowledge into molds which it has outgrown. I think this feeling alienates the outsider much more than any particular discrepancy . . . For it seems to him clear that, if our ancestors had known what we know about the universe, Christianity would never have existed at all.[42]

Lewis found that a historical perspective helpfully diagnosed a number of philosophical assumptions when applied to, say, certain areas of science. On the issue of the size of the earth in relation to the universe, Lewis noted: "There is no question here of knowledge having grown . . . The real question is why the spatial insignificance of the earth, after being known for centuries, should suddenly in the last century have become an argument against Christianity. I do not know why this has happened; but I am sure it does not mark an increased clarity of thought . . ."[43] Thus, he suggested that a knowledge of the history of science could help analyze a modern issue. Lewis believed that neither the facts nor the attempts to refute Christianity had been radically altered over immense stretches of time.

In his chapter "On the Reading of Old Books," he made a number of key observations. Decrying the habit of initially turning to secondary sources rather than primary sources, Lewis thought it was "topsy-turvy" to maintain a "preference for the modern books and this shyness of the old ones."[44] He regretted the obtrusive prevalence of this modernophilia in theological circles. Whereas Lewis preferred to have the reader first attend to the direct sources (with whatever guidance was necessary), he found a trend that substituted rumor for primary sources. He noted: "Where you find a little study circle of Christian laity you can be almost certain that they are studying not St. Luke or St. Paul or St. Augustine or Thomas Aquinas or Hooker or Butler, but Nicolas Berdyaev, Jacques Maritain, Reinhold Niebuhr, or Dorothy Sayers or even myself."

Lewis recommended this remedy: "But if he must read only the new or only the old, I would advise him to read the old. And I would give him this advice precisely because he is an amateur and therefore much less protected than the expert against the dangers of an exclusive contemporary diet. A new book is still on its trial and the amateur is not in a position to judge it. It has to be tested against the great body of Christian thought down the ages, and all its hidden implications . . . have to be brought to light."[45]

42 C. S. Lewis, *God in the Dock* (Grand Rapids: Eerdmans, 1970), 38.
43 Ibid., 39.
44 Lewis, op. cit., 201.
45 Idem.

Lewis continued with a metaphor similar to the one I have used above about entering the play after intermission. He asserted that if one enters a discussion group at 11:00, without knowing what has gone on from 8:00-11:00, one may interpret many things out of context. Inside jokes, laughter, references, and other nuances will not be appreciated. In the same way, Lewis continued, "you may be led to accept what you would have indignantly rejected if you knew its real significance."[46] The "only safety," according to Lewis, was to hold to the standard of plain ("mere" as the puritan Richard Baxter called it) Christianity "which puts the controversies of the moment in their proper perspective." This approach preserves a crucial perspective that is often wanting amidst today's ideological forays.

Lewis recommended the classics, the great books of Christianity. Among these he recommended Augustine, Aquinas, Boethius, Bunyan, Hooker, Pascal, Spenser, Butler, and others. The essays in this volume attempt to acquaint the reader with a few other greats, mainly from the Christian tradition with which I am most familiar. No doubt others could add to the debate by reviewing their own tradition.

Lewis warned that "[e]very age has its own outlook. It is specially good at seeing certain truths and specially liable to make certain mistakes. We all, therefore, need the books that will correct the characteristic mistakes of our own period. And that means the old books. All contemporary writers share to some extent the contemporary outlook—even those, like myself, who seem most opposed to it."[47] Lewis, more clearly than many moderns, observed "the characteristic blindness of the twentieth century. . . . None of us can fully escape this blindness, but we shall certainly increase it, and weaken our guard against it, if we read only modern books. Where they are true they will give us truths which we half knew already. Where they are false they will aggravate the error with which we are already dangerously ill."[48]

Lewis correctly saw the danger of holding the past in contempt and called for a fresh acquaintance with the best of the past. As these essays suggest, those who love C. S. Lewis may want to imitate his appreciation for the *paleo*. I, and many other fellow-Elders, want to concur with Lewis and others who have realized this. The theology of an earlier day has much to teach us. We might begin by admitting that there is a beam in our own eye—our presumption that we have superior insight.

Many Christians treat the past like a dead, and therefore irrelevant, ancestor. As a result, memory has little place in an age that has little vision. Rather than repressing memories about our predecessors and their virtue, remembering may be an undetected aid "for the living of these days"—unless, of course, we have definitively judged that our spiritual parents were so feeble, inferior, cowardly, or unenlightened as to be prevented from communing at the same table as we. That is the arrogance of the modern.

Agreeing with Solomon that "there is nothing new under the sun" (Eccl. 1:9), Christians in all ages can instruct those who live later. We, in turn, can learn much by standing on the shoulders of those who have preceded us. After all, if the "faith was handed down once and for all" (Jude 3), one may expect little change in core biblical truths over the centuries. Since the faith is essentially the same

---

46 Idem.
47 Ibid., 202.
48 Idem.

in all centuries, surely we can learn from other brothers and sisters in Christ. We will find some agreement with Chesterton who called the church a "democracy of the dead," meaning that (for those who love popular referenda) if we truly understand the unity of the church—both militant and triumphant—we will not deliberately disenfranchise those who have gone home to be with the Lord. They, too, have much to say in the referenda of today; though they are dead, they still speak (Heb. 11:4)—and we need to learn to listen. Perhaps fewer mistakes would be made if we returned free expression to those spiritual pioneers who have preceded us.

Most young adults only develop a deep appreciation for their parents when they are tested. That may be true in spiritual things as well. As one is tested by a very modern and often perplexing world, the Christian not only wants to know God's Word and will, but also on many occasions would like to ask his parents a few questions like: "What did you do when such and such happened? How did you handle a particular situation? What resources are available in regard to the following issues?"

The good news is that God has not left us totally without helpful advisors, but frequently we do not even know they exist or where to turn for help. Much of that is our own fault or due to our over-confident unwillingness to receive advice. Often modern Christians shut themselves off from helpful sources of direction by deciding from the outset that the knowledge of previous generations is of little or no value. Although the similarity is unintended, that is not altogether different from the 1960s slogan: "Don't trust anyone over thirty."

Funny that as most of us became "Thirtysomething," things changed. Similarly, it may be time to admit that we can trust some earlier Christians and beliefs—those that were well thought-out and scriptural—that are centuries old. Many earlier episodes of spiritual history may benefit evangelicals, if we can merely be healed of our phobia of anything older than thirty years old.

One contemporary thinker recently questioned whether there was value in knowing a medieval Christian thinker. Phrasing the important question this way, he queried: "But can a seven-hundred-year-old thinker still be relevant today? Students of logic will recognize the implication of the question as the fallacy of 'chronological snobbery.' 'New is true' and 'old is mold,' we are told. Logic informs us, however, that time has no necessary connection with truth. Or at least, if there were any kind of connection, then the time-honored thought ought to have the edge."[49]

Lord Acton spoke of the past as capable of teaching by illuminating "the instructions derived from the errors of great men."[50] He also noted: "The value of history is its certainty—against which opinion is broken." If we find that our parents were on to some things that we have not realized, or if perhaps their insights were deeper than the average paperback Christian book, then we should not be so arrogant as to cling to an uncritical bias for the modern. Jeremiah spoke of the "ancient paths" (Jer. 6:16)—those tried and trusted ruts of life that rebels sought to re-fill because they were routine. We may even discover, as C. S. Lewis did, that some of the ancient Christian examples are preferable to many unproven modern ones. As Lewis advised of a newer book or work, "It has to be tested against the great body of Christian thought down the ages, and all its hidden implications (often unsuspected by the author himself) have to be brought to light .

---

49 Norman Geisler, *Thomas Aquinas: An Evangelical Appraisal* (Grand Rapids: Baker, 1991), 11.
50 J. Rufus Fears, ed., *Selected Writings of Lord Action: Essays in Religion, Politics, and Morality* (Indianapolis: Liberty Press, 1988), 623.

. . The only safety is to have a standard of plain, central Christianity . . . which puts the controversies of the moment in their proper perspective. Such a standard can be acquired only from the old books. It is a good rule, after reading a new book, never to allow yourself another new one till you have read an old one in between."51

Lewis exhorted: "The only palliative is to keep the clean sea breeze of the centuries blowing through our minds, and this can be done only by reading old books. Not, of course, that there is any magic about the past. People were no cleverer then than they are now; they made as many mistakes as we. But not the same mistakes . . ."52

Nearly a century ago, G. K. Chesterton gave testimony about the value of rediscovering our past Christian heritage, when he found that the best truths had already been mined:

> I did, like all other solemn little boys, try to be in advance of the age. Like them I tried to be some ten minutes in advance of the truth. And I found that I was eighteen hundred years behind it . . . When I fancied that I stood alone I was really in the ridiculous position of being backed up by all Christendom. It may be, Heaven forgive me, that I did try to be original; but I only succeeded in inventing all by myself an inferior copy of the existing traditions of civilized religion . . . It might amuse a friend or an enemy to read how I gradually learnt from the truth of some stray legend or from the falsehood of some dominant philosophy, things that I might have learnt from my catechism—if I had ever learnt it . . . I found at last what I might have found in the nearest parish church.53

Lord Acton could have been helpful once again. He asked, "How is man superior to prejudice, passion, and interest?" His answer was: "By the study of History and the pursuit of the required character."54 Moreover, he recommended an option that is often ignored: "Resist your time— take a foothold outside it—see other times and ask yourself whether the time of our ancestors is fit for us."55

Above all members of Christ's Church, ordained officers must keep an eye on the distant goal for our churches. Accordingly, we must become somewhat time- and fad-resistant. We need to avoid the Sisyphusean treadmill of seeking to be ever-chic. I advise our elders not to be "always reinventing" (*semper reinventus*) the church that God has already created and endowed with such wisdom and godly protocols.

Sometimes even conservatives (not to mention liberals) seem too hasty to jump on the bandwagon for church-updating. For example, the mainline Presbyterian Church sometimes appears to want to be as far away from its old school Calvinistic heritage as possible. In 1996, the PCUSA had before it propositions to ordain homosexuals and to merge into the Church of Christ Uniting (COCU, a mega-ecumenical effort that would have instituted bishops). Fortunately, some of the more conservative positions held the day, even if narrowly in this

---

51 C. S. Lewis, *God in the Dock* (Grand Rapids: Eerdmans, 1970), 201.
52 Idem.
53 G. K. Chesterton, *Orthodoxy* (London: Lane, 1909), 16-17.
54 J. Rufus Fears, op. cit., 620.
55 Idem.

assembly. We commend that, while we repudiate the attempts to so transform the Presbyterian church into an *ecclesia modernus.*

Revisionism is an equal opportunity disease, though, one that can afflict conservatives as well as liberals. A few years back, I attended a conference in which a group was trying implicitly to redefine itself. Amidst this conservative group, I was surprised to hear its leaders so readily invoke the *Semper Reformandum* (perpetually being reformed) mantra. Having come out of a liberal denomination as a young man I learned to reach for my wallet to protect what little cash we had left whenever I heard that phrase. In most cases, the phrase "continually reforming" (besides being a poor Latin translation, rendered in the active voice instead of the passive gerundive; it should be "continually being reformed") signaled an attempt to move away from received truth. Of course, we realize that the past contains error and that no tradition is infallible. However, seldom has a church body been improved by the "continually updating" wing. More often than not, the alterations have been departures from the best expressions of orthodoxy. Hence I developed an instinctive distrust for the continual faddishness of the *Semper* wing.

Thus, I am surprised when I hear conservatives invoke that cant. Of equal interest, at the same conference, not a single speaker showed equal opportunity bias by stressing or citing the first part of the rubric: *Reformatus* ("having been reformed"). If one simply must be a *Semper Reformandum* advocate, then the least one could do to avoid total revisionism is to cite the first half of the motto ("having been reformed") as emphatically as he calls for updating.

Isn't that what the reformers did? Actually, I am not sure they were so open to revisionism. From my reading of Calvin and others, I cannot locate their invocation of *Semper Reformandum*; the reformers seemed to think that the church could simply be reformed to the eternal truths of the Word of God and gave little countenance to modernization dynamics. In fact, I cannot find anywhere that they used the *"Semper"* phrase. Can someone help me? Most likely it is just one of those vacuums in my theological education, but would someone cite for me where Calvin advocated the *Semper Reformandum*? It is abundantly clear that he called for *"Reformatus est,"* but I cannot put my finger on a call for *"Semper Reformandum"* by Calvin, Luther or Turretin. I cannot locate it in the great sixteenth and seventeenth century theologians. I see no charge to be "always hip" in the great Confessions. I cannot find this phrase or its paraphrase in Scottish or American Presbyterianism of the eighteenth century. I do not see it in Hodge, Bavinck, Wollebius, Ames, Perkins, Boston, Watson, etc. Perhaps I am just reading the wrong volumes. Or could it be that the *"Semper"* aspect is to theology what "unconditional positive regard" is to psychology: an invention of modernism to justify the *de facto* revisionism? I wonder. This phrase's moment of evolutionary appearance may be as instructive as its discovery.56

If, as I suspect, the *Semper Reformandum* addition is of relatively recent origin—and that it is a result of definite modernizing impulses—then perhaps my instinctive flinching from such vocabulary is warranted. Could it be that I was taught correctly in earlier years that *Semper Reformandum* was an inherently liberalizing phrase? B. B. Warfield once warned: "But let us

---

56 Five years ago *Premise* offered a prize for anyone who could show us an original use of this phrase prior to the year 1800. Still, no one has reported a sighting, possibly making a pre-1800 instance of *Semper Reformandum* less verified than either UFOs or the viability of Social Security in its present economic health. If this strand of *ur-progressivism* was so dominant early on, one wonders why it is so difficult to unearth multiple early instances.

equally loudly assert that progressive orthodoxy and retrogressive heterodoxy can scarcely be convertible terms."

We should have learned from Charles Spurgeon who warned earlier:

Macauley rightly said that theology is immutable; but these men are continually contradicting that opinion in the most practical manner, for their theology is fickle as the winds. Landmarks are laughed at, and fixed teaching is despised. 'Progress' is their watchword, and we hear it repeated *ad nauseam*. Very far are we from denying that men ought to make progress in the knowledge of the truth, for we are aiming at that ourselves . . . we trust that in some humble measure we are gaining it. But the words need interpreting—what is intended by 'progress' in this case? Which way does it go? It is too often progress *from the truth*, which, being interpreted, is progressing backwards. They talk of higher thought, but it is an ascending downwards. . . . their progress is a going from, not a going to, the place of our desires. Evidently, it is progress *from usefulness*. They invite us to follow them in their advance towards a barren Socinianism, for thither the new theology tends, or to something worse. Now, we know, at the present time, certain ancient chapels shut up, with grass growing in front of them, and over the door of them is the name *Unitarian Baptist Chapel*. . . . we have no desire to empty our pews in order to grow more grass. We have . . . not yet arrived at that consummation where the spiders are dwelling in delightful quietude in which the pews are more numerous than the people . . .[57]

Other readings for later or if obtainable
On the BCO chapters 8-9, read Thomas Smyth's "An Ecclesiastical Catechism: Officers of the Church," in Mark R. Brown, ed. *Order in the Offices* (Duncansville, PA: Classic Presbyterian Government Resources [807 Peachdale Lane, Duncansville, PA 16635], 1993).

The four books below were part of the southern Presbyterian church's attempt to train officers. They may still be available from John Knox Press or from a used book service (try Amazon.com or www.wjkbooks.com).

- Charlie W. Shedd, *The Pastoral Ministry of Church Officers* (Atlanta: John Knox Press, 1965). This work contains practical suggestions on home visitations, preparation for office, and the various shepherding functions of ordained officers.
- John Kennedy, *Presbyterian Authority and Discipline* (Richmond, VA: John Knox Press, 1960). This earlier work surveys matters of legality, authority, and order in discipline and government.
- Andrew Jumper, *The Noble Task* (Richmond, VA: John Knox Press, 1965).
- Andrew Jumper, *Chosen to Serve* (Richmond, VA: John Knox Press, 1961).

We are also happy to refer readers to our church's eBCO (http://capo.org/bco/part-1.html; updated before the 2000 GA). This electronic work contains links to historic documents that assist the student or Officer in learning more about earlier precedents and historic documents that permit us to understand polity matters within their contexts. When questions arise about original intent, especially if the meaning or history prior to 1973 is important, this is a helpful tool.

---

57 Charles Spurgeon, *An All-Round Ministry* (Edinburgh: Banner of Truth, 1986), 94-95.

Appendix Y: PCA General Assemblies and Study Committees

The following measures have been proposed or defeated in the past (References are to Minutes of the General Assembly by number of the Assembly and page number, e.g. 13-75 refers to p. 75 of the Minutes of the 13th GA), and before being needlessly resurrected one ought to know this past. One should also note that many of these proposals came to Assemblies with the full support of *Ad Interim* Committees. The items below have been proposed, and most of them have been defeated:

1) disallow higher courts to act for a lower court (13-75)   **Defeated 3-34**

2) to remove presbytery's power to dissolve churches unless consenting (13-77)**Defeated 16-21**

3) to erect the SJC (13-120)   **Deferred; not approved at first**

4) to approve *Ad Interim* Report **(13-121)**   **Referred back** with opinion of the GA viz:
   "**marks a radical departure** from the original tenets of the PCA"

5) to approve Philosophical Basis (an *in thesi* deliverance (14-105)   Approved;
   However, when a substitute not to approve was made, even with the Minority Report author himself not present, such substitute failed only 372-373 (14-102). There was no consensus or mandate on this, even *in thesi*, much less when this theory's implementations are acted on in subsequent years (See below). Also note how contradictory this is to #1 above and #14 below.

6) to have more fellowship oriented triennial assemblies (14-106)   **not approved; remanded**

7) re: judicial commissions, a substitute for the Committee (14-108) garnered 538 votes, but fell short of 2/3 of total registration (thus failing). As a result, the Assembly referred the "**defeated** motion and all matters concerning regional judicial commissions to the *Ad Interim* Committee." A mandate continued to elude this *Ad Interim* Committee.

8) to have a delegated Assembly (15-105)   **Rejected**; and ordered not to pursue

9) to erect SJC (15-106; see also #7 above)   Approved and sent down

NOTE: Also at this 15th Assembly a number of other measures were approved to be sent down to the presbyteries for their approval (Needing 2/3; percentages given in parentheses). Most were voted on in 1987-1988 as below:

10) to erect the SJC (16-90)   approved 29-13 (69%)

11) to change/reduce Nominating Committee (16-92)   **Defeated** 26-16 (62%)

12) to define "power," "authority," etc. (16-93)   **Defeated** 17-25 (45%)

13) to "clarify" relation of power between courts (16-94)   **Defeated** 16-25 (39%)

14) "A higher court cannot 'act for' a lower. . ." (16-95) **Defeated** 14-28 (33%)
15) to diminish connectionalism (16-96) **Defeated** 16-26 (38%)

16) to alter power/authority of Session (16-97) **Defeated** 17-25 (45%)

17) to define power as "only spiritual" and advisory-alone (16-99) **Defeated** 14-28 (33%)

18) to define GA power as advisory alone as above (16-100) **Defeated** 13-28 (31%)

19) to make higher court action contingent upon consent (16-101) **Defeated** 15-27 (35%)

20) to prevent Review and control from "acting for" (16-103) **Defeated** 14-28 (33%)

Note, a total of 22 different amendments to the BCO were voted on in this 1987-1988 year—half (11) from the *Ad Interim* Committee. All of the other 11 passed, while only *one of the eleven* proposed by the *Ad Interim* Committee passed, with nearly all of those failing to garner even a simple majority, much less the 2/3 needed to amend to BCO. Except for the erection of the SJC, all others failed, on the average only attracting the support of 39.4% of the presbyteries—certainly insufficient to base a claim for consensus support.

21) *Ad Interim* proposal to redefine role of Stated Clerk and AC (16-129) **Defeated**

22) *Ad Interim* redefinition of AC (16-134) Approved and sent down; Note #24 below

23) to amend BCO in line with #22 above (17-42) **Defeated**

24) to reduce committees of commissioners to "advisory" (18-107) **Defeated**

25) to change structure of GA and its reports (18-113) **Defeated by Indef. Postpone**

26) to give former moderators permanent seats in Assembly (19-122) **Defeated**

27) to have AC develop its own parliamentary procedures (19-122) **Defeated**

28) to allow RAO to be amended by less than a consensus (19-123) **Defeated**

29) to make committees of commissioners subservient to elected leadership on permanent committees (19-124) **Defeated**

30) to discourage Minority Reports (19-124) **Defeated**

31) to discourage new business from the floor (19-124) **Defeated**

32) to shorten the length of GA (19-124) **Defeated**

The 32 specific items above, which were aggressively pushed during 1986 and 1991, demonstrate that most of the ideas often bandied about, supposedly as accepted fact, *have been tried, have been extensively supported by some impressive leaders, but have not met the constitutional approval of the church.* Of these 32 ideas—which have caused much disruption in mission, created adversarial relationships, and have so harmed the church (such that the 19th Assembly even called for a moratorium on such efforts after defeating the proposals)—the only ones finally sustaining the broad, consensual approval of the church were:

a) the erection of the SJC (#3, #7, #9 above) which has generated no small part of controversy;

b) the approval of a philosophical statement (to which the Minority failed by only one vote in substituting its disapproval), which is marked by the Assembly as a "radical departure from the original tenets of the PCA."

The following ideas—(a) triennial assemblies more slanted toward non-deliberation, (b) defining church power as advisory only, (c) the squelching of Minority Reports, (d) the reduction of power of the committees of commissioners, (e) the diminution of the oversight by the higher courts, (f) the removal of "control" from Review and Control, (g) the centralization of power to an elite of elected officials or permanent committees, (h) the change in nominating procedures, and (i) attempts to "Revisit Structure"—have been consistently rejected as the church's consensus. These ideas, having been defeated, should not be foisted onto the church, even if a minority wishes.

During the 1990s, the PCA General Assembly turned to other study committees for guidance. In general, when consensus was found, the study committee's findings were approved. However, when findings involved changes to doctrinal standards, it was an uphill struggle to find approval. For example, in 1992 an *Ad Interim* Committee had been appointed to study divorce and remarriage. Specifically, it was charged to recommend if any causes for divorce were legitimate other than physical adultery or desertion by the unbeliever. The study committee determined that divorce might be permissible in the case of physical abuse by the spouse. The general findings were adopted, however, when it came time to amend WCF 24, the proposal failed to garner the requisite number of presbyteries; thus the measure failed to become part of our constitution.

Shortly thereafter, in response to concerns about the procedures and activity of the Standing Judicial Commission, an *Ad Interim* Committee was appointed to study judicial procedure. This *Ad Interim* Committee came to the 1995 General Assembly with certain procedural recommendations that were largely adopted. The explanation for the Assembly's approval of these may rest primarily in the fact that the *Ad Interim* Committee had true diversity, thus compelling it to reach consensus, and the Assembly was well aware of the potential for abuse among its own judiciary.58

---

58 Indeed, history had shown that in most cases, when a standing judicial body was erected, it would, over time, begin to think of itself as knowing better than the broader church. That was why early American Presbyterian courts were leery of ceding too much power to the hands of the few. The earliest commissions were also inclusive (that is, any member could attend if circumstances permitted), partitive (i.e., the part acted for the whole, never separate from it), and pragmatic; the first commissions did not exclude other members nor set doctrine.

The next major *Ad Interim* Committee to be appointed was the committee on Creation. Appointed because of a serious difference of opinion over the meaning of the WCF's phrase "in the space of six days" (WCF 4:1), this study committee presented its findings to the Tampa General Assembly in 2000. Its primary recommendation (i.e., that the Assembly hear its findings but not rush to conclusions so as to allow at least a year for study and reflection) was then summarily rejected, when a proposal from the floor to allow pluralism on the subject was hastily embraced.

The point of this brief discussion is to reinforce one clear idea: Whenever a higher court appoints a committee or a commission, that delegating body may certainly review, modify, or reject, if it so wishes, any part of the report from an *Ad Interim* Committee. Even if the *Ad Interim* Committee is comprised of venerable fathers in the faith, the Assembly and its commissioners may wish to alter, improve, and reject, in whole or in part, the work of a committee (see Appendix C by Mark Buckner below). It should also be noted that some *Ad Interim* Committees did find consensus and served the church well. *Ad Interim* Committees to study Freemasonry and Church-and-State matters were approved, and the church did not have to revisit those matters regularly.

Appendix C: Ten Tips for GA Newbies and Committees of Commissioners
By Mark A. Buckner

I have participated in PCA General Assemblies annually since 1994 and have been privileged to serve on Committees of Commissioners (the vehicle the PCA has designed to provide appropriate oversight for and review of the work of permanent committees and agencies) several times. As a neophyte Ruling Elder, this was a daunting task. All of you who attend should expect a maze of parliamentary confusion at first, various proposals that are difficult to follow without some acquaintance with the background of those issues, and a mountain of paperwork. Offsetting this, of course, is some tremendous fellowship and the gratification that comes from serving Christ in his church. Also, like most other complex tasks in life, it gets easier the more you attend. Below are ten tips to save first-timers a little time and heartache. I offer these simply as the fruit of previous counsel and from my own experience. My pastor tried to simplify things for me before I attended my first Assembly (among the helpful things shared was the Appendix Y above, "PCA General Assemblies and Study Committees," to illustrate that regardless of the presence of esteemed persons on committees, Elders should think for themselves, analyze, and approve what is best), and below are some of my suggestions based on various experiences.

First, the commissioner should review some book on parliamentary procedure. *Roberts' Rules of Order* is the standard guide (available online or in any large bookstore), and this can be misused by those with more experience, who can be tempted to 'lord it over' those who are less familiar with this technical procedure. Sometimes, when political zeal triumphs, true servant spiritedness is not always prominent in our Assemblies. One of the frequent areas of abuse is the use parliamentary procedure, which is good in the abstract, to prevent a neophyte commissioner from offering a good idea. And no one likes to be ruled out-of-order on a mere technicality with which he is not familiar. This caution is intended to stress two things: (1) General Assembly (GA) is, make no mistake, a political and parliamentary forum; it is NOT the annual missions retreat, and hardball is played on this field; and (2) the way to even the playing field is for commissioners to be forewarned and know the rudiments of parliamentary procedures. Pastors also have an obligation to assist and help them raise their proposals and ideas in the most effective ways possible.

Second, when the Handbook arrives (at least 30 days before GA opens according to our Rules of Assembly Operations [RAO]), the Ruling Elder should be directed to the matters that are primary and those that are secondary. He should think of reading through the Handbook once or twice. If he can only read it once, then primary matters must receive his attention; if he has time to read it twice, then he may read it in its entirety. In my experience, the following are **not matters of primary attention** and may be merely perused until/unless time permits. At first, then:

- Budgets should be considered only by those with expertise or with ample time.
- Reports from Ridgehaven, Board of Annuities, Covenant College, and Covenant Seminary are normally routine and can wait.
- Often the Standing Judicial Commission report is a labyrinth, and unless the Assembly is voting on a case or hearing a Minority Report on the floor, this is moot (sadly) anyway.

- We wish there was more real oversight on the reports of the four Permanent Committees (AC, MNA, MTW, and CE/P). However, most of their recommendations are so mundane as to leave the commissioners with little to do other than to approve minutes and budgets, re-elect coordinators, encourage support from all the churches, and set aside days of prayer for the various committees. To underscore this further, except for promotional and testimonial times at the Assembly, the reports of the three largest committees—involving key personnel and millions of dollars—seldom take more than a half hour on the floor. Thus, the commissioner may skip these pages in the Handbook until later. Of course, as long as leaders continue this format, which allows little real oversight or ownership, they probably should not complain about lack of financial support or zeal for their projects. Indeed, over the past two decades, the less the accountability allowed the more difficult it becomes to increase financial support for committees or agencies.

With this in mind, the commissioners SHOULD prioritize as **matters of primary attention**:

- The Nominating Committee report and seek to familiarize himself with nominees.
- The Overtures, which will be reported through the Bills and Overtures Committee.
- He should also read any substantive *Ad Interim* or study committee reports and recommendations. These are often lengthy and theological (good!), thus requiring time to absorb, critique, and consider amendments or alternative proposals.
- He should concentrate on Administrative recommendations related to property, personnel additions, and he should be vigilant about RAO and BCO changes.
- Any BCO or WCF changes that require a second approval must have 2/3 or 3/4 of the presbyteries supporting, and if any of these will be discussed at the Assembly (in one of the earliest sessions), the commissioner may wish to seek a briefing from his pastor.

Third, between receipt of the Handbook and the beginning of General Assembly, the commissioner should attempt to read and seek counsel as broadly as possible. He should not limit his input only to friends or past acquaintances. He might even wish to seek out criticism of key proposals from one or more who oppose the upcoming proposal. Iron still sharpens iron, and any Assembly that wishes to do its best work will benefit from biblical and fraternal review. Moreover, the commissioner would be wise to consider the financial implications of any decision, review it in light of first principles of our theology, note where interest groups or professional staff have vested interests, and compare these proposals against the backdrop of church history and the practices of other denominations. He might often wish to review the Caveat about Faddishness contained in Appendix F above to avoid a crisis hysteria.

Fourth, the Ruling Elder should understand that most matters come to the floor via an oversight group called a "committee of commissioners." This practice originated at the founding of the PCA and was an attempt to (1) prevent entrenched bureaucrats from dominating the decisions of the General Assembly (as had been done by the PCUS liberals), and (2) ensure that grass-roots Elders from each presbytery had ample opportunity to understand, scrutinize, review, and oversee key decisions. The institution and requirement to use these committees of commissioners is a wise one and has often helped to limit the control of the PCA by an elite. In 1991, there was an attempt to abolish these committees of commissioners—doubtless because some of the permanent staff and attendees at General Assemblies found them troublesome—and that was decisively rejected. Since that time, however, many of the various bureaucratic fiefdoms have found ways to minimize interference from or thorough oversight by these committees. It can be frustrating for first-time commissioners to serve on one of these and expect to actually give the quality of oversight that Elders customarily give in their local levels, only to be told that "it's really not their business; just trust the pros." Servant leadership may wish to proceed slower and seek to have as full support as possible rather than railroad inexperienced commissioners.

Fifth, if the commissioner serves on a committee of commissioners (hereafter C of C), the following should be understood:

- Read the RAO (the yellow pages at the rear of the BCO) to see the procedures and limitations for the C of C. Some mastery of these rules is critical if one wishes to serve well.

- Attend the Stated Clerk's briefing (time announced in the Handbook; normally at breakfast the opening day) to hear about procedures. Also, realize that should another elder suggest procedures, which seem to conflict with our rules or standards or that seem unwise, you, as a commissioner, may raise a question about that issue and may seek to have it clarified or improved, if possible. Don't, in other words, allow yourself to go down a parliamentary stream that is uncharted or unwise. Frequently, such procedural questions need to be raised sooner rather than later. It is acceptable to ask for the precedent or authority if a new or unwise procedure is suggested.

- As soon as the C of C meets, the first order is to elect its own chairman. A convener will have been appointed by the Stated Clerk to begin the proceedings. Any C of C may elect that man to be its permanent chairman or some other. Nominations are to be called for and may be made from the floor; or the C of C may vote to elect the convener as chairman. Either way, if one wishes to propose alternative leadership that is in order.

- Shortly after the election of a chairman and frequently after a devotional time, the C of C will hear presentations from permanent staff and coordinators as germane. These may be lengthy and, as expected, will lobby for the recommendations presented. It is possible even for non-members of the C of C to dominate the time and proceedings. Other guests may also attend (as per the RAO) and be heard or seated if room/time permits. Obviously, at some point, the C of C will have to restrict the testimony and presentations. While wanting to hear all relevant advice, guests—even of the highest order—are not to dominate or obstruct the proceedings; neither should staff or others. Accordingly, the C of C will have to guard its time and allow its own elected members ample time for discussion and consideration after all guests have been excused.

- Once the C of C begins, it may subdivide into subcommittees. Staff and permanent committee personnel may provide information during these sessions but should be restrained not to exert undue pressure. Once all preliminary and clarifying material is supplied, the C of C is to move into Executive Session (thus, excusing non-members of the C of C) and formulate its report and recommendations. Any C of C has the liberty to form its recommendations as it deems best after all the relevant testimony have been provided. These C of Cs should seek to give deference where possible to the work of permanent committees, however, they are ultimately responsible to represent Christ as Elders in the broader church, and they should seek to look after the interests of the Church instead of the interests only of one narrow faction or of the professional servants. At times, thus, the C of C will need to modify or limit the proposals that come before it. While they cannot generate new business, it would be an exercise in undue casuistry to suggest that they may not modify the business validly before them to conform to their best judgment. In keeping with the nature of a committee, members may certainly propose substitutes, amendments, and ask for further study on any matter properly before them.

- It is helpful if one serves on a C of C to write out any proposed amendments he wishes to make in advance (several versions are better than one!); he might even seek the counsel of others prior to offering such. And, as in any court of the church, every member may speak his mind and offer his counsel. He should also be diligent to listen to the counsel and concerns of others on his committee. A member may also offer—and sometimes the church is greatly helped by this—a Minority Report, if he thinks the majority seriously errs or if he thinks the church would be better served by having a different option on the floor prior to approving the Majority's Report. Our RAOs permit the presentation of Minority Reports, and the rules governing this protocol should be reviewed before Assembly, since one cannot always predict when he may be called on to present such alternative view. Normally, several members will contribute to a Minority Report, and as much consensus as possible among the minority should be sought. Just as in Sessions and Presbyteries, iron sharpens iron, so in the Assembly. No member should ever be intimidated out of offering his counsel or contending for conscientiously held beliefs. He may also speak to such issues as he wishes when the matter comes to the floor.

- Members of a C of C should also be aware that if recommendations are unanimous in the C of C, normally the Assembly will not debate or air those matters, opting instead for a short form of parliamentary procedure, which approves all items without objection in a single omnibus motion. So, speak and vote in the C of C or forever hold your peace!

Sixth, when motions come to the floor of the Assembly out of the C of C, the chairman will present all unanimous items under the omnibus motion. Then once those are summarily disposed of, he will normally take recommendations in order of sequence. The chairman's role can be a powerful one, as he is entitled to the final word on each recommendation immediately before the vote. This is especially important when the Assembly is narrowly divided or when a Minority Report is presented. After the vote on the floor, any commissioner may call for a division of the vote (if close and immediately after the vote), or may register a negative vote or a protest.

Seventh, the schedule of the General Assembly is printed in the docket of the Handbook. The first order is a worship service with Communion. Normally, the retiring moderator preaches a sermon, and immediately after that worship service the new moderator is elected. Any member may nominate someone for moderator, but often informal caucuses get together before Assembly to nominate their desired candidate. The office of moderator is designed, though, to have little influence in substantive decisions. Sometimes, the moderator will even yield the chair to previous moderators for a session or two. While the moderator is to be highly respected, since no one is perfect, a member of the Assembly may challenge his ruling, if one thinks he has moved away from the *terra firma* of good process. The proper motion for that is: "Mr. Moderator, I wish to appeal the ruling of the chair." That appeal is debatable, meaning that the one (and others) who raise this point of order may explain why they think the ruling is inadequate.

Eighth, the simplest reports come to the Assembly first. Thus, on the first full day (the opening day has little except the worship service and election of the moderator), reports from the Stated Clerk and the Inter Church Relations committee are presented (this normally features representatives from other denominations). Following these are the routine reports of the permanent committees and the Standing Judicial Commission. Often there is little discussion and little amendment of these reports; so little is debatable that the vast majority of these recommendations are often assumed under an omnibus motion to approve all matters from the C of C without dissent.

Ninth, as the week progresses, more important reports frequently come late on the docket and when the Assembly is fatigued. This can further lead to the tendency to spend very little time on very important subjects. The attendance may be lower when these vital matters are considered, or the hour may be late, or some commissioners with little patience may seek to rush the decision on a far-ranging matter. First-time attenders will have to discipline themselves to stay with the regiment, and it is in these 11th hour matters that the seasoned pros of many Assemblies can be most dominant. Ruling Elders need to stand and make their views known and advise the body.

Tenth: Five motions that let you know that desperation is setting in and something is afoot. I have seen the following employed several times and sometimes to the detriment of the church. A newby at General Assembly should sit up in his seat, stir himself from his nap, and know that something important is about to transpire if he hears the following:

1. The **moderator is asked to rule something out of order**—beside putting the moderator in a position of almost unchecked power, this request from the floor also usually annuls all previous procedure and work, which has been given to an issue or proposal.
2. **Parliamentarians** take to the floor or **announce their advice to the moderator**—again, our history warns us to be a little careful about procedural railroads, even if from the experts (Note, this is another reason that the Assembly may ultimately wish to rotate parliamentarians).
3. **Refer the matter to the CCB** (Committee on Constitutional Business)—this body of 8 men is only to give ADVICE anyway, and if one anticipates that they might rule more favorably on his proposal than it looks like it is receiving from the floor, it is very tempting to try to shift the venue in hopes that the matter will resurface with backing from another quarter.
4. **Refer the matter back** to the study committee and extend it for another year; or refer the matter back to the permanent committee with instructions that we can "trust the committee"—oversight apparently no longer being necessary for matters that flow from the staff. Regarding the pros, the implication is subtle but clear that to distrust them is impolite.
5. **Call for the Question**—this cuts off debate even if members have been standing in line to speak for a long time—and, more importantly, precludes additional perfecting, refining, and amending. If the Golden Rule is the standard, we might employ this tactic less.

Well, I hope to meet you at a General Assembly in the future. Perhaps these will save you a little time, catch you up to speed, and at least reflect some of the mistakes I hope not to repeat.

Appendix L: Sample from Lexington Presbyterian Church in Columbia, SC

A fine example of process that can be imitated is the reproducible bulletin insert from the Lexington PCA in Columbia, SC, on these two pages. Churches may tailor this to their own situation.

Officer Nomination Form

I have prayerfully considered the qualifications for officers in Christ's church and would like to offer the name of,

_____

in nomination for the office of

ELDER   DEACON
(Circle One)

In light of the biblical qualifications in 1 Timothy 3:1-14 and Titus 1:6-9, I have observed his consistency in the following areas:

(please check)

_____ His family life

_____ His heart for evangelism

_____ His aptitude for teaching in public or private (for elder only) in what context

_____ His love for others

_____ His love for the Word of God

_____ His faithfulness in serving others

_____ His faithfulness in worship

_____ His hospitality

_____ His generosity

I am confident of his qualifications for office, and I offer his name in nomination and will regularly pray for him and his family should he be elected to serve at Lexington Presbyterian Church.

I have spoken with the nominee and he is willing to be nominated for the office.

_____
(please sign your name)

Church Officers: Nomination and Election Procedures
Lexington Presbyterian Church, PCA

The Apostle Paul teaches us that the desire to serve as an officer in the church is a worthy ambition. He heartily endorses it, but he then explains that it is a demanding requirement of being an elder or deacon. So, the desire to be a spiritual leader in the church is a good thing, but not everyone is qualified to serve as an officer. Those who aspire to office in the church must meet the highest standards, and must be examined and tested (1 Timothy 3:15).

Paul describes the church as the "household of God . . . the church of the living God, the pillar and support of the truth" (1 Tim. 3:15). Those are strong statements, and if we believe them, we must embrace a high view of the church, and seek only the most qualified men to lead her. Officer nominations and elections have little to do with popularity and a lot to do with a person's consistent and deepening love for God above all things which nurtures a growing love and servant attitude toward his neighbor in the kingdom of God leadership is about loving God and neighbor, worshipping God and serving one's neighbor.

The Offices of Elder and Deacon

Elder – The office of elder is one of spiritual oversight and government of the church (Titus 1:5ff, 1 Tim. 3:1-7). In the NT elders are sometimes referred to as shepherds (Acts 20:28, 1 Peter 5:1-3) because they are charged with the care and nurture of the church just as a shepherd cares for his flock. Elders are also responsible for the teaching ministry of the church (1 Tim. 5:17-18). Thus, elders must both understand the truths of God's word, and be able to effectively minister in the body as one who encourages, edifies and when needed, confronts and rebukes.

Deacon – The office of deacon is one of service, extending mercy and sympathy to those in need, especially to those within the church. Deacons are first mentioned in Acts 6:1-6, as those chosen to minister to the physical needs within the church. The spiritual nature of the deacon's service of mercy is no less vital than the elder's rule; the health of the church is inseparably tied to both offices.

The duty of the office is threefold: 1) To minister to those in need and distress, 2) To administrate financial issues within the church (giving and distributions of gifts), and 3) To care for the church's property.

Any man assuming the office of elder or deacon must meet the qualifications listed in 1 Timothy 3:1-7, Titus 1:6-9 (elder) and 1 Timothy 3:8-13 (deacon). Both offices are perpetual—that is, for life, unless extraordinary circumstances allow or call for the dissolution of one's office.

Qualifications for Church Office

The qualifications for elder and deacon are listed by Paul in 1 Timothy and Titus 1. Generally and briefly, they are as follows:

Elder

Above Reproach: Is the candidate living in such a way that no one can point a finger at him for ungodly habits or actions?

Husband of One Wife: Literally, this means a "one-woman man." Is the candidate, if married, a loving and faithful husband; or if single, is he above reproach in his relationships with women? This qualification does not forbid a habitually divorced man from holding office. The focus is on a candidate's purity in thought, word and deed, toward women, and faithfulness to one's wife.

Temperate: Is the candidate self-controlled in all areas of his life? Does he over-indulge himself in any area?

Prudent: Is the candidate sound, reasonable and wise in his thoughts, words and deeds?

Respectable: Is the candidate respected by his peers, and is he a good model of Christianity for others?

Hospitable – "love for strangers." Does the candidate meet people well, and is his home open to minister to Christians, as well as non-Christians?

Able to Teach: Is the candidate able to communicate biblical truth to either small groups, large groups or individuals?

Not Addicted to Wine: Does he have any habits he cannot control, particularly in the area of food and drink?

Not Pugnacious: Is he prone to fighting and arguing, with family or friends?

Gentle, Uncontentious: Does he have an "even" temper, and a reasonable and teachable spirit?

Free from the love of money: Is the accumulation of material wealth a primary motivation and object of concern for him? Is he generous?

Manages His Household Well: Does he lead his wife and children well? Does he have the respect of his wife and children?

Not a New Convert: Does he have a track record of Christian maturity and growth in grace?

A Good Reputation With Those Outside the Church: Does he have a good reputation at his place of employment and in his neighborhood?

Able to Encourage Others by Sound Doctrine, and Refute Those Who Oppose It: Elders must be informed doctrinally. In the PCA, an Elder must understand and believe the system of doctrine summarized in *The Westminster Confession of Faith and Large and Shorter Catechisms.*

Deacon

Qualifications for deacon include some of those noted previously with the following additions:

Dignity: Is he respected for devotion to the Lord?

Not Double-tongued: Is he honest, does he tend to say one thing and mean another?

Loving What is Good: Does he look for, and expect, the best in other people? Are his values consistent with biblical values?

Hold to the deep truths of the faith: Deacons are not required to teach, but they must be committed to and believe *The Westminster Confession of Faith and Large and Shorter Catechisms.*

Procedure for Election of Officers

• Nomination—An officer must be nominated by a member of the congregation.

• Session Approval of Nominees—The elders in a congregation have the responsibility of evaluating all nominees initially for their fitness for service as an officer.

• Training and Examination—Nominees who accept the nomination to office are required to attend Officer Training Classes. The purpose of the class is to train, educate and examine nominees in the area of Christian Experience and call to the office, Theology, Church Government and Church History.

• Election—If the nominees are approved following their examination, they are presented to the church at a congregational meeting. Simple majority vote is required to elect the officers.

• Installation and Ordination—New Officers are installed and ordained according to the procedures in the PCA Book of Church Order, Chapter 24.

• Term of Service—Officers serve a period of three years, beginning the year of their election.

Your Responsibility

Each member should be aware of his responsibility to prayerfully nominate those men for office who demonstrate the biblical qualifications for office.

220 DAVID W. HALL

Appendix T: Timeline and Presby-Roots of the PCA

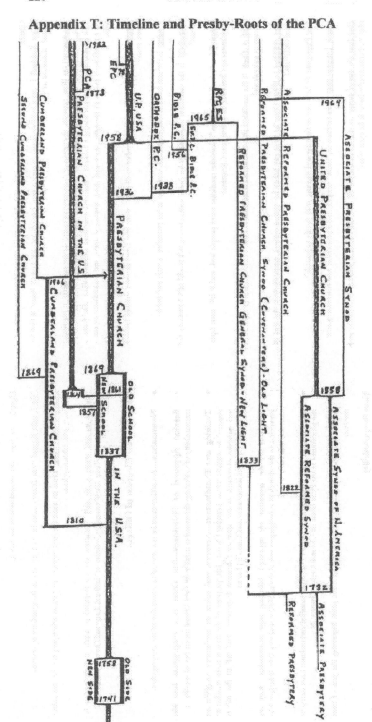

If readers wish to order directly select books from the author, please use this page.

Discount 20-33% off
Books by David Hall

#	TITLE	RETAIL	DISCOUNT PRICE
	The Arrogance of the Modern	21.99	16.99
	God and Caesar	14.99	9.99
	Paradigms in Polity	29.99	23.99
	Millennium of Jesus Christ	19.99	14.99
	Savior or Servant	19.99	14.99
	Manual for Officer Training	16.99	13.49
	Jus Divinum	19.99	15.99
	The Practice of Confessional Subscription	24.99	19.99
	The Legacy of John Calvin	12.99	9.99
	Add Shipping = $1.25 per book		

Mail checks (with this completed form) payable to:

David W. Hall
648 Goldenwood Court
Powder Springs, GA 30127

****

Other **Kindle** e-books (including *Holding Fast to Creation* and the recently released ***Questioning Politics*** [http://www.amazon.com/dp/B005VG3CTY]) by the author may be found at: http://www.amazon.com/David-W.-Hall/e/B001HPPL7E/ref=ntt_dp_epwbk_0

Or consult the author's **Amazon.com page** at:
http://www.amazon.com/gp/search/ref=sr_tc_2_0?rh=i%3Astripbooks%2Ck%3ADavid+W.+Hall&keywords=David+W.+Hall&ie=UTF8&qid=1318280819&sr=1-2-ent&field-contributor_id=B001HPPL7E#/ref=sr_pg_2?rh=n%3A283155%2Ck%3ADavid+W.+Hall%2Cp_82%3AB001HPPL7E&page=2&keywords=David+W.+Hall&ie=UTF8&qid=1318280828

Made in the USA
Columbia, SC
09 July 2022

63020048R00122